◆　　The Dance of Identities　　◆

INTERSECTIONS

ASIAN AND PACIFIC AMERICAN
TRANSCULTURAL STUDIES

Russell C. Leong
GENERAL EDITOR

BULLETPROOF: BUDDHISTS AND OTHER ESSAYS
Frank Chin

A RICEPAPER AIRPLANE
Gary Pak

NEW SPIRITUAL HOMES:
RELIGION AND ASIAN AMERICANS
David Yoo, ed.

WORDS MATTER:
CONVERSATIONS WITH ASIAN AMERICAN WRITERS
King-Kok Cheung, ed.

BLUES AND GREENS: A PRODUCE WORKER'S JOURNAL
Alan Chong Lau

MUSIC THROUGH THE DARK:
A TALE OF SURVIVAL IN CAMBODIA
Bree Lafrenier

TOMORROW'S MEMORIES: A DIARY, 1924–1928
Angeles Monrayo

FIGHTING TRADITION: A MARINE'S JOURNEY TO JUSTICE
Captain Bruce I. Yamashita, USMCR

THE 1.5 GENERATION:
BECOMING KOREAN AMERICAN IN HAWAI'I
Mary Yu Danico

THIS ISN'T A PICTURE I'M HOLDING: KUAN YIN
Kathy J. Philips

SPARROWS, BEDBUGS, AND BODY SHADOWS: A MEMOIR
Sheldon Lou

The Dance of Identities

*Korean Adoptees and Their Journey
toward Empowerment*

JOHN D. PALMER

University of Hawai'i Press
Honolulu

In association with UCLA
Asian American Studies Center
Los Angeles

Library of Congress Cataloging-in-Publication Data

Palmer, John D. (John David)
The dance of identities : Korean adoptees and their journey toward empowerment
/ John D. Palmer.
    p.   cm.—(Intersections : Asian and Pacific American transcultural studies)
Includes bibliographical references and index.
ISBN 978-0-8248-3371-8 (hardcover : alk. paper)
1. Interracial adoption—United States—Psychological aspects.   2. Intercountry
adoption—United States—Psychological aspects.   3. Adoptees—United States—
Psychology.   4. Korean Americans—Race identity.   5. Korean Americans—
Ethnic identity.   I. University of California, Los Angeles. Asian American Studies
Center.   II. Title.   III. Title: Korean adoptees and their journey toward empower-
ment.   IV. Series: Intersections (Honolulu, Hawaii)
HV875.64.P35 2011
362.734089'957—dc22
2010011683

Designed by Josie Herr

Printed by Sheridan Books, Inc.

Dedicated to my wife and sons
and my parents
David and Patricia Palmer

Contents

PREFACE

I was raised to believe in the American way of life—one that was founded upon the beliefs and values of meritocracy, freedom, and justice for all. With my classmates I pledged allegiance to the flag, learned about the great White explorers who discovered America and the founding fathers who fought for independence, and sang songs that upheld the belief that "this land was made for you and me" (Partridge 2002). It was then relatively easy living in the White middle-class culture because this was *the* way of life in the land of the free and the home of the brave. And life was good.

My parents, peers, and predominantly White community advocated a colorblind/adoption-blind philosophy that was sustained by the White middle-class culture. In elementary school, none of my teachers referred to me as the Korean one, much less the adopted one. It was predetermined that if we didn't talk about these aspects of my identity, then it wouldn't be an issue. Multiculturalism then meant learning about the "exotic" cultures in the world (e.g., Aborigines in Australia or Sioux Indians of the American Plains). The multicultural curriculum ultimately upheld the belief that White middle-class culture was "right" and every other culture was therefore different and abnormal. And I still did not have to worry about being different because I was considered a special member of the White middle-class since I had grown up in a predominantly White community that wanted to believe in a colorblind/adoption-blind philosophy.

However, whenever I looked in the mirror, I could see I was different. I was told time and again that the world would be a boring place if everybody looked and acted the same, yet I did not want to be different. I wanted to be like my White family and friends. I dedicated my life to speaking proper English, wearing fashionable clothes, playing sports, studying for admission into college, pursuing independence, and striving for a career that would establish a White middle-class lifestyle.

In spite of my efforts to "be like White,"[1] there were times when complete strangers, mostly White people, felt it their duty and privilege to point out that I was not a member of the White middle class. They would challenge my membership with intrusive questions: "Where did you learn to speak such good English?" "Where are you really from?" "Do you know karate?" The more White people asked me these questions, the more I tried to prove that I had in fact earned the right to be accepted as an authentic member of the White middle class.

Around my friends in particular I tried not only to act as White as possible, but also avoid all things related to Asian culture. When my friends joked about Asians or other people of color in front of me, I laughed with them. When they said, "But you're not like them, you're one of us," I was elated that they did not see me as Asian. I quickly learned that if I denied and rejected my racial differences, then I would at the very least gain recognition as an honorary member of the White middle class.

The consequence of living in the White middle-class culture was the denial and disempowerment of my racial and transracial adoptee identities. My parents, White middle-class Americans born and raised in the great state of Iowa, were told by the adoption agencies and social workers to raise me and my transracially adopted siblings in a manner no different from their two White biological children.[2] Their childrearing advice implied that my parents should follow a colorblind and adoption-blind philosophy so that all their children would feel loved and accepted.

In an attempt to keep me from losing all affiliation with my heritage, my parents made several attempts to connect me with Korean and transracial adoptee communities. For example, my mother took me to Saturday Korean-language school and Sunday school at the local Korean church. And every summer our family attended a weekend retreat for families who had adopted children from Korea and other countries.

My mother and a family friend, Dorothy Mattson (who had adopted five children from Korea), realized that their children (and other transracial adoptees attending the retreat) did not feel positive about their identities, especially as they entered their teenage years. Consequently, my mother began researching the first Korean culture camps. She and Dorothy initiated a culture camp in the summer of 1985 by hiring Korean Identity Matters (KIM), an organization developed by Doug Kim, a second-generation Korean American. Mr. Kim saw the need for Korean adoptees to develop a connection to their racial heritage (Parker 1995), due in part to his childhood experiences of attending Korean culture camps that taught Korean American (non-adopted) children about Korean culture and history. Therefore, he organized a staff consisting of 1.5 and second-generation Korean American university students to lead Korean culture camps around the United States.[3]

More than one hundred children attended the Iowans for International Adoption (IIA) camp each summer. My mother and Dorothy were pioneers in their efforts to introduce Korean culture to adoptees, as this was one of the very few culture camps in the nation at the time. They also realized, however, that teaching a group of Korean adoptees surface knowledge about Korean culture was a small endeavor in the face of a much larger problem. Making *bulgogi,* eating kimchee, and performing a traditional Korean fan dance were important in fostering a connection to and instilling pride in our racial heritage, but it was not enough to counteract the pressure to deny and reject our racial and transracial adoptee identities.[4]

My mother understood the larger picture of race and racism in the United States. She recognized that she was responsible for educating her transracially adopted children about individual racists who would attack their feelings about being Korean and Vietnamese. She acknowledged that race does matter in this world because the alternative was to support a cultural racism bent on upholding the notion that denying and disempowering her children's identities was the *right* way to raise transracially adopted children. She concluded that it was mainly cultural racism that forced her children to assimilate and mask their backgrounds in their desire to be recognized and accepted as members of the White middle class.

In 1994 the culture camp was renamed Korean Adoption Means Pride (KAMP) in an attempt to address the larger issues of race, racism, and identity. Dialogue sessions were formed that encouraged adoptees to voice their thoughts and experiences about being adopted and Korean. Most important, these sessions were closed to parents as the KAMP counselors, consisting of transracial adoptee young adults (post-high school), were the facilitators. This environment provided an opportunity for the adoptees to speak freely about race, racism, and identity issues without fear of upsetting their parents.[5]

Even though I attended Korean culture camp prior to the changes made in 1994, the camp allowed me to explore aspects of my identity during my teenage years. However, outside of camp I did not explore these issues because I was constantly worried about being ostracized by my White peers. Perhaps my greater fear was that I would finally realize I was not a White person. It was not until adulthood when I began an in-depth and critical exploration of my racial and transracial adoptee identities.

In my early twenties, after failing to gain full recognition and acceptance as an authentic member of the White middle class, I made the conscious choice to explore my identities. During my senior year of college I made my first journey back to Korea. Alone and confused, I felt Whiter than ever while I aimlessly walked the streets of Seoul. My Korean-language skills were limited to "hello" and "thank you," and the more I traveled throughout Korea, the more aware I became as to how little I knew about the culture. One memory that stands out was when I was eating *kimbap* at a street food cart.[6] The owner, a middle-aged woman, knew immediately that

I wasn't Korean. After I pointed to the *kimbap,* she brought the food to me and asked, "Are you Chinese? Are you Japanese?" With tears in my eyes I replied, "No, I'm American." This incident weighed heavily as I continued traveling around Korea because in the United States people would ask me the very same question, and I would always reply, "No, I'm Korean." The woman's question made me realize that I was neither here nor there; it proved that I was not really Korean.

The trip instilled in me a deep desire and need to learn more about Korean culture. After graduating from college and being out on my own, I began to explore what I perceived to be aspects of Korean culture. I joined a Korean church, enrolled in Saturday Korean-language classes there, and socialized with church members during weekend social gatherings. I soon discovered that I was not truly welcome. I was insulted at having to start language school with elementary schoolchildren (even the chairs were too small for me) and discouraged by the realization that these children knew more Korean language than I did. During social events I often stood alone as the Korean men in church mingled with each other and spoke in Korean. The older men often criticized and ostracized me for my lack of understanding of Korean culture, especially the Korean language. This angered me, and I wanted to shout that it was not my fault and point out that their children, who were growing up in the United States, also lacked Korean cultural skills. In the end, I left the church and vowed to return overflowing with Korean cultural knowledge, thus proving to them that, yes, I really *am* a Korean.

I decided to return to Korea—this time not as a tourist, but as a student of Korean culture. Over the course of three years I made every effort to assimilate into Korean culture. I formally studied Korean language, history, and culture at Yonsei University; I worked with the Syngman Rhee Presidential Papers under the mentoring of Dr. Young Ick Lew; I observed and interacted with Koreans whom I viewed as the "real thing." I consciously avoided all things I considered culturally White and American because I wanted to shed every aspect of that within me.

During my stay in Korea I also investigated aspects of my Korean adoptee identity. I visited my adoption agency in Seoul and traveled to Masan, where, I was told, my life began. I went to the orphanage, spoke with the director, and played with the children. To this day, visiting my orphanage remains the most difficult time of my identity journey. On my first visit I spent hours holding a baby boy who was about my age at the time of my stay in the orphanage. With tears rolling down my face, I prayed he would have a good life and, with great difficulty, returned him to his crib. And as I said good-bye, the older children clung to my arms and legs, begging me to take them with me. To this day I can still feel the grip of one little boy's arms around my neck as he refused to let go. I realized for the first time the real pain of my beginnings and consequently began a search for my birth family.

I had never thought too much about finding my birth family prior to my stay in Korea. My adoption records were minimal, to say the least, and I was often told of the difficulties involved in finding a birth family. Even before I began actively searching for my birth parents, I concluded that I would never be able to find them. And yet the thought of searching never really left me. At times I sat in the subway cars and buses looking at the faces of women whom I thought would be about the age of my mother— P. D. Eastman's (1960) book *Are You My Mother?* constantly flashed through my mind. I tried to look into their souls, searching for a hint of recognition in their faces, but I received only blank looks or, sometimes, hurtful glares in return. I eventually put an advertisement in a major newspaper and appeared on a television program dedicated to reuniting separated family members in Korea. Nothing ever came of these efforts, but I thought to myself, "At least I tried to find them; maybe it just was not meant to be."

After three years of living in Korea, it became apparent that I would never gain acceptance as an authentic Korean. Similar to the experiences I had while trying to be recognized as an authentic White, there was always someone reminding me that I did not fully belong in the Korean world. My identity was still caught in the middle of nowhere, as I spoke Korean with an English accent and constantly committed cultural faux pas that automatically branded me as the outsider. No matter how hard I tried to fit in, I was told that I did not belong.

At this point I felt as though I had no place to call home: Koreans did not recognize me as a Korean because I was raised by White parents in the United States, and Whites did not recognize and accept me as White because of my Korean phenotypes. I was lost in identity confusion and angry at the world for erecting such rigid racial and cultural barriers. I decided to return to my family who loved me and did not care whether I was Korean enough or American enough. They simply loved me for me.

Upon my return I felt more lost than ever in the United States and even within my own family, who could not accept the cultural changes I made. And the more I pushed them to acknowledge how I had altered my life, the more distance we placed between us. The conflict with my family made me feel more alone and isolated, and I wondered whether this identity journey had truly been worth all the pain I had caused—not just to myself, but also to the very people who loved me the most.

Then, I experienced an awakening when I attended the 1999 Gathering of Korean adult adoptees in Washington, D.C.[7] The 1999 Gathering provided me with new information and, most important, a connection to other Korean adoptees who were confronting similar identity issues. I felt empowered to speak out about my identity confusion at being caught in the midst of two cultures. The Korean adoptee community validated my voice by nodding their heads, seeming to understand what I was going through. Further, their questions made me feel as though what I had to say was important. I left the 1999 Gathering inspired to educate more Korean adoptees on the developing Korean adoptee community and was eager to begin conducting research on the Korean adoptee experience.

I was a Ph.D. candidate at the time of the 1999 Gathering, and many of my colleagues in graduate school encouraged me to research the experiences of Korean adoptees. They thought it would be innovative and would boost my academic career. I heeded their advice and my own academic ambitions as I began my first qualitative research project on the lives of Korean adopted young women (Palmer 2001b).

I soon discovered that I was not prepared either emotionally or professionally to undertake a large-scale study on the lives of Korean adoptees. First, I found interviewing Korean adopted young women to be emotionally painful (Rager 2005). I found myself caught up in their stories and wanted desperately to help and advocate for them (Palmer 2006, Young 2000). I began to view them as poor little orphans who needed my assistance, rather than as strong and resourceful young women. It became more apparent as I continued that I was still struggling with my own racial and transracial adoptee identity issues, and thus asked myself, Who am I to believe that I can produce non-exploitative, non-judgmental literature on Korean adoptees? Consequently, I opted to leave the research on Korean adoptees for another day.

Several years later, I accomplished three major things that have allowed me to return to my research on Korean adoptees. First, I earned my Ph.D. in 2001. During my Ph.D. candidacy years, as well as one year post-doctorate, I was able to develop and enhance my theoretical platform on identity development and hone my qualitative research skills. Second, I have challenged many of my own identity issues by accepting the fact that I will never be recognized as an authentic Korean no matter how much language and cultural assimilation I undertake. I have finally accepted that I am a "Korean American adoptee" and that I cannot change my life history as a Korean American adoptee. During those years in Seoul, I desperately wanted to deny my transracial adoptee identity because I believed this was the main reason I was never recognized as an authentic Korean. I no longer want to deny and reject who I am. I also realize that living between two cultures is a very powerful place to be, as I am able act as a bridge in bringing together cultural divides. Third, I have been teaching courses related to racial identity, racism, social justice activism, and qualitative research methods. This experience has provided me with a solid theoretical framework around the issues of race and has given me greater insight into issues of researcher identity and exploitation, and data collection, analysis, and interpretation.

This research project provided a new lens through which to view and reflect upon my own identity journey. The conversations with the Korean adoptees allowed me to view my internal and external struggles and presented me with a way to redefine identity development, empowered identities, and social justice activism. The design and theoretical framework of this study draws from my ethnographic research related to racial identity development, my culturally responsive pedagogy, and, most important, my own identity journey. Last, during the time of the study I married a Korean woman, Woolim Cho, and we were blessed with the birth of our three sons, David Mingyu, Jonathan Minhoo, and Henry Minjoon. These major life events have created new paths on my identity journey.

Acknowledgments

This work began in 1999 when I attended the first Gathering of Korean adult adoptees. I remain deeply grateful to the pioneers who organized the 1999 Gathering, as it came at a time when I was unsure where my identity journey was taking me. The 1999 Gathering allowed me to connect with others who could understand, to share my story without feeling ostracized, and, most important, to develop a voice that I hope can provide other adoptees with a starting point in their own identity explorations. From the first Gathering, and going forward, all of the adoptees, parents, and adoption agency workers that I met along the way have encouraged me to complete this work. I am especially indebted to and appreciative of all the leaders and members of the many adult adoptee groups.

I must first recognize all of the adoptees who agreed to be part of this study. Without their life stories and thoughts, this work could not have been completed. They shared with me many of their inner thoughts and sometimes shed tears of sorrow and joy during our conversations. I confess that after each conversation, I was emotionally drained and at times felt that I was not the right person to be conducting this type of research. Yet in the end their voices and actions continue to inspire my work and personal life. I wish I could name them here and give them the recognition they deserve for their critical insights and their fight for international/transracial adoptee issues on the local, national, and international scenes.

This work could not have been completed without the dedication, commitment, and support of my family, friends, and colleagues. Here, I wish to offer my gratitude to those who touched my life. I only hope that they will continue to inspire and comfort me throughout my lifetime. My sincerest thanks goes to my mother and father, who have continuously supported my endeavors and attempted to understand my angst even when I least deserved their support. My brothers and sisters were always there to lend emotional support. And a special recognition to my in-laws, Kee-Chul Cho, In-Soon Kim, and Dong-Hyun Cho, for their acceptance and understanding.

I am especially thankful to my colleagues for their support. D. Kay Johnston consistently offered valuable insight into the difficulties of publishing; Barbara Regenspan provided thoughtful revisions and sincere support; and Nisha Thapliyal was a wonderful sounding board on our daily commute. I also recognize Colgate University for their financial support of this work through several internal grants, one of which involved being a member of the Sio Diversity Chair Seminar, led by Rhonda Levine and Anne Freire Ashbaugh and attended by Pete Banner-Haley, Graham Hodges, and Steven Kepnes. Their critique of my work allowed me to explore new arenas in the field of race and racism. Moreover, without the dedication of editor Masako Ikeda this manuscript would never have made it to publication.

I need to acknowledge my friends David and Hyunju Kim Amos, Young Ha Cho and Kiyeon Han, Valerie Pang, Michelle Young, Alfredo Artiles, Eddie Moore, Jr., Lanese Aggrey, and Bettina Fabos for assisting me in my racial identity and social justice endeavors. And special recognition goes to Dr. Young Ick Lew for his continual mentorship and to Mrs. Keum Jae Lew, *Samonim,* who passed away while I was finishing this book, for her love and support.

Without my wife none of this is possible.

CHAPTER I

Dance of Identities

HANNA: [Korean] adoptees need to feel like they have [a] choice.
If you want to be 120 percent Korean, go ahead and change
your name and go to Korea. If you want to be 120 percent
American, that's fine too. But you can be something in the
middle if you want to. And for me, I call it a dance of identities
because I realized that I'm never only one or the other. I'm
always floating around.

In the summer of 1999 the first Gathering of Korean adult adoptees was
held in Washington, D.C.; more than four hundred Korean adoptees came
from around the world to share their life experiences, rejoice in their accomplishments, reveal their sorrows and pains, and develop lifelong connections. Some attendees admitted that this was their first time openly speaking
about their adoption stories; others shared their experiences of returning
to the Motherland; a few narrated their searches for birth families. Even
though the adoptees traveled to the 1999 Gathering through a variety of
identity paths, they shared the common bond of being transracial adoptees
from Korea. The connection that was created over this particular weekend soon spread worldwide. The powerful feelings that emerged led to a
significant increase in Korean adoptees joining established adoptee groups;
developing Korean adoptee groups in their local communities; organizing
Korean adoptee trips to Korea; volunteering at Korean culture camps; creating spaces for dialogue in chat rooms, discussion boards, and list serves;
preparing for the next Gatherings (the 2001 Gathering in Oslo, Norway,
and the 2004 and 2007 Gatherings in Seoul, Korea); and hosting mini-gatherings in various cities across the United States.

The significance of these groups and activities was that they were organized and informed by Korean adoptees.[1] Prior to the 1999 Gathering, some
Korean adoptees had claimed that parents and adoption agencies attempted
to control transracial adoption issues. These adoptees pointed out that the
agencies and parents mainly wanted to promote successful placements and
avoid dialogue about poor placement, lack of follow-up visits, and the
harm of promoting assimilation into the White middle-class culture. By creating an active Korean adoptee community, the adoptees could speak for

themselves and raise a new consciousness about transracial adoption, race relations, and White privilege and entitlement.

These active Korean adoptees discovered that their voices could not be silenced and marginalized by their parents, family members, friends, and adoption agencies. They shared their experiences without fear of being criticized as ungrateful, marginalized by racist and insensitive statements, belittled by those who viewed them solely as "poor little orphans" who needed a loving home, and censored by those who believed adoptees would give transracial adoption a bad name by speaking out about their experiences and political ideologies. Those who had been silenced finally felt free to speak their minds. And as more Korean adoptees felt empowered to release their stories and opinions into the Korean adoptee community, active members began to challenge institutional and cultural racism (i.e., a system of advantage based upon race; Tatum 1992) in the local communities.

My research is an attempt to understand these active Korean adoptees from their perspectives. Over the past several years I have dedicated my research to investigating the identity development of Korean adoptees and 1.5-generation Korean Americans (Palmer 2001a, 2001b, 2006, 2007). In my classes that explore issues of race, racism, and White privilege, I require all of my students to reflect upon their racial identity development. Throughout my work with racial and ethnic identity, it often seemed that the stage models restricted people to a certain category. The models are effective in providing a useful framework for students to investigate their identities and strive to advance to the next level, especially in an academic setting. However, the stage models are often unclear about how one moves from stage to stage. It appears that such movement is based more on maturity (i.e., from child to adolescent, to young adult, to adult) than self-reflection. Moreover, the final stage seems to conclude one's identity journey, which does not allow for growth beyond this stage, or show how major life changes may impact one's identity (e.g., marriage, parenthood, moving to a new community, death, etc.).

The dance of identities theory portrays the adoptees as taking their own identity journeys to discovering their identities for themselves (i.e., empowering their own identities). The theory does not allow for one adoptee to be a spokesperson for all Korean adoptees; it does not allow for one adoptee to claim that her/his journey is the right way to empowering one's identity; it does not allow for one adoptee to believe that her/his identity journey is any better than another's. Overall, I support the idea that it is the exploration of their identities that leads them toward their empowerment.

I am not implying that the Korean adoptees who participated in this study speak for all Korean and transracial adoptees. Readers may be led to believe that the adoptees in this study have completed their identity development or may assume that these adoptees believe they are somehow better than transracial adoptees who have yet to engage in a critical exploration of their identities.[2] However, because the Korean adoptees who participated in this study do not represent the majority, the book's purpose is not to illustrate how all transracial adoptees negotiate or should negotiate their identity development. Rather, illustrating adoptees' diverse experiences with issues of race and racism and their critical reflections is the main focus of this book and the core of the theoretical framework that guides this book.

Theoretical Framework—Dance of Identities

When I began this study, the theoretical framework was established from my own experiences as a Korean adoptee (as illustrated in the preface), my research agenda on racial identity development theory (Palmer 2001a, 2001b, 2006, 2007), and my culturally responsive pedagogy (Gay 2000, Ladson-Billings 1994). As a doctoral candidate at the University of Iowa, I was fascinated by racial identity theories, as they provided me a foundation upon which to base my life (Banks 1994; Cross 1971, 1978; Cross, Parham, and Helms 1991; Gay 1978, 1985, 1987, 1994; Helms 1984, 1990; J. Kim 1981, 2001; Phinney 1989, 1990, 1992, 2000; Sue, Mak, and Sue 1998; Sue and Sue 1971).

In graduate school, I first read Tatum's 1992 *Harvard Educational Review* article, "Talking about Race, Learning about Racism: The Application of Racial Identity Development Theory in the Classroom." I had just returned to the United States after spending three years in Korea attempting to discover what it meant to be Korean. The transition back into White American mainstream culture was difficult, as I no longer felt connected with my White cultural roots yet was still unsure what it meant to be Korean, transracially adopted, and American. When I read Tatum's article, I was struck by how it related to my life and my identity journey. I connected with her students' voices and their struggles to understand their racial identities.

The five major stages of the Black racial identity development model as outlined by Tatum (1992) are pre-encounter, encounter, immersion/emersion, internalization, and internalization-commitment. I recognized the pre-encounter stage as my attempt to gain acceptance in the White world, the encounter stage as my awakening caused by the collision of race and culture, the immersion/emersion stage as my exploration to understand what it means to be a Korean adoptee, and the internalization and internalization-commitment stages as my empowered identity and the desire to execute social justice agendas.

The pre-encounter stage is a time when the person of color has surrendered her/his racial self in an attempt to find acceptance in the White dominant culture. The pressure to fit in with the majority or to be viewed as a member of the dominant culture often forces these individuals to sacrifice their racial identity. Gay states that there is a "sense of unawareness, denial or disaffiliation, and unconscious and unquestioning dependence upon Eurocentric, mainstream cultural values and standards or self-definition" in the pre-encounter stage (1994, 152). J. Kim (1981, 2001) includes a stage before the pre-encounter where the U.S.-born Japanese American women in her study usually were immersed in the Japanese American culture and community prior to entering elementary school. However, when the Japanese American children entered school (the larger society) and were no longer surrounded by people who shared the same ethnic background, Kim noted that the girls began showing signs similar to the pre-encounter stage.

Once these pre-encounter people of color become aware that they are not accepted as full members of the White majority, either through direct racist incidents or learning more about their people's history, the encounter stage marks the moment they begin to "find themselves deliberately thinking about their ethnicity for the first time in their lives, or rethinking their existing beliefs and values about their ethnic identity and group membership" (Gay 1985, 46). Both Gay (1978) and J. Kim (1981, 2001) use the term "awakening" to define this stage because of the way in which the individual becomes aware of how her/his ethnic minority status plays a major role in her/his life. As a result, the person of color initiates a search for a racial affiliation to counteract racial discrimination and as a way to better understand her/his racial minority position in society. Kim found that the Japanese American women in her study were often confused and uncomfortable as they attempted to reconnect with Japanese Americans and Asian Americans due in part to feeling like outsiders and being ostracized by those communities.

Immersion/emersion is a time when the person of color becomes fully immersed in her/his racial identity. Some during this stage reject White supremacy and culture. More important, the person gains a greater understanding of what it means to be a member of her/his racial group. This may involve joining racial-affiliated clubs, advocating political movements for the advancement of her/his racial group, and destroying the "old identity" for complete transformation into the "new identity" (Cross 1991). Tatum (1997) concludes that when Black students racially self-segregate, they are making a conscious decision to surround themselves with other Black students in order to build a community or environment that enables them to act and behave in a manner that they find comfortable. Tatum then provides an answer to the common question, "Why are all the Black kids sitting together in the cafeteria?" by explaining that these students are not excluding Whites in particular; rather, they are immersing themselves in their racial identity in order to discover what it means to be Black. After learning about and self-reflecting on their racial identity, people of color emerge from their racially segregated positions with a newfound attitude and belief about the impact of race and racism in their lives. They emerge secure in the belief that they are not inferior to the White dominant culture. In the "internalization commitment" stage, Cross (1991) believes that the individual remains committed to promoting her/his own racial identity while at the same time building connections with other racial groups, particularly to the White dominant group. Gay (1994) views the final stage as the transformation of identity from the once angry self to an inner security and self-confidence. J. Kim (1981, 2001) believes Japanese Americans integrate their ethnic selves through all aspects of their lives and relate to other groups of people without rejecting their racial identities. Put another way, prevailing White values and institutions are not a threat to their identities. However, individuals continue to hold strong ethnic ties and attempt to build greater understanding with other racial and ethnic groups.

Throughout the racial identity development model the individual continues moving through the stages in search of a racial identity that is defined by her/his own experiences. This search might involve immersing oneself in the ethnic community, learning about ethnic culture through research-based literature, building relationships with others in the ethnic community, and connecting with media sources. Once an individual becomes comfortable with an ethnic self, s/he may reach the final stage. Phinney (1989) concludes that in the final stage, after the individual has acquired an ethnic acceptance, s/he then attempts to build relationships with other ethnic and racial groups.

While these models provide a solid foundation from which to investigate one's own racial identity development, I found these stages to be limiting in their descriptions of explaining a person's behavior in each stage. In the stage models I found it difficult to understand the reasons and the manner in which a person moves from one stage to the next. These models appeared to rank people from racially unconscious to racially autonomous, yet provided little insight into how one could empower one's racial identity, what an empowered identity actually looks like, and, perhaps most important, discovering how an empowered identity might lead to social justice activism. It is my intent to add to and challenge the ongoing discourse on identity development theories (Cross 1978; Gay 1978, 1985, 1987, 1994; Gee 2001;

Hardiman 2001; Helms 1984, 1990; J. Kim 1981, 2001; Phinney 1989, 1990, 1992, 2000; Sue, Mak, and Sue 1998; Sue and Sue 1971).

I am also able to connect my theoretical framework with my culturally responsive pedagogy. Since my undergraduate years, my teaching philosophy has evolved from a fundamental approach of multicultural education to a more multifaceted, culturally responsive pedagogy (Gay 2000). My teaching strategies revolve around three major concepts—*engage, empower,* and *enact.* I want students to critically *engage* the issues of race, racism, and racial identity through readings and critical dialogue. I promote the idea that exploring issues leads to building confidence in their understandings of the material, which ultimately *empowers* their identities. And from their empowered identity, they have the ability to *enact* social justice advocacy agendas in their lives and communities.

Enactment of the pursuit of social justice is not easily visible for most people in the current historical era. It became apparent to me that empowering pedagogical practices required allowing students complementary opportunities to practice enacting social justice theories. In my courses, I start by viewing social justice at the individual level by understanding how each student can consider enacting change within their local communities. Most often this takes the form of challenging the ideas of their family and friends. Then we enact change at the institutional level by implementing research projects or conducting service-learning projects after engaging with the critical social theory reflected in the literature review of the project write-ups.

I also make it clear to students that enacting social justice agendas is not always easy and that many times they will fail in their endeavors. I want to instill in them the foundation that will enable them to continue to challenge issues of injustice as they present themselves throughout life. Students need to realize that with empowerment comes the feeling of being connected to their communities and the responsibility to make the communities a better place for those around them.

I quickly learned from students' feedback that they desired some action, not just discussion of the issues. As a result, I now have the students share with the class their experiences of enacting social justice practice and involve the entire class by asking both the speaker and the class to reflect upon several issues related to a shared event. Students are required to think about how they would have responded differently before taking this class, what were the difficulties in raising these issues, how they felt afterward, and what they would do differently if given the opportunity to replay the situation. Reflection is a key component of enacting social justice agendas because it offers a space for students to both appreciate what has been accomplished and to consider more effective and/or more elegant actions for the future.

Overall, I want students to realize that as members of the educated elite they have a responsibility to improve their communities because they have the tools to make a difference. I instill in them the belief that change can happen and that they can take an active role in improving their communities. Students learn that enacting social justice agendas is not solely about advocating social change, but more about being active, good citizens by giving back to their communities.

At the initiation of this study I was intent upon establishing a theoretical framework that would illustrate how Korean adoptees moved from disempowerment to empowerment to social justice advocates. At first their journeys seemed to correspond with the established racial identity stages, my culturally responsive pedagogy, and my life story. Korean adoptees' identity development also resembled aspects of the early stages in the White identity model, due in part to their being raised in culturally White informed homes (Hardiman 2001; Helms 1984, 1990). These early stages depict an individual who lacks awareness of racial issues and tends to believe in a color-blind philosophy yet develops a fear of people of color based on stereotypes viewed in the media and learned through family and friends (Helms 1990). This fear leads to more distance and isolation from people of color. In addition, because Korean adoptees are people of color, they seem to experience individual racism in ways similar to those in the pre-encounter and encounter stages of the Asian American and Black identity model (Cross 1991; Gay 1987; J. Kim 1981, 2001; Tatum 1992). Some adoptees encountered similar identity questions as biracial/multiracial people because their culture typically does not match their physical appearance (Nakashima 2001).

It became apparent that Korean adoptees do not match any of the established racial identity models because of their unique experience of being people of color growing up in White homes. Indeed, biracial people and non-adopted people of color typically have at least one parent with whom they can racially identify, which may allow them access to certain racialized groups during the immersion stage. When Korean adoptees attempt to immerse themselves in the Asian and Korean communities, they often feel uncomfortable and shunned because they may not know the culture or may have grown up with negative stereotypes about Asians and Koreans (Palmer 2001b).

In addition, not having a parent with whom they can racially connect differentiates transracial Korean adoptees' lives from "children in the individualistic culture dominant in the United States" who desire individuation (Choi 2002, 469). The adoptees' experiences may appear parallel to the lives of most United States adolescents seeking independence from parents (i.e., separation-individuation), especially as they explore what it means to be Korean. However, their lives as adoptees raise certain issues of guilt and gratitude that may delay them from "attaining separation from parents and consolidating a sense of individuality" (Choi 2002, 468). And while these feelings of guilt and gratitude may resemble the experience of all adoptees, the Korean adoptees' struggles of being raised culturally White and viewed as racially Korean set them apart from same-race adoptees (R. Lee 2003, 2004).

The defining aspect of the Korean adoptees' identity became apparent to me from their reflections of living in-between and as part of two cultures. Directly from aspects of the adoptees' voices, a theoretical framework emerged that allowed me to illustrate the adoptees' identity journey as a dance of identities.[3] This "dance" involves the adoptee moving between and among three connected and simultaneously distinct identities—White cultural, Korean racial, and Korean transracial adoptee.

The White cultural identity is developed once they are adopted into White homes. And even though, as will be seen in this study, some adoptive parents provide opportunities for their transracially adopted children to explore aspects of Korean culture, the adoptees quickly realize that learning to be like White allows them certain privileges and acceptance within their homes and predominantly White communities.

The Korean racial identity is inherited at birth. Yet as they grow up in culturally White informed homes, this identity is silenced, especially as adoptees yearn to have their White cultural identity recognized and accepted in their family and community. This conflict between their racial and cultural identities often leads to confusion and angst. Indeed, as the world continues to view them as racially Korean, even though they are culturally White, the adoptees are left to ponder identity decisions that have no clear conclusions. Often, the adoptees feel that there are only two solutions to this quandary: completely rejecting everything associated with Whiteness and fully immersing themselves in discovering their Korean identities, or assimilating into their White cultural identities and foregoing everything related to their Korean identities. However, keep in mind that some Korean adoptees may never feel this confusion and angst and therefore remain attached solely to their White cultural identities.

Similar to Korean racial identity, the transracial adoptee identity is obtained without the adoptee's consent. While White cultural identity can be considered an acquired one, both the racial and transracial adoptee identities are forced upon the Korean adoptee. The desire to fit in and be like everybody else often leads transracial adoptees to suppress their transracial adoptee identities. However, comparable to their awakening to a racial identity, adoptees come to realize that by denying and disregarding their transracial adoptee identities, they often feel incomplete. As a result, some adoptees seek answers to their past lives, which include a birth parent search and reunion and/or connection with other Korean adoptees by joining adult adoptee groups, attending Gatherings, and blogging on line.

Overall, the dance of identities theory allows the individual to realize that there is no one path in engaging one's cultural, racial, and transracial adoptee identities. The individual chooses when and how to engage her/ his three identities. The activities the adoptee chooses to engage in and the extent to which she/he immerses herself/himself in her/his cultural, racial, and transracial adoptee identities are solely up to the individual; there are no rites of passages or developmental stages that each adoptee must transition through (Cross 1978, Gay 1994, J. Kim 2001). The theory does not intend to uphold the belief that adoptees must identify only with their racial identity or their transracial adoptee identity in order to be empowered. Indeed, the theory recognizes that solely identifying with a White cultural identity leads to the disempowerment of racial and transracial adoptee identities. Thus the theory implies that an empowered identity is developed through engaging and reflecting upon their racial, White cultural, and transracial adoptee identities. This engagement and reflection allows for the Korean adoptee to gain ownership of all three identities; they have discovered for themselves what it means to possess a cultural, racial, and transracial adoptee identity.

Purpose

Dance of Identities brings into question social constructions of race. The adoptees dispute, contemplate, resist, and defy the notion that there is an authentic Korean, authentic White, or authentic Korean adoptee. The adoptees force society to add new questions regarding terminology such as "sellout," "banana," and "White wannabe" as they challenge what it means to be Korean, Korean adoptee, Asian, and White at the same time.[4] Oparah, Shin, and Trenka open their edited work on transracial adoption by powerfully stating,

> We refuse to assimilate into white culture or to submit to narrow ideas about cultural authenticity in communities of color, choosing instead to name our own experience. In so doing, we reject the labels "apple," "banana," "oreo," and "coconut," recognizing that our experiences as adoptees of color are as authentic as those of non-adopted people of color. . . . We do not have to separate ourselves along the heavily policed borders of ethnicity nor do we need to

adapt to theories of identity advanced by non-adoptees. . . . Instead, we bring forth our unique creativity and spirituality as adoptees of color, to reinvent ourselves and the world. (2006, 14)

Following the passionate words of Oparah et al. and the other contributors, as a researcher and educator of color who focuses on race relations I feel it is imperative that readers realize this book adds another perspective to the complex nature of race and how we can address race from new angles. I fully understand why the race dialogue is embedded within Black-White issues. Wu states,

People speak of "American" as if it means "white" and "minority" as if it means "black." In that semantic formula, Asian Americans, neither black nor white, consequently are neither American nor minority. I am offended, both as an academic and as an Asian American. Asian Americans should be included for the sake of truthfulness, not merely to gratify our ego. Without us—and needless to say, without many others—everything about race is incomplete. (2002, 20)

The dialogue on race, racism, and White privilege must include the Asian voice as well as the Latina/Hispanic, Native American, and biracial/multiracial voices. I am adamant in the belief that in order to have a comprehensive dialogue on these issues, this dialogue must include the Asian diaspora, of which Korean adoptees are a significant part.

This book is larger than merely the Korean adoptee community because it has the potential to influence the identities of people of color, biracial/multiracial people, and Whites by adding another perspective to the complex nature of race. Specifically, transracial adoptees disrupt the deeply embedded notions of race on a global scale based on their lives as both in-between and part of multiple cultures. The classification of individuals into the static racial categories of Asian, Black, Latin American/Hispanic, Native American, and White disregards individuals' histories and multiple identities (Banks 1984, 1994; Takaki 1989, 1993). Reference to race remains one of the most common practices for ascribing group membership in a multiracial society because the visible characteristics of race tend to dominate cultural traits (Banks 1994; Bartolome and Macedo 1997; Omi and Winant 1986, 1993; Wu 2002). However, Korean adoptees are not typically recognized as authentic Asians within the Asian American communities due mainly to their experience of growing up disconnected from the Asian and Asian American communities. This detachment often results in Korean adoptees viewing themselves as neither Asian nor Asian American.

By listening to Korean adoptees' voices, I hope the reader will gain new insight into transracial adoption issues. In this way I am neither focusing on the pain and suffering of Korean adoptees nor seeking pity for the Korean adoptee community. This is my attempt to celebrate their triumphs, learn from their identity journeys and their self-empowerment, and reflect upon what they offer to race, racism, and racial identity dialogues.

From this social justice activist platform, it is my intent to portray the identity journeys of Korean adoptees from their perspectives. There were many times when I wanted to insert my own voice and advocate for the adoptees to seek out an identity journey similar to my own. I caught myself attempting to confine the adoptees' voices solely within established identity models. However, as a social justice advocate for historically marginalized people, particularly people of color and transracial adoptees, I had to climb down from my academic perch and allow the adoptees' stories to come alive, rather than become suffocated by my insights and political agendas. *Dance of Identities* allows for a diversity of experiences and identities to emerge as the adoptees reflect on their lives as Korean adoptees.

Within this book I provide implications for an improved understanding of transracial adoptees' identities that will support and encourage the identity development of these adoptees. The number of visas issued per year to "orphans coming to the United States" (technical term used by the Bureau of Citizenship and Immigration Services) has jumped from 8,102 in 1989 to 20,679 in 2006 (peaking at 22,884 in 2004). U.S. families adopted 265,677 children from other countries between 1971 and 2001. The number of Korean adoptees reached its peak in 1986 with 6,188 children adopted. Since 1955 more than 150,000 Korean children have been adopted by U.S. families. Children adopted from China have significantly increased from 201 in 1989 to 2,130 in 1995 (when the first considerable demographic shift took place) to 5,053 in 2002. Further, the number of adoptees from European countries admitted to the United States noticeably increased in the 1990s. In 1986 only 103 children were adopted from Europe. In 1991 that number jumped to 2,761, mainly from Romania, and in 2002, a total of 4,269 Russians and 1,122 Romanians were adopted into U.S. homes.[5]

In association with the increasing number of transracial adoptees in the United States, several publications have investigated this issue. Specifically, the 1999 Gathering influenced Korean adoptees and others to conduct empirical research on the Korean adoptees' experiences. Freundlich and Lieberthal (2000) requested information from Korean adoptees preparing to attend the 1999 Gathering and then reported their initial findings there. The researchers' final report was distributed via the Internet and illustrated a variety of interesting sociocultural variables. Notable was their finding that the vast majority of Korean adoptees identify with the White culture reflected in their upbringings. The study concluded with a proposal to study the following major themes: family dynamics, fitting in and being different, racial discrimination, and identity.

A few Korean adoptees have embarked upon research on Korean adoptees (Brian 2004, Flower Kim 2005, Hübinette 2005, Lieberman 2001, Meier 1998). Much of this research by Korean adoptees remains at the Ph.D. level and has not gone beyond academia. However, corresponding with the rapid rise of U.S. families adopting transracially and the rising number of transracial adoptees who are in their teenage and young adult years, the voices of transracial adoptees are being heard in other venues. *Seeds from a Silent Tree: An Anthology by Korean Adoptees* (Bishoff and Rankin 1997) was a groundbreaking work that generated interest in hearing firsthand accounts of Korean adoptees' experiences.[6] Several anthologies followed that touch upon many of the issues Korean adoptees encounter throughout their lives. *Voices from Another Place: A Collection of Works from a Generation Born in Korea and Adopted to Other Countries* (Cox 1999) and *After the Morning Calm: Reflections of Korean Adoptees* (Wilkinson and Fox 2002) both focus solely on Korean adoptees' reflections through essays and poems.

Korean adoptees have told their stories through autobiographical accounts: Thomas Park Clement's *The Unforgotten War (Dust of the Streets)* (1998); Elizabeth Kim's *Ten Thousand Sorrows* (2000); Katy Robinson's *A Single Square Picture: A Korean Adoptee's Search for Her Roots* (2002); Joanne Higginson's *Unlocking the Past* (2003); Jane Jeong Trenka's *The Language of Blood: A Memoir* (2003); Jeannine Vance's *Twins Found in a Box: Adapting to Adoption* (2003); and Sunny Jo's *From Morning Calm to Midnight Sun* (2005) are a few examples. These memoirs inform the general public of the various adoptee experiences from the perspectives of Korean adult adoptees. These books add keen insight into the struggles and highlights of being a biracial/multiracial transracial adoptee (Clement 1998, Eliz. Kim 2000) and the birth family search and reunion (Higginson 2003, Robinson 2002, Sunny Jo 2005, Trenka 2003, Vance 2003), and all provide connection to the development of a racial and transracial adoptee identity. These books are valuable sources for adoptees of all ages. They provide adoptees with the evidence that they are not alone as they develop a connection to the Korean adoptee community.

The above-named authors were revolutionary in releasing their stories to the public; prior to these narratives, the most readily available perspective on Korean adoptees was conveyed in the writings of adoptive parents and professionals who work with transracial adoptees—something that continues today. Some adoptive parents give specific attention to properly raising transracially adopted children (e.g., Evans 2001, Gray 2001, Klatzkin 2001, Melina 1986, Wadia-Ells 1995, Watkins and Fisher 1995) or publish within the children's literature genre, focusing on how parents can help their transracially adopted children understand their adoption (e.g., Brownell and Peacok 2000, Dorow 1997, McCutcheon and Paschkis 2001, Patton 2000, Petertyl and Chambers 1997). Other adoptive parents write about their experiences adopting and raising a transracially adopted child (Buchanan 2006, Demers 2004, McCabe 2003, Register 2005, Trevor 2006, Woodard 2002). While most of the literature written by adoptive parents seems to provide security and support for other adoptive parents in their decisions to transracially adopt and ultimately raise their children, it generally disregards the voices of transracial adoptees, in particular the experiences of teenage and adult transracial adoptees. Moreover, the parent authors seem to dismiss the larger issues of race, racism, and racial identity development. It even appears that there are more books by adoptive parents than by adoptees.

Since I first started working on this book, two powerful publications, edited by transracial adoptees, provided a new direction in understanding the transracial adoptee experience. *Outsiders Within: Writings on Transracial Adoption* (Trenka, Oparah, and Shin 2006) and *International Korean Adoption: A Fifty Year Practice* (Bergquist, Vonk, Kim, and Feit 2007) offer both personal insights into the experiences of these adoptees and theoretical and empirical research by scholars in the fields of social work, sociology, anthropology, psychology, and history. These two works move the transracial adoptee experience in a scholarly direction, which only enhances the personal accounts.

Throughout the years several non-Korean adoptee scholars have investigated the experiences and identity development of Korean adoptees (e.g., Fujimoto 2001; Huh 1997; Kallgren and Caudill 1993; D. S. Kim 1977, 1978; Ele. Kim 2001, 2004a, 2004b, 2005, 2007a, 2007b; Kim, Hong, and Kim 1979; W. J. Kim 1995; Koh 1981, 1993; R. Lee 2003, 2004; Trolley, Wallin, and Hansen 1995; Valk 1957; Whang 1976; Zuniga 1991). Most of this literature has focused on the adjustment of Korean adoptees in White homes, and while the research concluded that the majority of Korean adoptees adjusted to their new environments, most are nevertheless uncomfortable with their appearance, feel ashamed of their origins, and/or show little desire to learn about their birth culture, which often leads them to dissociate from anything related to Korea (Kallgren and Caudill 1993; D. S. Kim 1978; W. J. Kim 1995; R. Lee 2003, 2004). Some of the research attributed this negative attitude toward Korea to the inferior status minorities have in the United States and to the inadequate amount of positive exposure to their birth culture (D. S. Kim 1978; W. J. Kim 1995; R. Lee 2003, 2004). Consequently, these adoptees have little pride in being Korean and thus are inclined to join the White middle-class American culture because it is familiar and possesses higher status (D. S. Kim 1978; R. Lee 2003, 2004).

My book can act as a resource for transracial adoptees and those involved in their lives (e.g., parents, other family members, friends, teachers, social workers, and adoption agencies). As international transracial adoption continues to be an avenue whereby U.S. citizens build their families, there is a growing demand for qualitative and quantitative research that can help not only the transracial adoptee understand her/his life experiences, but also those who are closely associated with or interested in the institution of transracial adoption. I hope that I am able to provide transracial adoptees with a sense of security in their identity journeys, a feeling of self-worth and confidence in their backgrounds, and liberation from the coercion to choose a particular identity. I anticipate that this book will allow adolescent and adult transracial adoptees to recognize that they are not alone, that they are able to see others who also struggle with understanding their complex and often competing multiple identities. I also want them to witness how other transracial adoptees empower their identities through their own journeys and share with others along the way. While their journeys should not be regarded as the ideal road to empowerment, I hope readers will be able to reflect upon these stories and develop their own paths.

Research Methods

I began my study with a focus on the identity journeys of Korean adoptees active within the global Korean adoptee community. I was most interested in how these adoptees viewed their identities, the main influences on their identities, and the most significant events of their identity journeys. I first requested permission from leaders of Korean adoptee groups for individual interviews and then encouraged them to pass on my call for participants. I was generally well received and began scheduling phone interviews and on-site visits.[7]

In the summer of 2004 I attended the Gathering in Seoul. Some adoptees who had participated in my study asked why I chose not to conduct research during the conference. While I had considered conducting interviews at the Gathering, I decided that my presence as researcher would be intrusive, especially in relation to two groups: those attending a Gathering for the first time and those in Korea for the first time since their adoptions. In addition, I was attending the Gathering as a member and wanted to enjoy the conference from that perspective. Even though I engaged in several conversations and group discussions, I neither took formal notes nor conducted any formal interviews. Happenings from the Gathering do not appear in this book unless it is a reflection from one of the participating adoptees.

Some attendees at the 2004 Gathering discovered that I was conducting research on Korean adoptees. During and after the Gathering, a number of them inquired how they could participate in the study (some even sought advice on how to start their own Korean adoptee groups). I did not want to silence any adoptee who desired to share her/his story. I opted to include those who had contacted me and then requested that Korean adoptee developers of Web sites and list-serves post a call for participants. The number of adoptees rose to forty; since that time, two chose to withdraw, leaving me with a total of thirty-eight adoptees (see table 1).

The adoptees had grown up in various parts of the United States and Europe. At the time of the study they ranged in age from twenty to fifty one. Thirty-three are female and five are male. At the time of the interviews, seventeen were in their thirties, fifteen were in their twenties, and six were forty and older. Twenty-two were adopted in the 1970s, twelve were adopted in the 1980s, and four were adopted prior to 1970. With regards to their activity within the Korean adoptee community, all but four were involved in some type of Korean adoptee group, twenty had attended at least one of the major Gatherings, twenty-one had attended a mini-gathering (smaller Gatherings held throughout the year in different cities), twenty-eight had visited and/or lived in Korea, seventeen had conducted a birth family search, and seven had reunited with one or both of their birth parents.

I recognize that this group of thirty-eight Korean adoptees is a small portion of the 160,000-plus global Korean adoptee population. I further understand that numerous Korean adoptees in the world are not involved in any adoptee group, culture camp, list-serve, and/or Web site. I also want to clarify that not all of the adoptees speak to all of the chapters in this book. The book is organized into chapters according to major themes that emerged from the interviews and are grounded in the theory of the dance of identities.

Chapter Outlines

Chapter 2 illustrates how and why the adoptees assimilated to a White cultural identity, especially during the childhood and adolescent years. Assimilation came naturally, as the majority was surrounded by Whiteness on a daily basis. Some were filled with the idea that White is "right" and Asian "wrong." These adoptees developed a negative sense of themselves as Korean/Asian and expressed a desire to be accepted as White. Overall, the

Table 1 Demographics of the Adoptees

Name	Age	Gender	Age at Adoption	Year of Adoption	Member of Adult Adoptee Group	Attended Gathering	Visited Korea	Birth Family Search
Abby	24	Female	7m	1980	Yes	No	No	No
Alex	27	Male	4m	1979	Yes	No	Yes	Yes, not found
Amber	28	Female	1y 6m	1976	Yes	Yes, Seoul	Yes	Yes, not found
Angie	22	Female	1y 6m	1987	Yes, board	Yes, Seoul	Yes	Yes, not found
Bettina	32	Female	8m	1972	Yes, board	No	No	No
Brenda	50	Female	10y	1964	Yes, co-founder	Yes, D.C., Seoul	Yes	Stayed in contact
Brian	51	Male	7y	1960	Internet only	Yes, D.C.	No	No
Cathy	21	Female	8m	1983	No	No	No	No
Charlotte	36	Female	14y	1982	Yes	Yes, Seoul	Yes	Stayed in contact
Cindy	34	Female	1y 10m	1972	Yes, president	No	No	Yes, not found
Connie	29	Female	4m	1975	No	Yes, Seoul	Yes	No
Daniel	47	Male	2y	1959	Yes, president	Yes	Yes	No
Gloria	24	Female	4m	1980	No	No	Yes	Yes, not found
Halle	32	Female	5m	1972	Internet only	No	No	No
Hanna	32	Female	3y 6m	1975	Yes, founder	Yes, D.C., Oslo	Yes	No, found
Jackson	33	Male	6y	1971	No	Yes, D.C., Seoul	Yes	No, found
Jamie	33	Female	6m	1971	Yes, president	Yes, all	No	No
Jennifer	34	Female	6y	1976	Yes, president	Yes, D.C., Seoul	Yes	No, found
Joan	34	Female	1y 6m	1971	Yes	Yes, Seoul	Yes	Yes, not found

								Stayed in contact
Julie	37	Female	7y 6m	1974	No	No	Yes	No
Kara	30	Female	1y	1975	Yes	No	Yes	No
Karina	35	Female	1y 6m	1970	Yes	Yes, D.C.	Yes	Yes, not found
Katerina	31	Female	3y 8m	1977	Yes	Yes, D.C.	Yes	Yes, found
Keiza	32	Female	2y	1974	No	Yes, Seoul	Yes,	Yes, not found
Kelly	32	Female	4y 6m	1977	Yes	Yes, D.C.	Yes	No
Kendra	44	Female	1y	1961	Internet only	No	No	No
Kianna	33	Female	3y	1974	Yes	No	No	No
Kris	23	Female	2y 6m	1983	Yes, founder	No	Yes	Yes, found
Mary	20	Female	6m	1984	Yes	No	No	No
Michelle	21	Female	4m	1983	No	No	Yes	Yes, found
Robby	20	Male	6m	1984	Yes	No	No	No
Sadie	24	Female	5m	1980	No	No	No	Yes, not found
Sophie	28	Female	1y 6m	1977	Yes, board	Yes	Yes	No
Tammy	33	Female	9m	1972	Yes, board	Yes, Seoul	Yes	Yes, not found
Tess	22	Female	1y 6m	1987	Yes, board	Yes, Seoul	Yes	Yes, not found
Tonya	37	Female	8y	1975	Yes	Yes, D.C.	Yes	No
Tori	31	Female	3y 6m	1976	Yes	No	No	No
Woojung	29	Female	11y	1986	Yes	No	Yes	No

majority of the adoptees were happy in this state of "obliviousness." While there were times when their White cultural identity was challenged, for the most part they were able to gain acceptance as "one of us" (i.e., acceptance as an honorary White) at least within their families and communities.

Chapter 3 explores the moments when the adoptees' views on race and racism were shattered. In particular, the adoptees discuss how they came to realize the contradictions of their colorblind philosophy when their race collided with their culture. They separated from their Korean identities by living in the White middle class, yet the world continued to see them solely as Koreans/Asians. They did not know what it meant to be Korean because the adoptees were in denial about and/or rejected their racial and transracial adoptee identities. The awakening was a time when the Korean adoptees came to view their lives as in the middle of nowhere: they are not White because they are racially Korean, and they are not Korean because they are culturally White. In many ways, during this segment of their journey they were confused about how to identify themselves, since the world, their communities, and families were sending mixed messages. They were being raised to be colorblind in a race-conscious environment. And the more they attempted to run away from their Korean racial identity, the more they were told that they were not recognized as White.

Chapter 4 consists of the adoptees' voices as they discovered their racial and/or transracial adoptee identities. After awakening to the realization that they are in the midst of two cultures (being part of and distant from White and Korean culture), several adoptees engaged in activities that they believed would make them more culturally Korean, including attending Korean churches and joining the Korean Student Association on college campuses. Others chose to explore their transracial adoptee identities by joining Korean adoptee groups, conducting birth family searches, and questioning their parents about the adoption. The adoptees talked about their explorations as attempts to fill the holes in their lives and to feel whole and complete, because their awakenings led them to see how they lost control of their racial and transracial adoptee identities.

Chapter 5 delves into the many issues that arise when the Korean adoptees explored and reflected on their multiple identities—namely their White cultural, racial, and transracial adoptee identities. The tensions presented themselves in a number of areas, including within the Korean adoptee community and the institution of transracial adoption, and with parents and spouses. The adoptees reflected on how their relationships with parents and spouses became increasingly strained the more they involved themselves in Korean adoptee issues as well as in topics dealing with race, racism, and White privilege. They also discussed the many tensions within the Korean adoptee community, especially regarding the differing philosophies on the institution of transracial adoption.

Chapter 6 further illustrates the characteristics of the adoptees' empowered identities. Moreover, the chapter delineates the social justice activities carried out by empowered adoptees. They connected to other Korean adoptees by forming transracial and international adoptee groups and by mentoring the younger adoptees. Some saw the need to cross racial and cultural divides by reaching out to parents, prospective parents, and adoption agencies, as well as attempting to educate Koreans and Korean Americans about their lives as transracial adoptees.

Chapter 7 suggests that transracial adoptees, parents and adoption agencies, and social justice activists and educators first become more aware of the need to engage in an identity journey. I then suggest what can happen during this identity journey and conclude that the identity journeys can eventually lead to empowered identities. I am not saying that there is a need for Korean adoptees to "understand and appreciate their Korean identity" (Ele. Kim 2005, 54) or that they should become disgruntled with the institution of transracial adoption; rather, the dance of identity theory allows for adoptees to empower their journeys, to own it for themselves, and to decide what it means to be or not to be a Korean American adoptee. The main difference between the current racial identity development models and the dance of identity theory rests in the belief that there is no one starting place and thus no one ending place; there is no one direct path to empowerment—rather, empowering one's identity comes through engaged explorations and continuous reflections.

CHAPTER 2

Wanting to Be Like White

Dancing with a White Cultural Identity

CHARLOTTE: White washed! Well, because it's true. But when I talk about it there's no shame attached to it for me because it's a very natural process one goes through.

BRENDA: All these adoptees are White. I mean, they're Asian, but they're White. It's a sense of not resolving and being comfortable about the fact that you are totally White inside but you're Asian outside and those two haven't quite come together yet. I just say I am Korean by race but I am not Korean any other way.

Charlotte and Brenda, like several of the other adoptees, were challenged with offhand remarks about being bananas and more serious taunts of being sellouts. Most participants held fast to the belief that assimilation into the White middle-class culture of their adoptive parents was a natural, nearly unavoidable aspect of most Korean adoptees' life. The adoptees pointed out several contributing factors, namely cultural racism and the promotion of colorblind philosophy, that contribute to this natural process of assimilation (Rosaldo 1993). They also reflected on how assimilation was not their fault and that they should not be blamed (which they often were) for surrendering their Korean identities in favor of a White cultural identity, because they were not given any sustained and engaged opportunity to embrace their racial identity. Most adoptees discovered that embracing a White cultural identity led them to develop a negative self-perception of their racial and transracial identities.

Cultural Racism, Colorblind Philosophy, and Assimilation

While the attacks on September 11, 2001, the ongoing affirmative action debates in the U.S. Supreme Court, and the 2005 Hurricane Katrina disaster garnered some attention for the larger structures of racism that continue to haunt society, these forms of institutional and cultural racism are quickly labeled anomalies and can be solved in the court of public opinion. For example, in the aftermath of Hurricane Katrina, newspapers were reprimanded for their insensitivity when they depicted Black people caught on camera taking food and other supplies out of stores as "looting," whereas Whites, who were doing almost exactly the same thing, were seen as "finding supplies" (Kinney 2005). Public apologies were accepted as the media pointed the finger at individual editors and writers. Cover-ups steered the dialogue away from racial issues, and soon enough all was forgotten (Wise 2006). The questioners were silenced and the status quo continued to make others racially invisible.

Discussions about race and racism have also been silenced in schools and society through a colorblind approach centered on the logic that in order to treat people equally one should refuse to recognize race because doing so means admitting racial differences, and admitting racial differences leads one to act in discriminatory ways (Fine 1997, 2003; Lewis 2001; Tatum 1999). If everybody is colorblind, then the majority are led to believe that racists are those who act on prejudicial racial beliefs and that their actions are usually violent and destructive. Individual acts of racism are then portrayed in the media as carried out by individual racists who are often highlighted as members of an extremist White supremacy group. White supremacists certainly are not to be confused as representatives of the entire White race; rather, they are considered individuals with certain social and psychological problems. Those who commit such heinous acts are considered ignorant and not at all similar to the ordinary, colorblind White person. Cultural racism then allows people to believe that racism exists at the individual level; if one does not commit such crimes, then one is not a racist (Fine 1997, Derman-Sparks and Phillips 1997, Scheurich and Young 1997).

Some believe that racism is no longer evident in the United States—that we now live in a post-racial United States—due to the election of President Barack Obama. Millions watched Super Bowl XLI in 2007, where Lovie Smith, head coach of the Chicago Bears, and Tony Dungy, head coach of the Indianapolis Colts, were heralded as the first African American head coaches to make it to the Super Bowl. Coach Dungy will also be remembered as the first African American head coach to win the Super Bowl. People are bombarded with numerous examples that racism is "dead."

hooks contends that the belief that racism no longer exists is an attempt to "mask reality" and to further silence critical dialogues on cultural racism.

In contemporary society, white and black people alike believe that racism no longer exists. This erasure, however mythic, diffuses the representation of whiteness as terror in the black imagination. It allows for assimilation and forgetfulness. The eagerness with which contemporary society does away with racism, replacing this recognition with evocations of pluralism and diversity that further masks reality, is a response to the terror, but it has also become a way to perpetuate the terror by providing a cover, a hiding place. Black people still feel the terror, still associate it with whiteness, but are rarely able to articulate the varied ways we are terrorized because it is easy to silence by accusations of reverse racism or by suggesting that black folks who talk about the ways we are terrorized by whites are merely evoking victimization to demand special treatment. (1992, 345–346)

Cultural racism has a deep and profound influence on all people. The fact that the vast majority of people do not commit hate crimes does not mean that they are immune to the cultural racism that surrounds them on a daily basis. Tatum states, "None of us is completely innocent. Prejudice is an integral part of our socialization, and it is not our fault" (1997, 6).

Most people are unsure why their views on race and racism are shaped the way they are because they often do not question what they know and how they know it (Takaki 2003). Tatum further states that cultural racism exists in "the cultural images and messages that affirm the assumed superiority of Whites and the assumed inferiority of people of color" (1997, 6). Fine (1997) concludes that the institutions, in particular schools, uphold the standards of Whiteness as the good and right way to live; it is understood that everybody should want and strive for the same lifestyle. And West contends that Whiteness is developed as a way to control others, in particular Black people.

White supremacist ideology [i.e., cultural racism] is based first and foremost on the degradation of black bodies in order to control them. One of the best ways to instill fear in people is to terrorize them. Yet this fear is best sustained by convincing them that their bodies are ugly, their intellect is inherently underdeveloped, their culture is less civilized, and their future warrants less concern than other people. (1993, 85)

Cultural racism then forces people of color to surrender their racial and ethnic heritages in favor of assimilating into the White middle class and upholding White culture as the ideal. Rosaldo states,

North American notions of the "melting pot" make immigration a site of cultural stripping away. Seen from the dominant society's point of view, the process of immigration strips individuals of their former cultures, enabling them to become American citizens—transparent, just like you and me, "people without culture." Often called acculturation (though deculturation seems more apt), this process produces post-cultural citizens of the nation-state. In this view, social mobility and cultural loss become conflated, for to become middle class in North America is purportedly to become part of the culturally invisible mainstream. The immigrants, or at any rate their children or grandchildren supposedly become absorbed into a national culture that erases their meaningful past—autobiography, history, heritage, language, and all the rest of the so-called cultural baggage. (1993, 210)

Assimilation into the White middle class offers people of color the opportunity to become "part of the culturally invisible mainstream," yet simultaneously they are not allowed full access to all the privileges because they are still viewed as racial, ethnic, and cultural.

Colorblind ideology is a centerpiece of assimilation and cultural racism where racial differences should go unnoticed. The colorblind approach actually silences people's ideas about race, thus leaving most people unprepared to engage in a critical dialogue about race. White people are fearful that they may say the wrong thing and then be identified as racist. A person of color is fearful of saying the wrong thing and then being designated a radical angry person of color or, worse, accused of playing the infamous "race card." Most people do not want to speak openly about race, especially in racially diverse settings (Tatum 1992). This silence around issues of race is one of the main factors in the spread and sustainment of cultural racism (Fine 2003).

Assimilation as a Natural Process

Korean adoptees are not immune to cultural racism and colorblind philosophy. White adoptive parents who decide to open their homes to transracial adoptees are racially conscious, at least on a certain level. However, most adoptive parents grew up and live in the cultural racism that defines race relations in the United States. Many may uphold beliefs of cultural racism and colorblindness simply by raising and loving their transracially adopted child as their own. Several participating adoptees determined that the adoption agencies apparently did not value retention or learning of Korean culture; rather, social workers instructed parents to assimilate their children as quickly as possible into their White cultural worlds. Sophie remarked, "My parents were also the generation of assimilating your kids as fast as possible," and Bettina believed that "post-adoption services and exploring [Korean] culture and the language were not even on the radar screen when I was growing up."

Sophie and Bettina think their parents were led to believe that teaching aspects of Korean culture was unnecessary for their development and could actually cause more identity confusion. Consequently, most parents disregarded and sometimes even devalued Korean culture because they were told that being color-conscious would not allow their transracially adopted children to feel that they were full members of a White family.

By placing blame on the adoption agencies and social workers, Keiza could continue viewing her parents as good people. "I know my parents meant no harm. I know that it was a whole different time. It was a whole different mindset of assimilation." Overall, it appears that the institution of transracial adoption supported, at least at one time, assimilation as the best way to raise transracially adopted children in White homes.

Participants who were adopted in early childhood (older than four years old, as defined by the American Academy of Pediatrics) generally spoke about assimilation coming at the cost of their primary Korean culture (Ogbu 1992).[1] These adoptees endured hardship when they were forced to surrender their primary culture in favor of the culture expressed and exhibited by their White parents.

Charlotte is a biracial Korean and White woman who was adopted at the age of fourteen, along with her biological younger brother. She explained, "She [her adoptive mother] almost immediately after our arrival, . . . forbade us from speaking Korean to each other. And we were not allowed to keep in touch with anyone from Korea. She took away all our books and even dictionaries. I just could not believe it, it was just so surreal." Charlotte had many theories as to why her mother treated her and her brother this way. For one, she strongly believed that her adoptive mother had serious psychological problems and felt these problems could be solved with the love of a child. Specifically, Charlotte's mother was afraid of losing her adopted children to their birth family and culture; therefore, in Charlotte's view, she forced them to sever all ties to Korea in an attempt to lead them to believe they could never return to Korea.[2]

Brian and Woojung, who were also adopted in their early childhood years, talked about how losing the ability to speak Korean led to the loss of connection with their Korean racial identity. Most early childhood adoptees believed this sense of loss was unique in their lives, compared to those who were adopted as infants. Specifically, Brian and Woojung were somewhat aware of the disconnect to their Korean racial identities as they assimilated into their White families and communities.

BRIAN: Within a few years I completely forgot my native language. The idea back then in the sixties was the [adoption agency's] idea; bring them into a new culture and raise them in that new culture. There hadn't been that much of an attempt to retain any Korean heritage. I grew up essentially American.

WOOJUNG: I came to the U.S. and within six months I had lost my Korean speaking ability because my sister [her biological sister adopted at the same time] and I were encouraged to learn English, so we didn't speak Korean to each other at all. We were basically thrown into this culture and we immediately immersed ourselves in it so much that within three, four years I forgot that I was Korean.

Those adopted as children were able to recognize how they were losing their Korean culture in favor of their White middle-class culture. Brian and Woojung viewed assimilation as almost inevitable as the forces around adoptees pushed them to surrender their racial identity in order to be accepted into their new environment.

BRIAN: Each time we saw each other [referring to other Korean adoptees] we spoke less and less Korean and more English. We were all losing that identity.

WOOJUNG: I enjoyed school, actually, and I immersed myself in that culture pretty quickly. For a while I learned English and then did all the things that a young teenager would do.

Charlotte, who did not completely lose the ability to speak Korean and still holds on to many Korean cultural ways in her life, admitted that assimilation came quickly after her initial shock and resistance.

I was becoming like a Valley Girl, too Americanized. Back in those days, I didn't think about my adoption or talk to anyone about it. I was just trying really hard to fit in to the beach community and being the Asian Kelly Bundy. In the small beach town where everybody listened to Steve Miller nonstop, going to Grateful Dead concerts, I was becoming one of those people.

Even though Charlotte, Brian, and Woojung felt they were losing a connection with their racial identity, they all, in some form or another, held fast to the core belief that they are Korean/Asian. For example, Charlotte refers to her past life as the "Asian Kelly Bundy," and Woojung and Brian saw themselves losing their Korean cultural ways, but not their identity as Korean.

These childhood adoptees viewed the assimilation process as unstoppable. The power of wanting to fit in and be accepted was apparently overwhelming for them.[3] The desire to be accepted and even recognized as White was reinforced within their White families and communities. They could not change their Korean facial and body phenotypes; thus they believed that by acting White, they would gain some acceptance or be granted honorary White status (Tuan 1998). Kianna and Kelly, as well as many of the other adoptees, began to consider themselves White.

> KIANNA: I'm American. I'm as White as everybody else in my eyes. I dated White guys. That was it. I had no attraction whatsoever to Asians. And I just really didn't even think about trying to identify with them [Asians] whatsoever. It just wasn't important at all.

> KELLY: Probably just as an American. . . . I didn't identify as being Asian. . . . [I]t doesn't necessarily mean that I would have considered myself a Korean American growing up. . . . A lot of times you thought of yourself as White.

Clearly these adoptees were well aware that they were racially Asian, yet the push for assimilation seems to have come partially from the desire to fit in with the American (i.e., White) image. Kianna and Kelly both stated that they are American, and in their statements American equals White. Angie declared that the desire to be accepted as American led her to sometimes forget that she is physically Korean/Asian: "When I was younger, I forgot that even my sister [a Korean adoptee], . . . we forgot that we were Asian. We were so immersed in such a Caucasian culture, we just forgot."

I questioned how a Korean adoptee could forget having Asian features, because as Sophie and Daniel had pointed out, they could never truly forget they are Korean/Asian.

> SOPHIE: I obviously had it [racial identity] presented to me every time I looked into the mirror.

> DANIEL: I have two eyes; I can tell. You look in the mirror and you can tell. My adoptive family is Swedish and [sister's name, Korean adoptee] and I are in pictures with everybody and they're all six foot and blonde and we're not. I can tell.

Despite the mirror constantly reminding them that they are not White, several adoptees commented on how they simply forgot they were Korean/Asian because they were consumed with trying to gain acceptance as White, both culturally and racially. Ironically enough, as the following quotes detail, the mirror reminded them that they were, in fact, not White, but Korean/Asian. Connie and Robby, like several other adoptees, remarked,

> CONNIE: There were times that I would be in a big room and there would be a mirror and I would catch a glimpse of myself in the mirror and actually not realize that it was me. Because I was thinking, "Wow, that person looks really Asian," and it took me a second to really realize that's me looking at myself.

> ROBBY: Besides, when I looked in the mirror, I just assumed that I looked just like my parents and my family and all my friends. I didn't have a clue of what it meant to be Korean.

Connie's and Robby's statements bring light to why the adoptees may have forgotten that they are physically Korean/Asian: they had no real connection to Korean culture and strongly desired that their peers and community accept them as White. This desire even led some to want to change their outer appearance to look more physically White. Some adoptees in the study confessed that they wore blue contacts and dyed and/or curled their hair, and a few spoke of knowing Korean adoptees who opted for plastic surgery to change the shape of their eyes, nose, cheeks. According to Mary, "Even though my friend was adopted, we didn't sit around and talk about it [being adopted]. We were busy trying to curl our hair and fit into blue contacts."

Most adoptees declared that it was nearly impossible to change their phenotypes to look more White, hence they pursued other strategies to be accepted as White and ultimately were successful, at least in their surrounding communities (i.e., their comfort zones). Korean adoptees found safety and comfort within their White communities, even when, as Sophie points out, they may have been the only Korean/Asian in the community.

> The advantages, of course, of growing up in a small town of 600 people, everybody knows everybody and everybody knows your story so it wasn't like I was walking around town and people were saying, "What are you? Who are your parents? What is your situation?" Everybody already knew, so that anonymity was really great and safe.

Several adoptees concluded that it was easy to assimilate because the people in their immediate surroundings came to accept them, and the questions about race and adoption all but disappeared within their comfort zones. Some found comfort in the belief that their peers accepted them as White by not viewing them as any different; they were colorblind to the extent that the racial differences and transracial background did not seem to matter in their relationships.

This colorblind and adoption-blind attitude was reinforced by their peers' comments that the adoptees were not like the stereotypical Korean/Asian images found in portrayals in the media or in other public venues. Connie concluded, "I feel like a true-blooded American. And then other people would tell me that too. They said, 'I don't look at you as being Korean.' People tell me that all the time." Hanna spoke of the time she was trying to have a conversation with her White friend about racial differences and her friend stated, "I don't see you as being different." These comments reinforced the belief that race does not matter as long as they are accepted as a member, at least an honorary White member, in their White communities.[4] These colorblind comments apparently were the justification several adoptees needed to hear—that they had been fully accepted as racially transparent (Rosaldo 1993). Their friends did not see them as Asian or Korean. They were accepted into the community as one of them (i.e., White), at least in the colorblind eyes of those who knew them and their backgrounds.

Colorblind Approach to Race and Racism

The philosophy of avoiding dialogue about race and racism and promoting a colorblind approach contributed to the assimilation into the White middle-class mainstream. The adoptees were not willing to call their parents evil racists who restricted dialogues around issues of race, racism, and transracial adoption. The adoptees viewed their parents' attitudes toward race, racism, and transracial adoption as relatively normal, no different than most White people, and most adoptees viewed their parents as simply wanting to protect their children from the dangers found in the world.

Some adoptees believed that their parents were unable to understand the harmful effects of racism because of a lack of desire to even engage in such conversations. This indifference also stems from the belief that parents did not want their children to feel ostracized from the family due to their racial differences. Race was disregarded within the home, as Tori and Gloria discuss.

TORI: My mother was very much, "I'm colorblind and I don't see the difference."

GLORIA: In my family it [race] had always been ignored because they don't think difference matters. And I'd always felt this internal conflict. My parents kept saying that "race doesn't matter. We see the world as colorblind."

The colorblind approach seemed to silence questions about race, racism, and White privilege at home. Especially in homes where there were both biological (White) and transracially adopted children, most parents believed that they needed to be as colorblind as possible, as they did not want to show favoritism of one child over the other. Most parents do not want their transracially adopted children to feel as though they favor their biological children. Therefore, treating them all the same alleviates, in their view, any racial and biological favoritism.

When the Korean adoptees of this study ventured out on their own, beyond the comforts of family and friends, they discovered that most people are not colorblind; in fact, a majority of people were quick to point out that Korean adoptees are not White. However, like most parents wanting to protect their children, Julie's and Tori's parents were quick to advise them to roll with the punches and ignore racist comments.

JULIE: My dad is the one who basically told me, "If you can't fight them, join them. If they make fun of you, laugh with them. And sticks and stones may break your bones but words can never hurt you."

TORI: My mother's answer was of course to ignore it, turn the other cheek, and be the bigger person. And that was the mentality that I was raised with.

These comments illustrate how some parents are unable to clearly understand the psychological damage racist comments inflict on their children of color. Turning the other cheek and believing in the mantra that "words can never hurt you" is common advice for children being teased on the playground. Tatum (1997) believes that racist comments need to be addressed in critical dialogue, rather than silenced. Such dialogue will lead to a better understanding of the issues of race and racism, whereas silence will lead to greater fear of the racial other (see also Fine 2003). Yet the adoptees came to accept that their parents could never fully understand the overwhelming impact racial oppression had upon their children's lives. This may be due to their belief that parents viewed individual racism, especially at the elementary and middle school level, as similar to other forms of harmless teasing on the playground.

> JULIE: He [her father] always made it, "Well, you're being discriminated against, this is what you do. Look at the people who wear glasses—they get name-called too; what do they do? . . .You need to do the same thing that they do." That's the approach that I went away with in regards to discrimination.

> BETTINA: My parents would ask, "What did they say?" But I don't think they ever went to the school about it because it was just that they thought kids growing up get picked on by other kids and it's just a part of life. And they'd just say, "Well, just ignore it. Don't talk to them. Walk away."

> HALLE: It was very hard. In elementary school I got teased a lot by guys and they used to always call me "chink" eyes and used to always make the Asian jokes and just basically make fun of the way I look. I used to come home crying almost every day from school. My mom just [said], "Don't let them get to you." And she tried to make me feel better and say the same thing: "Kids can be cruel."

Several adoptees pointed out that their parents tried to connect to their child's experiences by equating the racist experiences of their children to a form of teasing they had experienced in school. In their advice, parents led the adoptees to believe that if they could endure the teasing, then someday they would be accepted by a colorblind world. However, Lewis clearly states why relating being teased, for example, for wearing glasses to being racially harassed is damaging.

> This strategy of deracializing incidents where racist slurs are used implies that they are like regular, everyday conflicts in which both parties should be held equally responsible; such a mode of addressing racist events makes it seem as if the victim is the one with the problem rather than the perpetrator (e.g., . . . "playing the race card"), as if they are making a big deal out of nothing. This functions as tolerance for racist slurring—implying the comments are like other put-downs that just happen to be racial. (2001, 790–791)

When Korean adoptees turned to their parents for advice on how to deal with racial harassment, some parents reacted as if their children were being overly sensitive and made them feel as if they were to blame and therefore needed to "get over" the problem. It appears as though these parents were caught in the same web of silence around racial issues, because they seemed to believe that racism involves only the overt violence displayed by White supremacist hate groups. Thus when the Korean adoptees talked about being racially harassed, their parents often viewed such incidents as harmless banter among children and best ignored. Such comments add to the silence around issues of race, racism, and White privilege, and as the adoptees further withdrew from approaching their parents, the parents may have concluded that their children were not encountering racism in their communities.

Silencing dialogue around race and a colorblind philosophy were forces that contributed to the Korean adoptees' desire to be accepted into the White middle-class mainstream. Several adoptees concluded that bringing up race and racism only caused more problems and thus tried to avoid and ignore the issues. They were often told that they had to be the bigger person by walking away from such ignorance.

In conjunction with ignoring issues of race and racism, the adoptees frequently discussed that dwelling on the issues could easily have led them to become "angry adoptees." Several discussed their interactions with and knowledge of certain adoptees who had become angry about their lives. Tori spoke of her fears that a deep investigation into her identities would result in turning against her family, friends, and community.

> There was another girl that I heard of who was adopted, and she turned. I use the phrase that my mother would say: she turned—meaning she no longer got along with her family. They blame it on the idea that she turned. I knew for the longest time growing up—I always had that sense of I don't want to be like that. I don't want to turn. I don't want to disappoint them [her parents]. I don't want them to feel bad about this, that, or the other thing.

Adoptees acknowledged that the Korean adoptees who chose to question transracial adoption and racism were soon viewed by their parents and other "well-adjusted" adoptees as deviating from the perceived "normal" Korean adoptee experience. The angry Korean adoptees were viewed as disgruntled about their lives due to factors outside the control of the parents and the adoption agencies. These adoptees were the ones who had turned against their "saviors." In order to remain fully accepted, some adoptees learned to deny the negatives and the racial contradictions in their lives. They did not want to be identified as disgruntled because it was better to remain colorblind and happy than color-conscious and angry.

The perception was that life was good in the racially unknown and unexplored. Korean adoptees did not have to face difficult questions related to their past, present, and future identities if they chose to ignore their racial and cultural differences and their transracial adoptee past. Some adoptees believed these explorations not only would lead them down a path toward anger and disgruntlement, but also that such investigations and questions were tell-tale signs of a lack of gratitude for their parents' love and good deeds.

Saved from the Streets of Seoul

"We saved you from the streets of Seoul" is a phrase that epitomizes the silencing of Korean adoptees' racial and transracial adoptee identities and promotes assimilation into the White cultural identity. This phrase gives rise to the belief that Korean adoptees are in need of saving, which sustains the long-lasting image of the "poor little orphan"; parents and White culture are the saviors, which signifies that Korean adoptees need to be eternally grateful; and the streets of Seoul are culturally inferior to White culture, which implies that the roads of their newly established White communities are paved with endless opportunities that would never have been available had they not been adopted by Whites.

The adoptees of this study were well aware that such comments coming from parents were not normal, and certainly most parents did not endorse these negative attitudes. While there certainly are parents who threaten to send their children back to Korea or state that they should never have adopted their children, especially when the child is acting defiantly, most of the adoptees in the study did not hear such statements. Rather, as they discussed in the interviews, such beliefs materialized on their own, based partially on the uncertainty of their lives as transracial adoptees (Landerholm 2001).

In their White families and communities the adoptees believed that noticing and reflecting on their racial and transracial adoptee identities would cause greater problems in their lives. Most adoptees were then made to feel that if they remained quiet about issues of racial differences and identity uncertainties, and if they upheld the belief that they had been saved from a life of turmoil and hardship in the Korean orphanages, then they would be loved and fully accepted in their families, schools, and communities. If, on the other hand, they chose to speak out about the inequalities, discrimination, racism, and White privilege, then they would be deemed ungrateful to their parents and the institutions that provided them with the means to access all the privileges and opportunities afforded in their White families and communities.

Most Korean adoptees were led to believe that their lives might have been filled with turmoil and strife in the Land of the Morning Calm[5] had their parents not rescued them from the orphanages. They were lucky to be given a chance to live in the land of opportunity and freedom. All of these beliefs sustain cultural racism and promote assimilation into a White cultural identity.

Poor Little Orphan

The image of an orphan is typically that of a child in need of a loving home. Taken a step further, one can imagine Little Orphan Annie or Oliver Twist, with their desperate and often dirty faces pressed against a window like a cute puppy waiting to be taken home. Some of the adoptees talked about how this orphan image followed them throughout most of their lives. They discussed times when strangers apologized, expressed pity, or even offered to be their new mother or father. Kelly commented, "A lot of people see us always as that kid. And it's hard for people to realize that adoptees grow up and we have opinions and thoughts on adoption that are valid. They always see us still as that little kid in that picture with the really sad look on our faces." What is interesting is that when Kelly began to speak out about the practice of transracial adoption and her experiences growing up as a transracial adoptee, her voice was often dismissed. Parents, adoption agencies, and the general public often viewed her, and other adoptees like her, as children without valid opinions and thoughts, based particularly on the "poor little orphan" image.

This image is disempowering in many ways. First, it promotes the idea that orphans are never truly able to take care of themselves and will always need some type of assistance. Second, the image does not allow orphans to grow up, which implies that they are perpetual children unable to speak for themselves. Finally, it reinforces the thinking that such poor little orphans will forever be scarred by their abandonment, thus it is better not to talk about the past, but only dream of the future.

Eternally Grateful

Even more disempowering than the above image is the recurring attitude that because parents and family members reached out and saved the "poor little orphan" from a life of despair, Korean adoptees should naturally be eternally grateful to their saviors. This mindset had a profound influence upon the Korean adoptees' racial, cultural, and transracial adoptee identities. Some spoke about how they did not feel they could ever question their adoption status, ask their parents why they chose to adopt, ask about their birth families, or challenge the institution of transracial adoption. If they ever did, then they were not properly grateful for all that was done for them. Brian and Hanna spoke on this topic.

> BRIAN: "You should be so grateful to be here." All of us [Korean adoptees] go through that some way or another. Or simply, we feel that we owe our parents something: "Thank you for all that you've given me." But the other times, [some parents] threw at you, "Little kid, you should be grateful, if it wasn't for us, you might be dead back there." That's a tough one to face.

> HANNA: She [a member of an adult adoptee group] shared a story where her adoptive mom said, "If it wasn't for me you would be a whore on the street."

These statements were meant to be hurtful and to silence adoptees, leading them to think that if they did not behave in a way their parents wanted, they risked being sent back to the "streets of Seoul." Therefore, several of the participants indicated that their adoptive parents wanted them to act like any normal American kid growing up on Main Street, U.S.A.

Brenda talked about how her mother enforced the belief that she should be forever grateful to her for adopting a hard-to-place child: "My mother, she adopted me for the reason of, 'As a Christian, I am going to rescue this poor little orphan and she better be so damn grateful to me for all I've done for her.' There's that sense of 'this child needs to be grateful.' We weren't allowed to make mistakes." The idea of making mistakes was brought up by some adoptees, particularly those who were adopted in childhood. Some came to believe that their places within their newly acquired families were fragile, and they could be sent back to Korea at any time for any mishap, great or small. As one can imagine, these particular adoptees were afraid to raise any issue—including any dialogue on racial mistreatment—that could have been perceived as a lack of gratitude toward their parents.

Some adoptees discussed how this sense of gratitude silenced questions about their birth families. Jamie felt that asking such questions would imply that adoptees were not grateful to their adoptive parents.

> One time when I was about seven I asked my mom about my birth mother. And I remember her telling me, basically the conjecture was,

"She probably loved you. She loves you very much. She probably thinks about you a lot." I remember crying, but I didn't want my mom to see me cry, . . . at the time I didn't know really what was going on. I don't think I thought about it too much because I was only seven. But now I realize what it was. Of course I felt sad, and I think maybe . . . I didn't want my mom to see me cry . . . because I . . . was worried that she wouldn't understand why I was sad. There was really no outlet for me to talk about that. I felt like there's no outlet for me to talk about my birth mother and what I thought of her. Looking back, my mom probably would have been okay with me talking about my birth mother to a certain extent. But I don't think I felt that comfort level with my mom.

The "comfort level" that Jamie refers to is not altogether clear in many of the dialogues. It seems that through their own thought processes, and possibly reflecting on their parents' inability to understand issues regarding race and racism, several adoptees chose not to openly discuss issues of birth parents and adoption with their parents. These adoptees did not feel comfortable discussing such issues with their parents because they did not want them to think they were ungrateful or did not love them.

Golden Paved Roads

The sense of obligation to their parents for saving them extended into the belief that life in Korea leads nowhere, whereas in their White communities, no matter how bad things might be, opportunities are limitless. Adoptees remained grateful for all their parents had given them, despite any shortcomings and hardships. A few revealed that they had been adopted into abusive (psychological and physical) homes, yet some nevertheless remained grateful to their parents for saving them from a life destined for despair in Korea. Brenda remarked,

My mother—I remember sitting there thinking my mother's motivation was not the best, but she did something that most people would not have done and that is she did adopt a [child] orphan disabled out of Korea and it is so hard to find families for older children and for children with disabilities. And I remember thinking at that time, I was sitting at my desk and I thought, "Oh, dear God, I am so thankful for the opportunities that I have been given, and I have the opportunities because my mother chose to give me a home and I am here at least in the states." If I had to choose whether I wanted to be here or in Korea or whatever, because I go back to Korea all the time,

I would choose to be here. I have an education, I have choices that I would never had had if I stayed in Korea. I called my mother up and I said, "We can't go back and change our past but I do thank you for adopting me because I have opportunities here that I would not have had if you not done that."

Brenda revealed several episodes of psychological abuse at the hands of her mother, yet she was nevertheless able to put this aside and see her mother and her life in the United States as better than anything she would have experienced in Korea.

Julie also experienced difficult times in her adopted home, but she still felt this was far better than living in Korea: "No matter what situation that you're from, you're living in America. We [Korean adoptees] still feel luckier. . . . I've had discussions with other Korean adoptees about that. I was always grateful; even though I went through some hard things, I was still very grateful."

When I first started working on this project, I concluded that Brenda and Julie, as well as adoptees like them, had been silenced by the overall image of the United States as far superior to Korea. This notion is reinforced by the growing number of Koreans studying in the United States and of Korean families immigrating here. However, after listening to several Korean adoptees' stories, especially Brenda's and others who were adopted as children, I realized that their beliefs were informed not simply by media perceptions that promote the United States as culturally and financially superior to Korea. Additionally, these adoptees tend to hold on to memories of hardship in Korea, whether in the orphanages or with their birth parents, and most concluded that life in the United States was a vast improvement over their experiences in Korea. The time spent in their White communities reinforced the belief that they were better off in their adopted homes, hence they were happy to assimilate into their White cultural identity.

Adoption Papers

The manner in which adoptive parents and adoption agencies handled the papers of their children also influenced Korean adoptees' views on assimilating into their White cultural identity. Granted, many adoptees had been abandoned, thus their adoption papers lack crucial information and leave many questions unanswered. This lack of information led Tori to believe that it was hopeless to even begin to investigate her identities.

For me, growing up, it was always really interesting because I was older, to boot. All of my records, of course, simply say "no data, no data on file, no record." And so, early on, when I knew that, I never needed to go into [the] whole . . . reunion of birth parents. I never went in that direction because in seeing that paper, especially . . . the fact that it kept saying "no data, no data, no data," I just automatically figured, well, that means that there is no data. That means it's hopeless. And again, because I didn't have a horribly bad family . . . I didn't want to run away from them. These were the loving people who I knew I could always come home and cry to. I never thought that I needed to run away from them, and [since] it was technically no data, well then, what, pray tell, would I need? And I never really looked at it again.

Tori's thoughts reveal how easy it was to silence her Korean racial and transracial adoptee identities, and that adoptees might come to accept this lack of information as irrefutable, and therefore there is no need to even try to uncover the unknown. Tori also indicates that added to the hopelessness of discovering the past is the belief that there is no need to search when life in one's adoptive home is relatively secure and happy. Digging into the past and attempting to identify with their racial and transracial adoptee identities would only disrupt this comfortable world order.

The adoptees discussed how the adoption agencies and parents often withheld information from them. Abby was aware of several adoptees who had been told that the building housing their records had burned down: "There were a lot of fires going around in Korea. That's what they [adoption agency] said: 'There was a fire and the place went out of business.'" While there may be a number of legitimate reasons for not releasing information to them, the adoptees believed the agencies withheld information to persuade them to believe it was pointless to look into their pasts, because they would find nothing there. Joan stated,

When I went [to Korea] in 2001, I actually talked to some people at [the adoption agency] about it [adoption records]. First of all, they said for a long time a lot of folks lied to the adoptees because they really didn't want them to look for their families or they didn't want them to see the records where it was just so minimal. They were ashamed. They would rather tell the adoptee that they had nothing or the records were burned or whatever, than actually just disclose the truth.

Many of the adoptees believed that by withholding information, both their parents and the adoption agencies were trying to protect them because they had the adoptees' best interests in mind. However, some of the adoptees felt the agencies and parents did so out of fear that the adoptees would someday discover the truth not only about their adoptions, but about the oppressive nature of the institution of transracial adoption that is sustained by a sense of White privilege and entitlement. Tammy expressed the anger she felt when she discovered the lack of information in her adoption records.

> Looking through my file, there was nothing in there. The people that I was over there with . . . were joking, "Tammy, we need to place a couple of bets to see who has the thinnest file," because we were all adopted around the same time. And I was, "Yeah, yeah, yeah, okay," just as a joke. And so I look through it and it was my vaccination card, my police report that said they had found me in the subway station, and then the list of foster mothers . . . with mine highlighted. And then on the back, just scribbled on the back, was my [adoptive] dad's name and his address in [town name]. I was looking at it and thinking that this is a goddamn sale's slip. I can't even believe that it can be just reduced to this. It's a receipt.

A few of the adoptees believed that one of the main reasons for withholding documents and information was their parents' fear of losing their adopted child. Brian clarified this point: "Some adoptive parents, especially the mothers, feel very threatened when this [adoption paper issue] comes along. A lot of them will hide their children's adoption papers. It's very interesting. There's a friction, but for the mothers it's a very threatening thing. But where they're coming from is, 'I don't want to lose my child.'" In addition, some of the adoptees rationalized that one of the underlying reasons for White parents to adopt transracially was the sense of security that their children would not have the opportunity to return to their birth families. By telling Korean adoptees that it was hopeless, next to impossible, or that Korean culture forbids them from finding out about their histories, parents and agencies led the adoptees to believe that they were the "chosen ones" and should therefore have no desire to uncover their pasts, but only think about their bright futures.

Assimilation into a White Identity: White Is Right, Korean Is Wrong

In assimilating into the White culture of their surroundings, most adoptees came to view Whiteness as the model, the norm, the right way to live (Fine 2003).[6] The negative perceptions they received about their adoption backgrounds from parents and adoption agencies, and their belief that they were saved from a hopeless life in Korea fueled their views that "White is right" and "Korean is wrong." As a result, the majority of adoptees distanced themselves from their racial and transracial adoptee identities.

This distancing was also influenced by their parents' belief in assimilation and their desire that the children not feel out of place. Sadie and Jackson discussed how their parents did not expose them to Korean culture growing up.

> SADIE: I can't say how active I was in any Asian culture activities or anything like that. I do remember my parents sending us to Korean culture camps. . . . They just sent us [her and her Korean adopted brother] twice.

> Jackson: I don't remember how old I was, maybe seven or eight years old; they [his parents] took me to some Korean evening or something that some organization arranged. They took me there just to taste some Korean food. But that was it. That was all I had during my upbringing.

Some of the adoptees reasoned that their parents did not introduce Korean culture because they wanted the children to feel that they were fully accepted in their White families and communities. Connie concluded that ignoring racial differences (i.e., being colorblind) and believing in assimilation (i.e., cultural racism) were viewed as in the best interests of adoptees, so they would feel welcome in their White families and communities.

> For all intents and purposes I was like a little American girl, so why introduce me to this other culture? They felt that I already looked different, so let me be as normal, as American or normal as I could. And that was what they were going to teach me. That's how they were going to raise me. They thought that was the best thing for me—"We don't want to raise her in Korean culture because she lives in America and she already looks different, so we don't want her to be identified as different in other ways." And that's how they felt about it.

This particular quote reveals the mindset of some adoptive families in raising their children. The philosophy of disregarding race and of viewing White as "normal" and other ethnicities as abnormal inhibited the adoptees' development of both their racial and transracial adoptee identities. Connie, like others, was told that in order to be American she had to surrender her racial identity, because being American (or normal) meant acting like White, which also implied that one cannot be both American and Korean.

It appeared that the more comfortable the adoptees became in their White families and communities, the more uncomfortable they became with their Korean and Asian heritage. Some concluded that their unease was due in part to the negativity that is associated with being Korean/Asian. The stereotypes of Asians depicted in the media played a powerful role in the adoptees' desire to dissociate themselves from the Asian and Asian American population. They were unable to identify with the Korean/Asian characters, mainly FOBs (fresh off the boat—immigrants who are stereotyped as forever foreigners due to their lack of knowledge of American popular culture and who tend to follow the culture of their ethnic heritage), overachievers in school, talented musicians, exotic females, asexual males, or martial arts experts (Palmer 1999; Pang 1997; Zhou 1997a, 1997b). Charlotte believed that adoptees' desire to be White was a way to avoid being identified as Korean/Asian.

> I've seen this not only with adoptees, but Asian Americans who grew up in predominantly White communities, where you don't see people like yourself very often. And people need role models and cool people to be able to claim some pride. And growing up, Long Duck Dong was the only Asian male image I ever had, and your people are always portrayed in such [a] degrading and insulting manner, and when you're young and insecure and you're trying to find your place these images have an impact on how you see yourself.

As a result of some of these negative images of Koreans/Asians in the media, several adoptees talked about how they feared being grouped with people who are completely foreign to them. In the process, Kendra came to loathe Koreans/Asians due in part to these negative images: "Beauty isn't White, but that's how I looked at it. White equals everything right. And Asian equals everything that I don't want to be. And that's so negative. That self-image is so negative because when I looked into the mirror and saw what I saw, that to me was a negative. I was a negative."

The principal damage of assimilation into White culture is revealed here. By uncritically assimilating into White culture, the adoptees developed a negative perception of their Korean/Asian heritage. Some hated their looks, and some spoke of their attempts to avoid all things Korean/Asian. As she began to internalize many of these harmful stereotypes, Kendra felt she had to separate from the Korean/Asian stereotypes, and expressed the anxiety she felt when she was mistakenly identified as a Korean/Asian.

It was a complete denial of being Asian. An utter, utter denial of it and to the point where I would actively look to reject people who look like me. I was embarrassed by when they spoke to me. I was embarrassed by their accent. I was embarrassed by the way they dressed, the foods they cooked, the whole thing. I did not want people, my friends, to identify me as one of them.

Connie also discussed feeling uncomfortable about being around Koreans/Asians.

In my high school there were probably, in my graduating class, . . . over five hundred people, and there were three other Asians besides me. But they were all really Asian. They had their Asian names. I never really hung out with them. I actually shied away from Asian people until recently. I don't think scared is the right word, but not comfortable around other Asians.

Because some of the adoptees feared being labeled by their White friends and peers as members of the Korean/Asian community, they saw their heritage as a hindrance, an impediment to their complete acceptance and assimilation into their White communities. Consequently, they developed an even stronger desire to be White and lost contact with their racial and transracial adoptee identities.

The adoptees moved even further into the White culturally informed communities because this was a comfortable environment for them. Tori pointed out how the desire to be White and not Korean is overwhelming for most Korean adoptees: "Pardon stealing the expression, but too many of us are still hiding in the closet here because . . . it's just the fact that we're still seeking validation and acceptance . . . from White folks and so we're trying to be White. I used to joke about the fact that I was a banana: yellow on the outside, white on the inside."

The adoptees were not explicitly encouraged to completely avoid all things Korean/Asian in their pursuit of assimilation and acceptance in their White families and communities; however, living in White environments allowed them to disregard and deny their Korean racial and transracial adoptee identities. And since parents and communities believed that recognizing racial differences would further ostracize Korean adoptees from their environments, the adoptees received little to no positive reinforcement about their racial identity. Assimilation led to disempowerment and a disconnection with their racial identity, which eventually led adoptees to connect almost exclusively with their White cultural identity.

Most Korean adoptees were quick to accept this cultural identity. By doing so, they believed that they would remain acceptable members of the normalized and dominant group, as long as they did not challenge the existing order. They did not complain about racism and racial discrimination; instead, they worked harder to overcome their differences by distancing themselves from their Korean/Asian heritage and upholding Whiteness as supreme. They felt they should remain forever grateful to their parents for saving them from a life of certain despair, far from Korea, where they could have ended up as beggars, gangsters, or prostitutes. These particular adoptees were made to believe that they had been given the greatest gift ever: a life of acceptance in the White middle class.

It was relatively easy for most adoptees to assimilate into the White culture in which they were raised. Through cultural racism, they grew up in an environment that fostered a fear of investigating issues of race because their parents had yet to consider their own White privileges and entitlements (McIntosh 1992) and had "been socialized to think of the United States as a just society" (Tatum 1992, 5).

The plethora of identity issues that arise from transracial adoptions may not have been fully thought through by many of the parents. Even in loving and supportive homes, their children questioned these issues of identity as they pertained to cultural racism. However, most adoptees in this study do not blame their parents for their perceived lack of knowledge and understanding of these issues. They accepted that their parents did the best that they could given the resources available to them at the time.

In the interviews, most of the adoptees discussed a time in their lives when they realized they were in denial about their racial and transracial adoptee identities. This awakening typically occurred when the adoptees realized that their race did not match their culture, and when they saw that they were not accepted as White. Tatum states, "Why are young people of color thinking about themselves in terms of race or ethnicity? Because the rest of the world is viewing them that way" (1999, 28). Even though the majority of adoptees viewed themselves as White, they were continually reminded that they were, in fact, not.

CHAPTER 3

Opening Pandora's Box

Dancing in Between and Nowhere at All

TORI: I felt even more out of place and this sense of loss. I don't fit in with all the White folks that I've always known. And then culturally I don't feel like I fit in with all these Asians that I supposedly blend with physically. And so that left me with a whole lot of nothing.

CATHY: I think everybody [Korean adoptees], whether they've had an identity crisis or not, [has] had the experience of we look Korean but we're not of the Korean community, we're not from a Korean social background. But on the other hand, we are from a White social background, but we're not White.

At some point in their lives the Korean adoptees of this study encountered a racial experience that sent them into a spiral of angst and uncertainty. Underlying this debilitating pain from being called a "gook" or "chink" was the shattering of their sense of reality—that the world is not colorblind. In 1903 W. E. B. DuBois stated that Blacks were constantly compelled to develop and struggle with "second-sight in this American world,—a world which yields him no true self-consciousness, but only lets him see himself through the revelation of the other world" (2004 [1903], 38). The individual develops what DuBois coined the "double consciousness," where there is "this sense of always looking at one's self through the eyes of others, of measuring one's soul by the tape of a world that looks on in amused contempt and pity" (38). Thinking about identity journeys in this way, Korean adoptees are typically compelled to accept and recognize that most of the world perceives them through their Korean racial identity, while generally ignoring their White cultural identity. However, the adoptees are generally not accepted as "authentic" Koreans/Asians within the Korean, Asian, and Asian American communities because of their culturally White upbringings.

This identity confusion is often deemed a "crisis" because it causes a great deal of pain and anger when adoptees' worldviews are contradicted and destroyed. Having lived within the cultural racism that promoted strict delineations of racial and cultural categories, most were forced to choose between being White or Korean/Asian; they could not be both. Rosaldo confirms these feelings.

> Race relations in North America involve a blend of assimilationist efforts, raw prejudice, and cultural containment that revolves around a concerted effort to keep each culture pure and in its place. Members of racial minority groups receive a peculiar message: either join the mainstream or stay in your ghettos, barrios, and reservations, but don't try to be both mobile and cultural. (1993, 212)

Most adoptees succumbed to the pressure to deny their racial and transracial adoptee identities because they wanted to fit in with their families and communities, and because they viewed Korean/Asian culture as abnormal and inferior to White culture. When acts of racial harassment and discrimination forced them to see that assimilation did not always lead to full acceptance, they felt they had been deceived into believing in a colorblind society.

Several adoptees, however, did not view these experiences as an identity crisis. This collision was not a negative; rather, it was the spark that sent them on their journeys to discover their unique identities. Instead of using the phrase "identity crisis"—a negative term that implies a destructive time in one's life—several adoptees called it an "identity awakening."[1] For them, an awakening signified the initiation of understanding their White cultural identity, as well as the beginning of a critical exploration of their racial and transracial adoptee identities.

"Oh, My God, I'm Really Korean!"

In retrospect, the adoptees realized that their parents had not always lived up to a colorblind philosophy. Specifically, the adoptees saw that when their parents attempted to introduce aspects of Korean culture, they recognized that race does indeed matter. A few adoptees also concluded that most of their parents' attempts to bring Korean culture into their lives reinforced the attitude that Korean culture is secondary to White culture, is inferior and exotic, is solely for the Korean adoptee, and should be experienced only outside of the home. In other words, even though parents claimed that they did not recognize racial differences, sending the adoptee to Korean culture camp or language school was something done only for and by the adoptee.

Contradictory Messages

Hanna discussed how her parents' attempts reinforced a cultural racism that sees White as right and the norm, whereas Korean is secondary and inferior.

I remember I went and bought a can of kimchee to take home. And I opened it and my mom was saying, "That stinks, throw that out." That actually, again in hindsight, really hurt my feelings. It wasn't meant or intended to be like a slight on me. But, when I have been really reflecting a lot back on these experiences . . . they were subtle but yet they were very powerful for me because I felt she was rejecting a part of who I was.

When Hanna attempted to bring in a part of Korean culture, her mother quickly diminished it; kimchee, as well as other aspects of Korean culture, were to be kept (both literally and metaphorically) out of sight and therefore out of mind. Tori also talked about how kimchee was perceived in the house:

Another piece of that whole entire pie is that my mother . . . we would be at the store and she'd give me the big kimchee and I felt, at the time when I was little, I felt it was more this branding. It was just marking, as saying, yes, we acknowledge the fact that you are not like your family. And my mother would say, "Go put that [kimchee] in the refrigerator downstairs because it smells." There was almost, again, [a] closeting of things because it's, "Here is your kimchee," which is stinky and bad, "and it goes downstairs."

There was an overarching belief that Korean culture was not welcome in the house. While their parents may at times have attempted to tolerate this cultural difference, some parents sent a subtle message that Korean adopted children were allowed to live in the house, but their racial heritage would remain inferior to that of their White parents.

Beyond seeing Korean culture as inferior to White culture, Hanna's and Tori's parents implicitly viewed Korean culture as valuable only to their Korean adopted children. Some adoptees discovered that when (or if) they decided to investigate Korean culture, they were left to their own devices. Some mentioned that their parents located Korean culture camps and language schools or introduced a Korean person to them. However, as Kara pointed out, most adoptees noticed that their parents seemed to take only a minor interest in Korean culture.

I remember one time my mom had some culture camp brochures for kids adopted from Korea, but it was like they were sending me away; it wasn't like they were experiencing it with me. It was more, "Well, if you want to do this, we'll ship you off and you can learn about your culture for a week." But to me it was more embarrassing. When you're a teenager all you want to do is assimilate.

This is another example of the contradictory messages that the adoptees received. They were supposed to uphold a colorblind philosophy by ignoring racial differences, yet they were also told that they are racially different from their White families and communities and should therefore learn about their birth heritage. These messages led Joan and Sophie to resist anything relating to Korean culture.

> JOAN: I remember my parents asking me if I wanted to learn more about my heritage. When I was a teenager they offered it [Korean culture] to me and I declined the offer. I actually was very stubborn about the whole thing.

> SOPHIE: At a young age, my parents asked me one time if I wanted to go to Korean culture camp and I was adamant in saying "No." But obviously it had a little bit to do with the fact that I didn't have any reflection of who I was and any understanding of why that would be important for me growing up in [a] small town because from what I remember it was, "Why do I need to do this special camp when nobody else in this town is doing a special camp?" or "Why do I have to pretend I'm different or do something special?" And they never brought it up again.

I was intrigued by the adoptees revealing their negative feelings toward Korean culture as children because those who had had little exposure to Korean culture growing up often wished that their parents had provided opportunities for them to interact with Koreans and Korean culture. The adoptees who had been given opportunities to attend Korean culture camps, churches, and language schools often resisted because they did not want to be identified as different from their White families and peers. Exposing adoptees to Korean culture was seen not only as a recognition of racial differences, but also of Korean culture as being available solely to the adoptees because they were not viewed as *fully* White. One could conclude, therefore, that there does not seem to be one correct way to introduce Korean culture into the adoptees' lives because, on one hand, it was forced upon them, and, on the other, there was not enough exposure. However, through our conversations, it became apparent that adoptees felt parents needed to allow them to embark on their identity journeys on their own, while at the same time providing opportunities for the adoptees to investigate their identities.

In other words, there seemed to be a power struggle over who had control over the adoptees' identity journeys.

For example, the adoptees who attended culture camps as children and teenagers recognized that the camps were organized by the parents and adoption agencies. In reflection, Cathy and Alex dismissed critical investigation into their racial and transracial adoptee identities because the camps seemed to provide a stereotypical perspective of Korean culture.

> CATHY: We have a Korean teaching staff coming over from Korea. And there's Hangul class, music class, dance class, taekwondo; they can choose between taekwondo or dance, and then we have recreation time. They stick all the parents in the kitchen to cook Korean food with the supervision of Mrs. Kim. So we have a Korean lunch. It's pretty much learning the basics. I mean, I wouldn't say that I have anything of a firm grasp of the Korean language or Hangul. It was nice just to learn about Korean culture.[2]

> ALEX: It was my summer camp. I think the most exciting thing . . . was those Friday lunches because that was the only time I got to eat some kimchee and some *bulgogi.*

The adoptees realized that cultural competence in the Korean community may not have been their parents' main purpose in introducing Korean culture to them, which led some adoptees to conclude that their parents' sporadic and at times insincere approaches to Korean culture sent contradictory messages about race and culture. On the one hand, they were raised to ignore their racial identity through a colorblind philosophy; on the other hand, because their parents felt they needed to learn about Korean culture, adoptees received the message that they were, in fact, racially Korean (i.e., not White).

Birth of a Child

One of the more interesting identity awakenings occurred when Korean adoptees had children themselves.[3] The birth of a child initiated reflection on a variety of issues concerning their identities, in particular their racial identity. For Cindy and Brenda the births of their first children allowed them, for the first time, to see their Korean physical features as beautiful, because for most of their lives they had been led to believe that White was the standard of beauty. West confirms these adoptees' beliefs: "The myths offer distorted, dehumanized creatures whose bodies—color of skin, shape of nose and lips [and eyes], type of hair, size of hips—are already distinguished from the white norm of beauty" (1993, 83). The birth of their children allowed them to accept the fact that they are Korean and they are beautiful.

> CINDY: When my son was born, I just looked at him and I had this overwhelming feeling that he was beautiful. That he was Asian and Asian looking and he was beautiful. And I hadn't experienced that before. I thought being Asian was not good, because I didn't see beauty in the Asian face and Asian features. He's so Asian and he's so beautiful; that was the turning point for me. He had beautiful eyes and they were my eyes.

> BRENDA: I was always told for so many years, for the first years of my life, how I had so many things wrong with me. And then having my daughter, I thought my daughter was the most beautiful baby I had ever seen in my life. I used to just [lie] there and just watch her because she was so beautiful to me, and I remember thinking, how could something so beautiful come from something so ugly? And she was a turning point . . . maybe God wasn't so bad and he rewarded me with something that was so beautiful, and she was so perfect.

Both women clearly express the harmful impact that assimilation had on their self-perceptions. The pain is still evident, as they even now see themselves as "ugly." However, once they had given birth to their Asian-looking children, both used the phrase "turning point" to describe how their negative thoughts about being Korean dissipated—they saw their children as beautiful with the Korean phenotypes they had received from their mothers (both women had White spouses).

These mothers were then forced to reevaluate their racial identity because they had passed this identity on to their children. They soon realized that someday their children would ask questions about what it means to be racially Korean. They worried that they would not be able to answer these questions because for most of their lives they had completely ignored—and in some cases actively resisted—anything related to Korea. Cindy and Karina feel that as parents, they do not want their children to experience similar negative feelings about their racial identity.

> CINDY: Having this connection to the past through him [her son], I realized that I should really try to find some things out so that I can pass them on to him. Because [of] my experience growing up

and not having that connection to my Korean identity and not having exposure to Korean people or any pride in being Korean, I wanted to give him some of that connection to his Korean identity. And I thought it would make it easier for him.

KARINA: My dad's statement was, "Your oldest daughter, she's just like you." And it made me think, who am I like? I've got these children and they're like me. Who do I resemble? Who am I like? . . . It came to a point where, I'm Korean and I want to share this with my kids. . . . I didn't have the Korean pride growing up, but I wanted them to have pride in being Korean.

For most of the adoptees who had become parents, their children were the only biological connection they had (at least to whom they knew they were connected). More important than the biological connection was the conviction these adoptees felt in not wanting their children to endure the same identity confusion that they had experienced.

They wanted their children to develop a sense of pride in their racial selves—something most of these parents were unable to attain in their attempts to assimilate into their White communities. These parents were able to recognize how important it was to stress the significance of both cultures—Korean and White—in their households beginning at the birth of their children and continuing on a daily basis.

Leaving Their Comfort Zones

The awakening to their racial and transracial identities led several adoptees to reflect on how others saw them; they reasoned that if they were aware of how they stood out among a crowd of White people, then others certainly would view them as being racially different from the White majority. Safe within their comfort zones (i.e., within the communities where they grew up or had established themselves), Korean adoptees were able to dismiss many of these thoughts of being recognized as racially different. However, once they stepped outside these comfort zones, they awakened to the fact that they were not accepted as White.

Several adoptees spoke of how strangers had made it clear that they are not White. Michelle and Hanna viewed their awakenings as the realization that most people could not see their White cultural identities and instead focused mostly on their racial identity.

MICHELLE: I did not notice being Korean until I got here [college] because—and it sounds terrible—but it was . . . I got bombarded with e-mails about being in the multicultural club, about being in the Asian club. . . . Both times I was set up with the—I hate saying this—the non-White admissions counselor, and she happened to be Asian. I would rather just not have that.[4]

HANNA: I remember getting off the airplane and walking down, and in hindsight this guy was pretty accurate because he walks up to me and he opens up this booklet, and it's a map of Korea and he [told] me, "Sign this petition for your country." In hindsight, most people would think I'm Chinese or something else, but I remember my reaction was, "I'm not Korean. I'm American."

With more people recognizing them as Korean/Asian, especially outside their comfort zones, the adoptees were confronted with the reality that they are not White. Some eventually realized that no matter how much they might have believed in and adhered to aspects of White culture, their Korean racial identity would always be recognized while their White cultural identity typically would go unnoticed.

"Oh, My God, I'm Not Korean!"

Through the assimilation process, most adoptees denied and disregarded almost all aspects of Korean culture and therefore grew up with little to no knowledge about it.[5] However, when they were recognized as Korean, and yet were unable to associate with what it meant to be Korean, some felt embarrassed about their lack of knowledge of Korean culture. Some adoptees associated with non-Korean people who often knew more about Korean culture than they did, which in turn made the adoptees feel both inferior and somewhat ignorant. For example, Michelle came to realize that she needed to connect to Korean culture because of her White friend.

We were talking about taekwondo and how he [a White friend] knew more about Korea than me. He knew the writings because he had been in taekwondo so long and he knew certain other facts. And having him know more than me, I just felt that this is sad. And he wasn't of Korean descent; he's actually Caucasian. It's because he knew the sport. But I felt that [it's] pretty sad that I don't know this and he knows more than I knew. I know that I shouldn't feel sad. It's just I should welcome that new information, but it was more like maybe I should learn something about the country myself.

This situation speaks volumes about the privileges that White people have in consuming other cultures. Some scholars view this as cultural colonialism or cultural imperialism, while others see Whites attaching themselves to other cultures because they do not feel that White is a culture (Apple 1997, Fine 1997, S. Lee 2005, Said 1993).

Witnessing Whites taking ownership of Korean culture often coerced the adoptees into trying to gain entry into their local Korean community. However, Amber and Tammy felt like imposters because they were viewed as lacking cultural knowledge of the community.

AMBER: When I would meet my Korean friends' parents for the first time, they'd always want to speak to me in Korean and I'd have to explain I don't speak Korean. It was the biggest shame because I couldn't speak Korean. I'd always have to explain: "I'm adopted, my parents are White Americans, they don't speak Korean, [and] they never taught it to me." And so they'd at least be forgiving of the sin that I didn't speak Korean. But then there'd be that shift there that I wasn't a real Korean.

TAMMY: It's just having Korean people come up and speak to me in Korean. I remember it happened maybe once or twice. I went to D.C. for some choir trip in high school and this woman began speaking Korean to me and I got really mad. I said, "I don't speak Korean." And she said, "Your parents didn't make you learn it, right?" And I said, "My parents are White." And then I walked away. The friend that I was with, he's Caucasian; he said, "You didn't . . . have to be so mean to her." I was just pissed. And I knew that if I really explained he wouldn't understand anyway.

These feelings of inadequacy in negotiating Korean cultural terrain weighed heavily on several adoptees. Many felt that they were looked down upon, even openly criticized, for not knowing how to speak Korean or for being unfamiliar with aspects of Korean culture. Some felt they were unfairly blamed. Some adoptees also apparently were angry because they had to reveal their transracial adoptee identity in order to gain some forgiveness for not having a connection with their racial identity. Perhaps they were also angry that they were recognized as Korean, while their White cultural identity was completely ignored.

For many of the Korean adoptees the awakening to their racial and transracial adoptee identities occurred when they left home to attend college. This was their first time around a significantly larger population of Korean

Americans, Asian Americans, and international students from Asia. In this new atmosphere, and with the belief that they should know more about what it means to be Korean, some attempted to join their college's Korean Students Association (KSA). Bettina and Tori spoke of their attempts to join the KSA.

> BETTINA: When I went to college I started having an identity crisis. I didn't really feel like I fit in with the KSA because most of the people were native Korean speakers and I didn't know anything about the language and the customs.

> TORI: I thought to myself, "Okay, I am going to join the Korean Student Association." Honestly, I've joked about it to this day—I should have joined the Iranian Student Association; it would have been the same thing. It would have been the same difference, because I got there and the majority of the students are directly from Korea. I walked out there onto the quad, they're talking in Korean, they're playing Korean hand games, and I'm feeling completely like I didn't fit in there either.

While not all the adoptees attempted to join KSA or, for that matter, attended college, the point is that some felt inadequate when attempting to join the Korean community. There were certainly times when Koreans pointed out to the adoptees that they were not authentic Koreans, yet more often than not it was the Korean adoptee who determined for her/himself that s/he did not belong within the Korean community.

It is also interesting how the adoptees quickly pointed out that Koreans in the KSA came directly from Korea and they viewed them as "authentic." These were the Koreans some of the adoptees sought out to help them connect with Korean culture. However, due mainly to a cultural divide, the adoptees found it difficult to develop strong relationships with these "authentic" Koreans, especially romantic ones. Kris and Charlotte attributed this divide to their negative experiences with and perceptions of Koreans.

> KRIS: There was a group of Koreans [in high school] who were fresh off the boat—fobbie, as we called them. But they always stuck together. There was a group of about ten of them. A lot of my White friends asked, "Do you ever hang out with them?" And I said, "No." I don't think I can relate to them because they all speak Korean and I don't. They all have that cultural background and they all eat kimchee and they all do this and that. I don't think I [could] really hang out with them or [find]

myself being friends with them. I was friendly with them, and in the beginning they were asking me, "Who are you?" because they could tell that I was Korean. I dated a boy in that group and it was really very difficult. It was my first and only Asian boyfriend. And . . . needless to say it didn't work out. I think a lot of it was because he'd feel uncomfortable bringing me around with all of his Korean friends and they would be drinking *soju*[6] and speaking in Korean. I could do the *soju* part, but not the speaking in Korean.

CHARLOTTE: I consciously or maybe subconsciously avoided Asian men, in particular Korean men, because of my background. I knew that they would never accept me. There have been maybe one or two Korean guys who expressed an interest. But I knew that never in a million years would their parents bother with me. I think pretty highly of myself; why would I put myself through that? Where, as far as I know, none of my White boyfriends ever made an issue out of it. Whereas [with] the Koreans it just goes on and on and . . . my Korean American girlfriend's mother kept on making disparaging remarks about me. So imagine trying to date or marry one. So that ruled out Korean guys altogether [in] my book.

Possibly fearful of being rejected due to their adoptive backgrounds, the adoptees talked about their weariness of developing intimate relationships with those they perceived as authentic Koreans. Their relationships with Koreans appeared, at least on the surface, on the level of acquaintance-ship—those who could provide them with Korean cultural knowledge. This sensation of "dancing in between and nowhere at all" led the majority of the adoptees in this study to search for connections, a place where they could find comfort in their identities—where they believed their outer appearance would match their inner feelings.

Opening Pandora's Box: Initial Exploration of Their Racial and Transracial Adoptee Identities

JULIE: I honestly didn't know where to begin, and I wasn't sure if I wanted to tackle it and open up Pandora's box. I was actually afraid. I've held back on opening that door because I wasn't quite sure if I really wanted to trigger any memories because I just didn't feel like I wanted to go there. I'm still very wary of the emotional aspect of this and opening Pandora's box.

For the most part these identity questions occurred during adolescence, when the adoptees, like most teenagers in the United States, had doubts about their identities and place in society (Goldstein 2007). For almost all of the adoptees their identity awakenings led them to search for connections with their racial and transracial adoptee identities in the hopes of finding where they truly belonged. However, their initial attempts to explore their identities often led to more confusion and uncertainty. For some, this crossroads led them to revert to their White cultural identity. Others were determined to be accepted for their racial identity. Still others developed relationships for the first time with Korean adoptees who were also questioning and reflecting on their identities, which allowed them to feel secure in their transracial adoptee identity. Opening Pandora's box should not be seen as engaging in an exploration of their racial and transracial adoptee identities; rather, it is the result of their identity awakenings and thus should be viewed as a time when the adoptees first test their identities.

Awakening to a Racial Identity: First Visit to the Motherland

Twenty-eight of the adoptees made at least one trip back to Korea: five traveled on an adoption agency-sponsored tour, two were members of Korean government-sponsored trips, three were part of a group visit, two studied at a university in Seoul, a few traveled with their mothers, one traveled on her own, and two traveled through a university-sponsored study abroad program. The following are examples of the ways in which the adoptees described their first trips to Korea.

> CONNIE: I had just been to Korea in May of 2003, and that was my first trip back. I was there for almost two weeks and I stayed with a friend of mine [a Korean adoptee] who was living there. That was my first introduction to being in Korea.

> SOPHIE: I've been back to Korea once. I went back three years ago and I was there for a month. I did an international summer school program where adoptees go back to Korea for the first time and then they provide essentially a tour and school setting.

> JOAN: I spent two weeks in Korea. And, that was . . . hard, actually. Because I did it all alone, I wasn't really prepared. I really didn't have anyone. I did it completely on my own and I had no contacts there. I contacted the [adoption agency] office and I got a tour of the orphanage that I came from and that was about

it. I explored a lot of Seoul and outside of Seoul. I did a lot of exploration in that sense.

KRIS: The first time I visited Korea was the summer of my senior year of high school. I went on a Motherland Tour with my parents. They did the whole showing the orphanages, going to [the adoption agency], going to [an] unwed mother's home, which was really amazing, and doing the tour of Korea, seeing all the touristy sites. We actually went back to my orphanage and brought back presents and talked to the director.

These reflections illustrate the diversity of the adoptees' experiences in returning to Korea for the first time since their adoptions. The dialogues highlight how each had different expectations, dreams, and hopes about their first return to Korea. And although their trips were short-lived, all of the adoptees discussed how the experiences had a profound effect on their identities.[7]

One of the major awakenings to their racial identity that occurred during these first trips to Korea was the comfort of being around people who looked like them. Indeed, nearly all of the participants grew up in predominantly White small towns, so simply being in a place where they were in the racial majority allowed them to connect with their racial identity. Connie discussed how this was the first time that she could actually blend in with the crowd.

My first experience going to Korea, the first couple of days I was there, it was just so weird because I was thinking, "Oh, my God, I've never been around this many Asian people ever. We must be here for an Asian conference because why else would so many Asian people be all together." I thought it was weird, but at the same time it was such a relief to blend in and not be the sole Asian person. It was so nice to blend in with everybody else.

Most spoke of how the feeling of being constantly watched suddenly disappeared because they were now part of the racial majority. Several mentioned that the fear of being called a racial epithet disappeared as they walked around Korea. A few attempted to connect their feelings of being part of the racial majority with what their White family members and peers must feel on a daily basis in the United States. Some were able to understand why their parents, friends, and community members often promoted a color-blind philosophy. It was relatively easy to uphold such a philosophy when one became a member of the majority race, because the colorblind philosophy views everyone as the majority (Lewis 2001).

However, this feeling of belonging was short-lived for most adoptees. Jackson and Connie realized that they were not considered Korean because they did not know how to navigate through Korean culture—they could not speak the language and, most important, they did not feel culturally Korean.

> JACKSON: It's weird because I felt like a tourist in a place where I should almost feel like home. People were asking me, "Didn't you feel like you were home?" And I told them, "No." When I walked around in Seoul, I remember the first day, my brother [biological brother, also adopted] and I walked out from the hotel and . . . just walked around for a little bit and everybody looks Korean, but I don't feel I'm Korean. That whole thing . . . [is] weird because everybody looks like me but I still feel like I'm not one of them.

> CONNIE: I was also very aware that I stood out. For example, I would be on the subway and my friend and I would be speaking English and everybody would be looking at us like, "What are you saying? Because you look Korean, but you're not speaking Korean." And then when people would come up to me and ask me something in Korean, I would say, "I don't know what you are saying."

This awakening to the fact that they were not accepted as Korean by Koreans often led to disappointment and even anger toward Koreans. Some adoptees said their trips to Korea left them feeling that they had been rejected twice by Koreans: first when Korean society upheld rigid beliefs in bloodlines that restricted adopting someone else's child, and then when they returned to Korea, only to be treated with disdain for not knowing Korean language and culture and looked down upon, almost pitied, by some Koreans for being an adoptee.

Expectations then played a major role in their experiences in Korea. It was rather interesting how these adoptees prepared for their first trips to Korea. Some did not have big expectations prior to their trip; they simply wanted to visit the land of their origin, but did not necessarily believe it would be a life-changing event. Others admitted that they tried to put up a serene front, when in reality they were anxious about a number of things.

Almost all of the adoptees (except those adopted as children) stated that for all their lives they had, to some degree, imagined and fantasized about life in Korea. Kara dreamed of a perfect world, and when she experienced Korea firsthand, her fantasies were largely shattered.

> I did go over to Korea for the first time this past year. It was amazing. At first I hated it and I felt so guilty, after thirty years of imagining what you think Korea is going to be like, you can't even know. I mean, it was everything that I thought it was and nothing that I thought it was. The first few days I hated it. I felt so guilty and so bad. I thought this was terrible, this is awful, I hate this place.

The expectation that a visit to the Motherland would allow adoptees to finally feel at home often led to disappointment and more confusion. Keiza and Amber were not prepared for the range of emotions that would surface during their visits.

> KEIZA: Deciding to go to Korea was humongous. It was a turning point. Since that trip, my life just has not been the same. I've really struggled with my identity and who am I, the whole where am I from [question].

> AMBER: People ask me about that trip and I can't sum it up in one sentence. I mean, it was horrible and it was wonderful all at the same time.

The majority of the adoptees who traveled to Korea opened Pandora's box and revealed what they had attempted to hide and exposed their fantasies as unreal. Michelle and Charlotte had a lot of difficulty making sense of their newly informed identities.

> MICHELLE: After my Korean trip, I didn't care. That was partly because [of] my reaction to the situation that was over there at the time. I didn't want to learn anything about Korea anymore. If someone brought up, "How was your trip?" I got a little hostile and turned away.

> CHARLOTTE: The first time was just traumatic; I mean, I had so many mixed-up thoughts and feelings and I was just really, really confused and just feeling really, really sad, just comparing my life to that of my friends who had stayed in Korea. I can't even figure out what actually happened. I just crashed after the first trip. So the first trip was really, really hard.

By opening Pandora's box, several adoptees were forced to see that they are neither Korean nor White. The contradictions, confusions, and uncertainties left many wondering if they should stop searching for the unknown and simply be happy living with a White cultural identity, even if it meant denying their racial and transracial adoptee identities. Nevertheless, opening this part of their lives often led to more questions about their past lives, especially their transracial adoptee identity. Thus several of the adoptees began opening up their adoption papers, speaking with adoption agencies, and questioning their parents about the adoption.

Adoption Agencies, Adoption Papers, and Learning about the Past

For the adoptees who traveled to Korea, part of the itinerary included visits to their adoption agencies and orphanages. These visits often spurred a strong desire to search for birth families. However, the paperwork for most adoptees was minimal at best. Joan noted the impact her "empty" history had on her identity.

> When they pulled out my records, when I went to go see [the adoption agency], they told me that they didn't have any of the original files at all. They really had nothing for me. And so that was really hard. I just think going back to your Motherland brings up a lot of questions. It was really hard to imagine myself in the country where my birth mother may or may not be there. I just thought I would be able to get a little bit more knowledge from the orphanage. I really didn't get a whole lot from them either. They really didn't greet me with open arms at all. In fact, I was supposed to stay there for three weeks and I cut my trip short. I just went home. I was tired. I was also really heartbroken. When I went to the orphanage and they told me that they didn't have anything, I was like a little lost puppy. I just remember only certain points of . . . being completely alone in the city and I remember being so devastated after my meeting at [the adoption agency]. I was just so crushed.

Joan's disappointing experience was similar to many of the adoptees in this study. They went to Korea with expectations, hoping to find some connection to Korea and in particular their birth families. However, when they were met with empty files and coldness from their adoption agencies, it shattered their dreams.

These meetings with adoption agencies were understandably emotional for most of the adoptees. Keiza stated that she did not really expect anything to come of the initial meeting; however, it uncovered emotions that she was unprepared for.

I was totally content in my little perfect world that I grew up in. When I went to Korea for the first time . . . they had me go to my agency, and this woman pulled out my file and there it was, I mean, this old, yellowed paper, this brown file, that had my name on it, that had the same documents in it that I had copies of and had the same picture in there that I had of myself. And she asked me, "Do you want to find your Korean family?" I mean, I hadn't even thought about that; that's not why I was there, and if I [said] no now, [I'd] never have the chance to even change my mind. I just said, "Okay, yes." So she said write your contact information down. I did that. She gave me, without any proof or documentation, . . . pieces of information that I had never had. I mean, she told me that my birth mother was dead. I mean, she told me all these things that had no basis whatsoever. I just left there being totally confused and not knowing if she was just making up some story because I was there or if this really was true. I just didn't know what to think.

Several important aspects can be gleaned from Keiza's story that reflect many of the adoptees' experiences with their adoption agencies: first, there is a sense that if the adoptee did not act immediately, all information could be lost; second, adoption files were often inconsistent; and third, because the adoption files were often viewed as unreliable, most adoptees were generally suspicious of the information given to them.

Most adoptees went to their adoption agencies because they believed it was the expected and normal thing to do while in Korea, even if they did not believe anything would come of it. When they were given information that contradicted previous knowledge, they often viewed it as a half-truth or as a ploy to dissuade them from searching for their birth parents. Alex spoke at length about being exposed to additional background knowledge about his birth parents.

Here's a big part of my first trip back. I had always been told that I had been abandoned when I was a day old and found on a church doorstep in a basket, no note and no knowledge of my parents. Therefore, the idea of [a] search was never a big thing for me. I just figured [it was] too hard for me to do. And I [didn't] want to go back and break up any families or anything like that. But then when we went to [the adoption agency] and I looked at my file, at first, I thought, "This isn't my file!" They said, "No, no, it's you." The file is very different from the one I have at home. I was born in a hospital. It had information on my birth mother. It probably didn't sink in until I got back from Korea; that's when I started really thinking more about searching. That was a big transition period for me. For twenty-one years I had figured there is no way I'm ever going to be able to find my birth parents and therefore there's no point in searching. Then, boom, I was given this other information. I didn't know what to do with it at first. And I still had that feeling that there's no point in searching.

It is interesting that Alex's adoption story is often retold in the U.S. mainstream media: he was left at a church in a basket. Several adoptees had similar stereotypical notions about their abandonment. Some adoptees, however, were told of being found eating out of garbage bins, walking aimlessly, or begging on the streets.

The adoptees who were able to gain new information about their histories reacted in different ways, yet most viewed it as a means of taking control of their adoption stories. Rather than passively receiving the stories that had been told to them, they could now actively discover them for themselves. This awakening in some ways was the beginning of their journey toward empowerment, because from the beginning most adoptees had been told that it was fruitless to search for answers to their past. Some were told that a fire had destroyed all the paperwork or that record keeping was minimal because that was way the system worked at the time of their adoptions.

More damaging were the stories adoptees heard about birth families refusing to meet with them due in part to embarrassment and the shame it would bring to the birth families. It appeared that the full truth was hidden from the adoptees, which only perpetuated the notion that adoptees must forever be protected, always treated like lost orphans.

Hanna's story epitomizes the notion that information should be withheld from adoptees until they come of age (and it is difficult to determine what that age actually is).

I had come home for October break and I remember it got very quiet and very serious. My parents said, "There is something that we need to tell you." And I'm thinking, "Oh, what did I do wrong?" I was trying to think about what I did to get into trouble. And my parents pulled out a letter from my paternal grandfather from Korea. He had written this letter when I was about thirteen or fourteen. [My family was] divided at that time, [with] my brother and my mom saying wait until she's older, my dad and my sister saying tell her right now. And my parents ended up consulting . . . another adult adopted person.

I don't think she was necessarily a Korean adoptee. But she said wait until she's a little bit older. And so that's what they did. It was very profound for me because, first of all, the feeling of it was, I knew I was . . . from Korea. It was like my fairytale book seeing this letter, and there was this grainy picture of my paternal grandparents. It was almost like these fairytale figures stepping out of the book and being real. And I was thinking, "This is so out of control." And I remember my parents later on saying that they were surprised that I really didn't do anything about that. It was a little too much. I wasn't really ready to digest that information. When I read this letter at nineteen, there was this incredible pull towards Korea. I really should go there. But then I thought, "Why do I want to go there? Is it just because I got this letter? What would I want to go for?" I couldn't answer those questions and I feel fortunate that I didn't really act on it right away because I had not begun to process my own adoption experience. My adoption story had always been something told to me. And I think at different times in my development I integrated different parts of it, and I remember very distinctly at around eleven or twelve thinking, "Korea is really far away. It's a whole other language. I'll never find those people anyway." And pretty much that was it, extinguished. I didn't think of biological people related to me until this letter walked into my life. And even then I wasn't ready to handle that.

Hanna's parents and older siblings ultimately chose, partially based on the opinion of one adoptee, to withhold Hanna's past from her. And when this information was given to her at the age of nineteen, five years after they had received the letter, Hanna was still confused, still not sure what to do with it. Hanna's story shows how Korean adoptees' stories are often not their own. By withholding information, families convey to the Korean adoptees that they are not ready to control their own identities.

It is not my intent to minimize any Korean adoptee's story, nor do I want to challenge parents' and adoption agencies' decisions to withhold information from the adoptees. What I would like readers to glean from these excerpts is that for most of their lives their adoption stories were presented to them (i.e., they had no control over their stories). Once they began to learn more about their pasts, some adoptees were encouraged to seek answers for themselves and on their own terms.

Each of the adoptees dealt with this new information in their own way. Some, like Keiza, refused to accept it as true. Others, like Alex, Hanna, and Kris, while reluctant to fully acknowledge such startling information, were intrigued by the possibility of locating their birth parent(s). Kris stated,

The first time I went to Korea, we went back to the orphanage and found out that . . . my records [given to her parents when she was adopted], which . . . said "abandoned" or "information unknown" on them, weren't actually true. I guess it said that [I'd] been dropped off at a police station and I had no identifying information; I was abandoned. That was it—"Unknown information." But when we went there [to her orphanage for the first time], the director of the orphanage . . . I guess it had been such a long time that he'd probably seen hundreds of thousands of children go by and maybe forgot the falsified story. He said, "You weren't abandoned. Your birth mother came to me." Then he proceeded to tell me this whole new story that I [had] never heard before. He said that I had actually spent time with her for the first year and a half of my life and had been going in and out of the orphanage for the last couple of months. That was just a shock [in] itself. And at that point I was thinking, "Oh, my gosh! Is she alive? Where is she? Where does she live?" And he said, "She's still alive. She lives in [city name]. She has a new husband." And I was saying, "Oh my God."

It is difficult to imagine the range of emotions that these adoptees experienced when they discovered that what they had believed all their lives was suddenly exposed as false. Some were angry at being lied to their entire lives. Others became very curious about the possibility of meeting their birth parent(s). Whatever the emotion, it is apparent from Julie's account below that this new information allowed her to develop an attachment to her beginnings and to her racial identity.

I do know one thing that has meant a tremendous amount to me in regards to my awakening, as far as who I am as a Korean, was when my mom gave me my case history report of who I am. The social worker gave a list of my height, my weight, where I was found, and what my personality was. The fact that they had that bit of history prior to my adoption made me feel whole because I don't have infant pictures that I can go back to. I don't have any real identity. I don't feel like I have an identity with anybody. So when she gave that to me, that is when I really felt like I'm really Korean. This is who I am on this piece of paper. That was emotional for me. I was crying; I mean, I bawled when I got it because it was a connection that I needed to reconnect [to]. I no longer ignore who I am as a Korean because this is who I am. It started with this piece of paper and this history. When she gave that to me that was huge. I mean, that's when

I became more open to being active about my culture, who I am as a Korean, and what Koreans do and their traditions and all that stuff.

Whether their stories were based on fairytales or terrible beginnings, the overall theme rests in the fact that their stories were consistently told to them, and embedded in most of these stories was the implicit notion that it was pointless to search for connections to their past. For most of their lives the adoptees had been told that no information existed, which rendered a birth family search useless. This strong dissociation with their past led to a disconnection with their racial identity. An awakening to their identities meant becoming aware of how their race and transracial adoptee background informed and influenced their everyday lives. However, discovering their identity was not solely about an awareness of the fact that they were Korean; it was also about discovering what it meant to be a transracial adoptee and the issues related to being one.

Awakening to a Korean Adoptee Community

For many of the Korean adoptees, meeting others like them was the first awakening to their racial and transracial adoptee identities. Most discussed turning to transracial adoptee groups for information, bonding, and understanding as they took their first steps with their identities. However, before examining how meeting Korean adoptees inspired them to investigate their identities, we must first ask this: what inspired them to reach out to transracial adoptees in the first place? This is an important question, because it allows us to understand the spark that encouraged them to seek a connection with their identities. The adoptees' answers centered on two main factors: their mothers and the Internet.

Mothers as the spark. For some adoptees, the awakening to a transracial adoptee identity was initiated by their mothers. Mary stated, "The summer before I came here [to college], my mom actually found [a Korean adoptee group] on line. I came to their summer barbecue and met everybody and decided I liked the group and joined." Jamie's story is also interesting: her mother happened to run into another parent who had adopted a child from Korea, and this initiated an interest in Jamie to begin investigating her transracial adoptee identity.

[My mother is] talking to this guy and making all the arrangements [for docking a boat at the harbor] and at the end she said, "Oh, can I get your name just in case something goes?" He said his name was Jin. And she said, "Oh, well that's a different name; what kind of name is that?" And he said it was Korean. And it turned out, of course, she said, "Oh, my daughter is Korean." And they had the whole conversation. He was the harbor master's son and he had been adopted [from Korea]. He wasn't there when she got [there], but she talked to the harbor master. They were talking about us. And he said that Jin had written down the reservation information, but then also added a note, "Her daughter's a Korean adoptee," with an exclamation point. They started comparing notes on us. And basically she was telling me this story. I didn't become interested in meeting other Korean adoptees until my mom told me about this conversation. And that's when I suddenly realized, that . . . there are more people out there. I never thought about it until then.

It is interesting, at first glance, that Mary's and Jamie's mothers were more informed about or perhaps more aware of Korean adoptee issues than their children. However, adoptive mothers do not have to navigate all the emotions that surface when discussing issues related to the transracial adoption experience. Moreover, when adoptive mothers investigate these issues, it is nonthreatening, to a certain extent, to their White racial identities.

Korean adoptees, on the other hand, live with these issues daily, and some try to hide from any dangers that might arise if they choose to explore their racial and transracial adoptee identities. The adoptees often viewed opening this Pandora's box as both scary and risky because of stories they had heard about angry adoptees or those who had turned against their parents. Avoiding these identities allowed most adoptees to remain content with their White cultural identity.

Most adoptees believed that actively involved adoptive mothers (as well as mothers who encouraged transracial adoptees to connect with these issues) should be applauded for their efforts because these mothers encouraged the children to take the first steps toward empowering their identities. However, some of the participants wanted to caution that at times such efforts can be viewed as a form of colonizing in that some adoptive mothers (and advocates) tend to take on the issues as their own, due in part to their enthusiasm, without realizing the difficulty that some adoptees may have in navigating through many of the issues associated with transracial adoption.

Connecting on the Internet. In the late 1990s the Internet craze swept the globe. Online groups were formed around almost every issue imaginable (Fabos 2004). The Internet became a spark for many of the adoptees in this study to begin investigating their racial and transracial adoptee identities on their own, and, more important, they could explore with anonymity. This allowed them to ask specific questions without embarrassment or fear of being attacked for their perceived ignorance. Moreover, they could read others' stories and draw connections to their own stories without feeling obligated to share them before they were ready.

The Internet brought Korean adoptees together from around the world. Web sites were developed by Korean adoptees and adoption agencies. Internet communities were developed solely for Korean adoptees and for all those who were connected to the Korean adoptee community (e.g., parents, spouses, friends, extended family, potential adoptive parents). Amber and Karina reflected on their online experiences.

> AMBER: I went on line. I was just doing the whole Internet surfing thing. . . . I started looking for Korean adoptees. And then I thought, "What if my adoption agency is on line? What information can I get?" And it really just started from there. I found out about all this stuff and it was slowly, through reading all this information, through seeing the other Korean adoptee organization that had already formed, what they were doing, who the members were, that I really started to get in touch with other people and got actively involved with the online community. And it's through my own sheer will of becoming educated. I mean, I had no idea that there [were] that many [Korean adoptees] out there until a few years ago.

> KARINA: When we first got the Internet—that's how I started searching. I looked at the [adoption agency] Web site and I started to discover chat rooms and I met [another Korean adoptee] on line. The Internet has been a big key in connecting adoptees, whether they're just searching for other people that are like them from the outside anonymously or looking for a community. And, do you know how many more Web sites, how many more list serves that have come out just keeping everybody in the loop of what's going on and stuff? A lot.

The Internet was one of the most common means for the global Korean adoptee community to come together. Even though such groups had been forming before the World Wide Web came into existence, the Internet certainly had a profound impact upon this community. The Internet was a key source for many adoptees not only to find more information, but also to meet Korean adoptees worldwide.

1999 Gathering

While the Internet offered a space for Korean adoptees to interact across distances and in relative anonymity, the 1999 Gathering was a place where they could come together to rejoice, share, and develop a Korean adoptee community. Several participants who attended this first Gathering were awakening to the fact that they were not alone. Karina and Brian came to realize and accept the significance of their transracial adoptee identity.

> KARINA: The 1999 Gathering. . . was the piece that really sent my life; that was Pandora's box, it was the international Gathering. I remember one of the first things was getting in the elevator and looking around and seeing all Korean adoptees in the elevator. This was an "Ah ha!" moment. It's, "Wow, look at this, this is so cool, we're the majority." I remember that was the first thing I said. We're the majority in the elevator, and then as I looked around the hotel, we're the majority of this hotel. I mean, it was just this mass [of] people; I have never been in a group of adoptees, a group of Korean people more than probably five until that experience. It was just an incredible experience. The biggest piece for me was connecting with other people. I can look at the picture and just say, "I can remember this day and I remember the feeling of belonging." There wasn't something wrong with me.

> BRIAN: When I was in D.C. in 1999, there was a Korean adoptee Gathering. And it was the most eye-awakening event. It was a grand awakening simply to see so many others like me. You have these wonderful little networks where you can contact, swap information, and if I ever felt alone, like there's no other adoptee out there who understands me, I can never lament. I can never say that statement without hypocrisy. There are tons of me out there. It's a grand feeling, I belong to this fraternity and it's a wonderful sense of belonging. Ever since then, wherever I move I try to find other Korean adoptees.

Karina's and Brian's comments echo those adoptees who had returned to Korea; they felt empowered simply by being around so many others who looked like them, and possibly the awe-inspiring feeling of being part of the racial majority. Most of the adoptees had grown up in places where they were one of the only racial minorities within the area, and several of them mentioned how they had become accustomed to always feeling that they stood out in a crowd. For Jackson and Tonya, the 1999 Gathering, where they finally found themselves part of the racial majority, allowed them, for perhaps the first time, to feel connected to a group of people both racially and culturally.

> JACKSON: I think after the first Gathering in '99, I obviously became more aware that there are actually groups out there for adopted Koreans. I mean, it was just being able to talk with other people who had similar experiences, especially for those who didn't grow up with other adoptees around them.

> TONYA: I was quite excited just to have the experience of meeting with Korean adoptees. It [the 1999 Gathering] was exciting. It was energizing. It was fun to hear that a lot of the Korean women have the big calves, and there were several of us who kept food under our bed when we first came to America—just to know that my experience wasn't that different from anybody else. That somebody else related to the experience that I went through. It was definitely energizing. I would definitely say that was one of the reasons why it was so exciting and energizing to be there, because we have shared experiences and we didn't have to explain ourselves; we just knew.

They had their thoughts and experiences validated by others who could truly empathize with them. For most of their lives, the majority of the adoptees felt that no one could understand what they were going through. Especially during their initial contact with other adult adoptees, Cindy, Amber, and Charlotte experienced this strong feeling of finally being connected to other people.

> CINDY: I remember the sense of relief at finally being with a group of people that I belonged with, that I fit in with similar experiences and we're all culturally, most of us at least, are culturally White and look the way that we do.

> AMBER: Whenever you meet somebody else who's been through the same experience, then you immediately feel that sense of understanding that nobody else can give you. We were all exploring our Korean roots and finally getting the opportunity to see that there are literally thousands of other Korean adoptees

out there. So meeting other adoptees reinforces the idea [that] we're not alone because we have this common experience.

CHARLOTTE: I think that overall it made me feel more connected and it's made me feel like I'm one of the grains of sand, as opposed to always just sticking out all by myself.

The awakening to a Korean adoptee community allowed these participants who had attended the 1999 Gathering to gain a strong sense of belonging both racially and culturally. The attendees understood the dilemma of being transracial adoptees from Korea, and from that affinity most felt that they could begin to take ownership of their racial and transracial adoptee identities by exploring for themselves what it means to be a Korean adoptee.

The sense that their realities were suddenly shattered was not uncommon for the adoptees. What is intriguing is the way this awakening influenced some adoptees to initiate their identity journeys toward empowerment. Throughout their lives they felt they had been lied to or protected from the truth. When the adoptees began to make sense of their adoptions by themselves and on their own terms, they were able to seek answers about their adoption. When they dug deeper into their pasts, some discovered new and alarming information, while others were told that no information could be found. Presented either with new information or an empty file, the adoptees displayed a wide range of emotions, from anger to grief to resentment to disconnection. Some wanted to return to a place where they would not be forced to explain their unique identities—a time when people accepted and judged them for who they were, not what they looked like. Yet their identity awakenings forced them to recognize their racial and transracial adoptee identities as important aspects of their lives. Some Korean adoptees made the conscious choice to critically explore all that was inside Pandora's box.

CHAPTER 4

Engaging and Reflecting

Dancing with a Racial Identity and
Transracial Adoptee Identity

> TORI: The answer has to be about me being brave enough, if you
> will, to throw my own mental closet doors open and then
> rummage around long enough in there to fix myself from the
> inside out. It's not a fix that's going to happen by somebody
> handing me culture. It's not going to be fixed by any of those
> things. But it's going to be me actively acknowledging these
> false feelings of the past, connecting with other people, and
> truly feeling a sense of more self-esteem from within.

Dancing with a White cultural identity is a time when Korean adoptees are
lulled into a state of denial and disempowerment about their racial and
transracial adoptee identities as they grow up within the status quo of their
culturally White-informed homes and communities that promote assimilation, a colorblind philosophy, and silenced dialogues around issues of race,
racism, and White privilege. Later, there is an awakening, when the adoptees acknowledge that their racial and transracial adoptee identities cannot
be denied and disregarded, because the world is *not* colorblind, and assimilation into their White communities is limited because they are *not* racially
White. For the adoptees in this study, the awakening most often occurred
when they left their comfort zones, when they were forced to reflect on their
identities, or when they were reminded that the early part of their lives is a
mystery. This initial awakening and the opening of Pandora's box led most
of the adoptees to critically explore either or both their racial and transracial adoptee identities.

In this chapter I attempt to illustrate their engaged explorations of these
identities. As they set out to discover what the identities meant to them,
there was no direct path that all of the participants followed, as each reacted
to certain situations differently. For example, for some, traveling to Korea
could be considered an awakening to their racial identity, while for others such a visit might be viewed as an engaged exploration of their transracial adoptee identity. The main point to keep in mind is that through

these engaged explorations and critical reflections the adoptees were able to empower their identities.

Dancing with a Racial Identity

Cultural racism led most adoptees to believe that they could not be both White and Korean; in many ways they were forced to choose one or the other, hence many chose to identify with their White cultural identity because they felt that Korean culture was only for authentic Koreans. However, when they awoke to the fact that the world did not view them as White, most of the adoptees attempted to incorporate Korean culture in their everyday lives. Joan believed that matching her race with her culture would allow her to establish an attachment to her racial identity.

> It was starting to bring some peace for me in terms of the more I knew about the culture or the more I learned about the culture, the more I just felt a little bit more at ease with who I am. Because for a very long time, even though I had a good life, I always felt like I was living a phony life. I was living a fake life because it just seemed so surreal. So, once I started exposing myself to Korean culture and having Asian friends and learning more about the culture and . . . everything of the sort, I started to feel a little bit more peace inside, which is something that I definitely needed.

A connection with Korean culture allowed some adoptees to feel that they were more attached to their racial heritage. As they began immersing themselves in what they determined to be sites of Korean culture, they felt a little less awkward, less of an outsider, which in the end allowed most to feel a positive connection with their racial identity. These cultural connections were mainly related to aspects of food and language. Some began to eat and prepare Korean food and seek out authentic Koreans to teach them the language. Some viewed Korea as the ultimate site to gain access to Korean culture, leading them to visit for short or long stays or seek permanent residence in Korea. In college, some majored in Korean or Asian studies and attempted to join Korean Student Associations. Others looked into joining their local Korean communities.

Attending Culture Camps

Only twelve adoptees in the study attended Korean culture camps during their pre-teenage and teenage years. What is more interesting is that of the nineteen participants who were adopted between 1976 and 1987, nine attended culture camp, whereas of the nineteen participants who were adopted between 1959 and 1975, only three did so.[1] This may represent a shift in philosophy on how to raise transracial adoptees. Parents of the more recent wave of Korean adoptees were encouraged to provide opportunities for their children to engage in the culture of their birth country. Hanna and Karina, who fall into the more recent adoptee category, recalled some of the activities their parents involved them in.

> HANNA: We didn't do anything too formal. It's funny, I remember my mom taking me to a culture afternoon, and there were other Korean adopted kids there and I learned this Korean song, the rabbit song, "San Tokki" [Mountain rabbit]. My mom has no recollection of taking me to this thing. I might have been seven or eight years old.

> KARINA: When I was young, four or five, I'm thinking it was Korean culture camp that we went to because my sister and I went. I remember singing, "Head, shoulders, knees, and toes." Doesn't everybody know that? My mom took us down there, and I must have been four or five because I have pictures of me in this little *hanbok*.[2]

Largely through the development of Korean culture camps from the late 1980s until today, more Korean adoptees in the United States have been given the opportunity to learn aspects of Korean culture. This increase in awareness also parallels the increasing number of Korean adoptees during the 1980s (in 1986, the peak year, 6,188 Korean adoptees were admitted into the United States). A recognizable cultural and generational gap exists between the first wave of Korean adoptees and those who came after 1975 based on access to Korean culture camps.

What is interesting is that the first wave of adoptees did not resent their experiences. One might think that such differences in experience would lead to animosity or perhaps jealousy, but this was not the case. The first wave did wish that they had had more exposure to culture camps, opportunities to visit Korea, and the networks of Korean adoptees that exist today. However, as seen in Sophie's and Hanna's comments, they did not regret their experiences, because they were able to view their lives from a sense of their own accomplishments.

> SOPHIE: Would it have been beneficial for my parents to make me go to culture camp? Perhaps, but at the same time, I'm very proud

of the journeys that I've come on in my racial identity. It was one that I took on my own when I was ready and it wasn't forced on me. It was my own journey and I really enjoy that.

HANNA: I think there's a distinction between "that would have been really nice" versus "I really wouldn't have needed that because that wouldn't have made such a difference in my life." I think sometimes when I say it would have been good if I had a chance to do more cultural things, it's more . . . that it would have been great to have around. I'm not a worse person because I never had it. Sure, in hindsight, I wish I had started Korean language a lot sooner and had access to all that cultural stuff.

One of the major differences between the first wave and the subsequent one was the opportunity to engage with Korean culture. Both sets of Korean adoptees appeared to have assimilated into the White culture of their parents and communities and then awakened to their racial and transracial adoptee identities some time during adolescence or early adulthood. The post-1975 adoptee generation seemed to have had more access to Korean culture. Their experience with that culture and the questioning of their identities happened earlier in their lives. However, culture camps that continue to endorse a curriculum that excludes critical dialogue and investigation of the adoptees' multiple and complex identities could contribute to a false sense of control and security in their identities.[3] Therefore, I cannot conclude whether Korean culture camps had any significant impact upon the adoptees' identities.

Of the twelve adoptees who attended culture camp in their youth, seven went only once. While all seven claimed to have pleasant memories of singing songs and playing Korean games, they were unable to recall why they went only the one time. It appears that the parents may have believed that an introduction to Korean culture was a one-shot deal or that exposing their children to the culture might lead to cultural confusion. This attitude parallels the way in which multicultural education is implemented in schools today as sporadic celebrations of culture (Pang 2004).

In addition to the lack of continuous engagement with Korean culture, most adoptees, as Julie points out below, were able to see the stereotypes that prevailed within the camps, but they were not likely to question the harmful effects on the adoptees' identities because they believed exposure to stereotypes was better than none at all.

Exposure to some culture is better than exposure to no culture. And if you are Korean, then it's better to have been exposed to some part of Korean culture, even if it's stereotypical, than to no part of Korean culture and with the child asking, "I wonder what it was like?" I just believe that some exposure is helpful and beneficial. They are American parents, so not all of them are going to even know what's stereotypical and what's not.

In reflection, the adoptees who were not exposed to Korean culture camps wished that they had had the opportunity. Michelle and Bettina believed that the culture camps, whether dynamic at critically investigating their identities or not, would have provided a foundation for them to explore these identities. In other words, going to culture camp—however flawed it might have been—was perceived as being better for their identity development than having no exposure to culture camp at all.

MICHELLE: I do know that a big part of going back to camp was keeping [in touch] with your friends. Another big part, . . . though, was that they were all Korean. It was important for me to have that feeling at that time. I liked being around the same almond-eyed shaped, black haired kids and just feeling that everyone here—I know it sounds terrible, but they always say it's good to be different or to be unique, but I just loved being there and being able to fit in. And as far as how much we actually learned about the culture while we were there, a lot of it was meeting them halfway. What I mean by that is every year the same fifth-grade class would do the same dance or learn *Hangul*. Every year you go up another step and that got a little tedious. Maybe just being familiar with the culture is enough.

BETTINA: I don't know anything about the language. I can't read it. And the customs, I don't know anything about them. I really don't know anything about Korea even now, although I'm starting to look into it. People who adopted kids from foreign countries can give them cultural lessons, language, and all those sorts of things; I wish that I had [had] that. I think it just would have been easier interacting with [Korean] people if I had grown up with post-adoption services. If I had [had] cultural information at least I would have had a starting point to talk to people about, or I would have understood what they were talking about or how they felt about me. I just feel that I would have had a better launching point.

In retrospect, these adoptees were aware of the limited access to Korean culture. However, they still believed these camps helped them understand and connect with their identities. Sophie, Tess, and Keiza recognized that adoptees who have opportunities to attend culture camp and explore other aspects of Korean culture seem to have a better grasp on their identities.

> SOPHIE: I found that when I talk to these kids [attending culture camp], fourteen, fifteen, sixteen [year-olds], they seem much more centered in their identity issues than I did at fifteen years old. And that's possibly because their parents have been making them go to these Korean culture camps. They're around other adoptees, not just adoptees, but Asian people, so that they can get a reflection of who they are. Being around other adoptees at the age of thirteen, when they're interested in each other and starting to blossom, and the fact that they can look at another Asian male at the age of thirteen and find them attractive, I didn't have that. I didn't know what that was like. So when I look at them, they're very stable, much more stable than I was when I was at fourteen years old.

> TESS: Last year was the first time I ever worked at a culture camp. And talking to these teens that are in high school or even in junior high, I was amazed. At that age I didn't even think about that. I have kids coming up to me and they're asking, "When can we eat Korean food?" They're more curious; I think that's the big thing, is letting them just be aware of things. That is my big thing; I wish that [had] happened to me at that age. I wish that I was more aware of things concerning culture and background.

> KEIZA: I think I felt like I was just clueless about Korean culture because several of the people [in a tour group to Korea] had been to culture camps. There was the twenty-five and over crowd and then a lot of eighteen-year-olds. A lot of the eighteen-year-olds had gone to culture camp and been back to Korea with their families already. It was a very different experience for them. They were more versed in the culture and the language. They were able to say things to [Korean] people. And the older ones, we were just like, that would have been nice to know.

However, several adoptees recognized the lack of genuine investigation into identity development at culture camps. Keiza and Karina concluded that a lack of critical dialogue around issues of identity and transracial adoption caused more identity confusion for the campers because they were unable to relate their experiences to their lives outside culture camp.

> KEIZA: Honestly, I don't know the answer. Having talked with more people who've been to culture camps, I don't think culture camps are the answer because it really is a super false environment. When is anybody ever going to be in that environment in real life?

> KARINA: They [teenage Korean adoptees] don't want to be at camp learning about Korean culture, because they've been there for twelve years now and they don't ever change the program. I finally have tried to change it. But camp gives them a false sense of security. There are a couple of kids that I've seen that have grown up at camp, and at camp they're these outgoing, self-confident kids, they're leaders, and then they go home and they are completely the opposite. They don't leave their room. They don't associate with anybody else. It's really, in my opinion, from what I've just seen at culture camp, there's a very big false sense of security for these kids. It's not the real world.

These comments reflect the attitude that the adoptees who had the opportunity to attend culture camp might have gained a strong sense of self during their time at camp simply due to being around other adoptees and learning aspects of Korean culture. However, once they returned to their White families and friends, Kianna and Woojung felt isolated and were unable to share their experiences with anyone.

> KIANNA: It's just amazing how some of my friends . . . don't even grasp the ideas of being adopted and being adopted into a Caucasian family. They just don't understand why I think the way that I do sometimes or why I make comments about certain things. It's just amazing.

> WOOJUNG: [When] I was about seventeen, I just felt really isolated and alienated. I had all these friends and at school I was doing well and fine, but at the same time I just felt like my so-called American friends or White friends [had] no idea about the turmoil I was going through about my Asian American identity and being adopted.

Feeling that their experiences were short-lived and had no bearing on their lives outside of the culture camps, Halle and Tori resisted even attending in the first place, because doing so would have meant actively admitting that they are not White.

> HALLE: It was just one summer that I went and I think my parents realized it was a big mistake. I just had no desire to connect with other Asians because I wanted to fit in so much with being White. I think that's why I didn't like the Korean camp. I didn't want to be Korean. I was very confused. When I went to the Korean heritage camp, that was when I was anti-Korean, and I didn't want anything to do with it and I didn't really give it a chance.

> TORI: I [was] sent off to Korean culture day camp with these other kids and, let me just tell you, that was [a] shock. All of sudden it was culture shock. . . . "Oh, my God, all these Asians." So, I didn't feel this sense of community of "Wow, a whole entire bunch of people who are like me." No, I actually felt the opposite. And I [didn't] have Korean culture up until [that] moment and then all of a sudden it's all shoved down my throat with, make origami and learn a couple of words in Korean. [It was] completely out of context [with] my everyday reality.

Some adoptees recognized the lack of critical dialogue and investigation of the Korean adoptees' racial and transracial adoptee identities at these culture camps. Nevertheless, they still strongly supported the need for such camps. Many of the adoptees were actively involved in culture camps as organizers, board members, or mentors, which allowed them to design the camps to include spaces for dialogue about racial and transracial adoptee issues. All were in favor of culture camps that provided a venue for adoptees to meet others like them, experience aspects of Korean culture, and, at the very least, recognize that their racial and transracial adoptee identities are important.

Making Korean Friends

Most of the adoptees seeking to connect with their racial identity began by establishing relationships with their local Korean communities. Some attended a Korean church in their area in an attempt to meet people who they felt were authentic Koreans. Others were introduced to Koreans by colleagues or friends. A few started conversations with local Korean grocery store or restaurant proprietors. All were looking for people who could help them learn more about what it means to be Korean.

ROBBY: I want to make Korean friends now. For the most part I didn't really start making any actual Korean friends until the end of last year and this year, when I started taking the language class and meeting more language partners.

TAMMY: My husband is going to school and there are a lot of Asian students. A really good friend of mine, who was a colleague of his, started teaching me Korean. She has a daughter that's six months younger than my son, and she was staying home at the same time. So we'd get together all the time and we'd go have lunch in Korean restaurants and she'd just tell me all about Korea.

MARY: I've been really interested in meeting a lot of language partners and keeping in touch with them and just hanging out with them and seeing what it was like—the language and culture, the history and food. I mean, this year was the first time I ever had kimchee. But it was funny because I was with my language partner and she was like, "This is kimchee." But if I had grown up differently maybe I would know that already. Our relationship was pretty formal, just as a language partner. But now, we've hung out more and we talk more and we're actually friends . . . and we can talk about other things. I've talked to her a little bit about my adoption experience and then I asked her what she thinks about it. She understands and respects that. She doesn't look down on me. But I need to really speak more Korean with her.

One can hear the uncertainty in the adoptees' voices regarding their relationships with people they considered authentic Koreans. Although they were learning new aspects of Korean culture from these friends or, for some, at camps, some still recognized that the Korean culture was not yet their own.

In other words, they did not "own" Korean culture; they still did not know what it meant to be Korean because they were culturally White. Consequently, some adoptees sought a sustained and direct connection to Korean culture by revisiting Korea—not as tourists, but more as someone seeking to understand what it means to be Korean.

Visiting and Living in Korea

For most adoptees their first return trips to Korea were awakenings to their racial and transracial adoptee identities, which then sparked a desire to establish a stronger connection with these identities. This yearning further prompted ten of the adoptees to make multiple follow-up trips to Korea (three were preparing for their second trips at the time of this study).

During their second and subsequent trips to Korea, Woojung and Alex attempted to establish stronger connections to being Korean by living as Koreans. While there, they moved beyond the tourist perspective to learn more about Korean culture and what it means to be Korean.

> WOOJUNG: As a sophomore in college, I went on an exchange program for a semester to Yonsei University [in Seoul], and then that's when I really picked up a lot [of] Korean because [I] spoke it every day.

> ALEX: The second and third time I went back I had a lot more free time where I would just get on the subway and go anywhere.

Alex also pointed out that most adoptees need sustained exposure to Korean culture because their short visits, while insightful, provided only glimpses, and they quickly returned to their White culturally informed lives upon leaving Korea: "I've had good trips back to Korea. However, only being there for two weeks at a time, by the time you are leaving you're just starting to get comfortable. So that's why I'd really like to go back for a longer, extended period of time. It still seems like little tour groups and I'm not really experiencing Korea and any culture."

Six of the adoptees stayed in Korea for longer than a month. Charlotte and Woojung studied at Yonsei University in Seoul. Woojung and Katerina both taught English in Korea for almost two years. Katerina and Joan volunteered at orphanages in Korea. Hanna went on multiple trips and during each one visited with her birth family. On her third trip to Korea, Kris stayed with her birth mother. It is interesting that of these six adoptees, five had reestablished relationships with their birth families. Charlotte had been adopted at the age of fourteen and Woojung at eleven, and both were able to maintain contact with their birth families. Katerina, Kris, and Hanna were able to reunite with their birth families. Their relationships with birth families allowed them to feel connected to their racial identity and facilitated multiple trips to Korea.

Learning Korean Language

Most of the adoptees stated that throughout their lives they felt that they were not authentic Koreans because they did not possess Korean cultural knowledge, particularly skill in the Korean language. Amber and Abby felt a sense of shame and loss.

AMBER: Tell all your other friends about how difficult it is to be a Korean person who grows up in another country, surrounded by White people and not speaking to Korean people. And then when we go back to our motherland that they treat us badly because we don't speak Korean. "Hello! Whose fault is that?"

ABBY: Korean people come up to me and say, "Oh, you don't even speak your own language" all the time. I don't get upset by that because it's just they're stupid, they don't really know what they are saying.

Because they felt ostracized from the Korean community for being unable to speak Korean, most adoptees concluded that learning to speak the language was one way to feel closer to Korean culture. More important, they believed that gaining Korean-language skills would allow them to be recognized as Koreans and thus move toward empowering their racial identity. As Abby and Tori indicate, becoming fluent in Korean would allow them access to the Korean community, which was often closed to them.

ABBY: Language connects you back to who you are and your culture and how you can express yourself. You can express yourself. I could go to Korea and just do whatever. I can go and try to find my birth mother on my own. I could make friends in Korean on my own. I could live there. No problem. Also, people admit that a lot of their problems and issues such as relating with Korean [birth] parents is the language barrier. The language is so big.

TORI: I've read anthologies of other Asian adoptees and I know that for so many folks connecting back to their Korean culture and Korean language has been really pivotal. I think for a little while I wanted that, but I think it's because I thought that maybe if I had that then it would fill some void or I would feel . . . connected to something.

Charlotte and Woojung, both adopted at an older age, lost their Korean-language skills as they quickly assimilated into their White culturally informed lives. However, once they were awakened to their racial identity, they regained that skill.

CHARLOTTE: After having been through that [living in the United States] for almost two years, I could no longer speak or understand

Korean, which I found shocking because my English was nowhere near perfect, and the way I found out was when I came home from school one day and my adopted mother wanted to surprise me. She'd gotten some Korean cable and they had all these Korean soap opera programs. When I walked in she had a big smile on her face and she said, "Surprise!" and there's this Korean soap opera on the TV. I couldn't understand it and I was horrified. So I sat and watched it, and watched it, and watched it [for] . . . maybe twenty minutes or half an hour [and] all of sudden I heard . . . one word that clicked, and from then on it was like being in one of those Star Wars machines where you go through the time zone, . . . and things click and then all of [a] sudden you understand everything. I've studied some linguistics; I can't explain what happened, but I think when someone or something is actively repressing some memory or language or identity or whatever, it just disappears.

WOOJUNG: What happened was, the summer of my freshman year [of high school], my parents promised me that if I had saved up, then I could go visit my family in Korea for the summer. So I got a job. I was busing tables at a restaurant. So I saved up. Then I went back to Korea and it was actually a big shock because I couldn't speak Korean. I couldn't understand Korean. And when I came back from that trip—it was only a two-week trip—I told myself that I would relearn Korean, which was very hard because I didn't have anyone to speak with. In high school, when I turned about sixteen, when I got my license, I used to drive about an hour across town to where there's a Korean church and on Saturdays I would take Korean classes with a bunch of little kids. Then when I indicated how serious I was about this, my mother hired a tutor from the university, a Korean exchange student. She came down and spoke to me in Korean, which only lasted for about three or four months because then she went back [to Korea]. I just made small efforts. Then I found Korean tapes and listened to them everyday so that it would come back.

Possibly the strongest motivation for both Charlotte and Woojung to relearn Korean was the desire to reestablish relationships with their birth families. And although both stated that they lost their Korean language within the first couple months in their adoptive homes, both were able to regain fluency in the language. However, for most of the Korean adoptees, especially those whose first language is English, learning the Korean language proved difficult for a number of reasons.

Only a few of the adoptees attempted to learn the language in formal situations. During the time of the study, Mary and Robby were enrolled in Korean-language classes at their university as they were preparing for a study-abroad semester in Seoul. Connie was enrolled in a continuing-education class at her local junior college. Jamie, in preparation for her trip to Korea, enrolled in a university extension course. Halle took a Korean-language and history course while she was an undergraduate. Tonya started taking a class offered by the local Korean church. A few of the adoptees were exposed to the basics of the Korean language as children when they attended culture camp.

It seemed as if the adoptees were embarrassed at not knowing how to speak Korean or about Korean culture, which made them not only feel inadequate, but also forced them to see that they are not racially Korean. This then compelled Kris and Kendra to give up their attempts to connect with their racial identity.

> KRIS: I tried to learn Korean, actually, in college. I never got past the elementary stage of it. I took it for about two and a half years. I know the basic conversational Korean, but I definitely need to take [my] share of the blame. I don't feel like I've learned a tremendous amount.

> KENDRA: I tried to learn the language; that didn't last very long. At some point, I realized that this is not who I am either. And that there's probably nothing ever in my life that is going to make me culturally Korean.

At one time many of the adoptees had believed that becoming fluent in Korean would solve all of their identity uncertainties. However, for most their lack of fluency in Korean solidified their identities as culturally White individuals who happen to look racially Korean.

A connection to their racial identity was constantly being negotiated between others' (especially Koreans and Korean Americans) recognition of the transracial adoptees' identities and their own feelings of inadequacy with and distance from Korean culture. Indeed, the adoptees did not see themselves as authentic Koreans because they did not possess Korean culture, especially Korean language. The lack of Korean cultural skills led the adoptees to believe that they could not gain full entry into the Korean and Korean American communities. When they attempted to do so, they often felt like outsiders due to the cultural differences. Being unable to connect with the community members, some of the adoptees sensed they were being ostracized because they did not possess the Korean cultural skills to be full members.

For several adoptees, cultural differences and a sense of rejection from the community impelled them to distance themselves even further from their White cultural upbringing, shunning anything associated with their Whiteness; at the same time, they attempted to assimilate into the Korean culture. However, no matter how hard they tried to become Korean, their efforts apparently were not enough for them to be recognized as Koreans both in the Korean community and in their own minds.

On the other hand, several adoptees believed that the knowledge they had gained about Korean culture was enough for them, and they found comfort in that. They did not feel terribly distant from their racial heritage and accepted the reality that they would never be accepted as Koreans. However, they were no longer ashamed of this, due in part to the realization that their identity was found not just in their racial identity, but also their transracial adoptee identity.

Dancing with a Transracial Adoptee Identity

Most of the adoptees had had some type of contact with other Korean and transracial adoptees during their early childhood. Fourteen of the adoptees had other immediate family members who had been adopted from Korea—five were adopted with a biological sibling. Four had a Korean adoptee relative, and two had transracially adopted siblings not from Korea. Many also recalled other Korean adoptees in their schools or that their parents had befriended other parents in their communities with Korean adoptees. I should also note that not all of the adoptees in this study could claim to have investigated and reflected on their transracial adoptee identity. Some were just beginning to locate this identity, while others had been dancing with it for years. All of the adoptees have considered their transracial adoptee identity at some point in their lives. Thus it is important to better understand how they navigated this significant aspect of their identities.

Mary and Cathy spoke about meeting other Korean adoptees at culture camps and about other types of get-togethers for transracial adoptees sponsored by adoption agencies or adoptive parent groups.

> MARY: My best friend growing up is also Korean adopted, so we
> both felt the same way about things. We didn't really think we

were that different. Our parents actually introduced us when we were little because we were both adopted.

CATHY: We went to a Korean culture camp every summer. I have some good friends who I've been going to camp with. We actually came on the same plane together. I met them at camp and we've been best friends since.

Kris and Cindy discussed how their relationships with Korean adoptees were formed around their commonality, yet they often did not talk about what it meant to be transracial adoptees.

KRIS: Although my parents were connected to this adoptive parents group, the contact was very limited, like once a month, if that. There was only a handful of people in that group, so maybe . . . five or six kids who were Korean adoptees, and all of us were around the same age, but far enough apart that we didn't hang out together so much.

CINDY: My cousin is also adopted from Korea. She's not my biological cousin, but she was adopted from Korea. We grew up together. We were very close when we were young, but we never, ever discussed being adopted or our experiences or our families or anything.

Several adoptees explored their transracial adoptee identity by immersing themselves in active Korean adoptee communities. They posted their thoughts and experiences on Web sites and list-serves, mentored teenagers, and volunteered to speak on panels. Some adoptees formed groups in their colleges and communities. Others became social workers for adoption agencies and adoptee counselors. A few were involved in writing and researching issues related to transracial adoption.

Connecting with Other Korean Adoptees—Gatherings, Groups, and Online Forums

I mark the 1999 Gathering as a major turning point for the global Korean adoptee community. The Gathering certainly awoke many of them to their racial and transracial adoptee identities and in the process made them aware of the strong need for a sustained and dynamic transracial adoptee community. As many of the Gathering attendees returned to their predominantly and culturally White informed communities, they craved interaction with other Korean adoptees. Throughout the United States, Europe, South Korea, and other parts of the world, Korean and other transracial adoptee groups were formed.

Established communities of Korean adoptees existed prior to the 1999 Gathering. In fact, Also-Known-As, Inc., in New York City, a transracial adoptee group formed in 1996, was a cosponsor of the 1999 Gathering. According to the 2004 Gathering conference handbook, thirteen groups were formed before 1999—eight in Europe, four in the United States, and one in South Korea. The first Korean adoptee group, Adopted Koreans' Association, was formed in Sweden in 1985, and the first in the United States, Minnesota Adopted Koreans (MAK), was formed in Minneapolis-St. Paul in 1990.[4]

In spite of these efforts to form adoptee groups, the majority of the adoptees grew up feeling completely alone. They did not fully fit in with their White families, peers, and communities because they are Korean, and they did not fit in with the Korean/Asian communities because they were culturally White. Even though Mary, Tonya, and Keiza were able to build strong and trusting relationships with their families and friends, they believed these important people could not understand what it meant to be a transracial adoptee, culturally White, and racially Korean.

> MARY: I think even if you meet an adopted person and you don't really click that well, you still have an understanding just because you are adopted. It's just the knowledge that you share. I can talk about it with my family and my friends, who are all really great, but they just won't quite understand it.

> TONYA: I mean, most people who haven't been [transracially] adopted haven't experienced some of the racial tensions that may have happened in their small towns. It's just different. Just to have somebody relate, to say, "Hey, I understand, that's what I went through." That was very nice.

> KEIZA: It was comforting finding other people that had been through similar experiences. I don't think I could have predicted how amazing that experience would be, but it has been. I mean, I have just, in recent years, . . . made some of the best friends of my life and they are Korean adoptees.

The Korean adoptee community provided many of the adoptees with a strong feeling of being understood. Jamie, Tori, and Connie were then able to talk about their experiences with people who could relate to and understand their lives.

> JAMIE: I finally was talking to people who knew. I never really considered that I could share this part of my life with somebody else and not have to explain the whole story like I would have to other people; I was born in Korea, but then I was adopted, that whole song and dance. And so it was just interesting to be with people who had a similar experience.

> TORI: All of sudden I just realized that everybody out there who's transracially adopted, who fit a similar demographic to me, people who do not match their racial identity with their adopted family—it was these folks, as well as maybe biracial children, that I shared a community with. It was sharing that feeling of being stuck in that no man's land of two different races and maybe or maybe not being accepted by either side.

> CONNIE: I mean, it was great to be around so many other adopted Korean people that had the same experiences. I think that the only people [that] can really understand my feelings when I share things about the conference are other Korean adoptees. Finally, here's this group of people that know exactly what my life has been like, and I know what their life has been like growing up with brothers and sisters with blonde hair and looking completely different. That was definitely the best part of it, . . . just being around other people like me.

Beyond finding a connection with others who could understand and relate to their experiences, this community also provided a safe place where most adoptees could feel they would not be judged. They could safely raise questions and engage in critical dialogue about the complexity of their identities.

Within these conversations, adoptees would raise the topics of racism and White privilege; they also questioned the institution of transracial adoption. Never before had they felt a sense of comfort in discussing these issues because before joining the group they were often met with resistance from their families, peers, and communities. They were likely deemed ungrateful or accused of playing the race card by the people whom adoptees believed could not truly understand their lives. However, as Kendra, Tammy, and Tori point out, the Korean adoptee community allowed them to feel that their experiences were finally being recognized and appreciated.

KENDRA: I finally have managed to . . . reach out and make some connections with some real adoptees. . . . That was just the hugest part because I found other people that understood. And, I've never had that before. I could get on here [the Web site forum] and say whatever I wanted to say and they understood that. I didn't have to defend myself, or explain myself. At least some of the ones that responded, they understood. Never before have I ever had that. It has been a huge part of learning to accept myself, learning to be proud of who I am.

TAMMY: I took my first trip back to Korea last summer and so I wrote this article for [a] newsletter. And at our annual event I had one guy come up to me and [say], "[Tammy,] I got the newsletter, it's nice to have you back writing. And I said, "Thanks. What did you think?" because for me to write it was a big step because it made me feel really vulnerable. I was thinking [he was] going to say, "You shouldn't feel that way" or try to talk me out of my feelings. But he said, "[Tammy,] that's exactly how I felt."

TORI: I think that the importance is to provide a forum where people can actively connect. Because I think it is about coming out and making yourself vulnerable and revealing every last thing that has ever made you feel bad about yourself and then you are going to have to speak those words and you are going to have to share them with others; that's terrifying.

Within the group they were free to tell their life stories with the strong belief that people could understand their lives. They believed they would not be judged or belittled for sharing their stories. Several adoptees discovered that the members of the adoptee groups could provide answers and suggestions to questions and concerns.

By connecting on multiple levels with other adoptees, the community could provide a sense of family. This feeling was partially built on the adoptees' newly acquired sense of finally belonging to a community, but it also comes from a sense of not fully belonging in their adoptive families. Some adoptees did not feel they were completely accepted by their families, and Cindy and Hanna believe a sense of family is not universal among adoptees.

CINDY: I think for some adoptees their experiences with their adoptive families have been tolerable at best and negative in some cases. I think that we all have a need of wanting to belong, of wanting to make permanent connections and strong relationships. Seeking out that family is even stronger for them. And I've heard people say, "I'm so glad that we got together; I just need to be with my people."

HANNA: I think that for some other adoptees it's being connected to the community itself and almost creating a new family, which I think has been very interesting as well. I think it's really remarkable, too, that in some ways we have become surrogate families for people who maybe didn't feel like they really belonged in their adoptive family at some level. But here they feel like these are my peers, this is who I am now and I want to surround myself with that. It's this aspect of being connected and feeling attachment to stuff. It's about getting connected either through knowledge or by people or being connected to something that has a history. And again, it's that aspect of being part of a continuum, of being part of something that has existed before you and will continue to exist after you.

Most adoptees were involved in a Korean adoptee group. Some members joined to gather information about traveling to Korea, to gain insight into birth searches, and to connect with other Korean adoptees. For Karina, Cindy, and Sophie the main function of the group was to offer an abundance of knowledge and information about dancing with their transracial adoptee identity.

KARINA: The main function is to offer adoptees different opportunities to get together, to expose them to resources that are out there, and to provide a networking service. One of the things that they do is they're a service organization. Two, they offer a networking service as far as, say somebody's going to move here, an adoptee, and she wants to get involved in adoptee organizations. Then they can hook them up with people in this area. And then, three, it's just a social organization by giving people the opportunity to get together and get their fix.

CINDY: Most of the time you feel a little like an alien, like you're the only one of your kind. So seeing that there is a group of people out there . . . like you and listening to some of their experiences and some of the ways that they have explored their Korean-ness and dealt with the whole Korean adoptee issue gave me some direction to my efforts in that area. I was able to see the options, [see] that I could do everything from going to Korea, living in Korea, or just eating Korean food.

SOPHIE: It's connecting, networking, supporting, educating. I think it's all those. Organizing social functions for adoptees to get to together, especially if you've never been around adoptees before and meet some new people and have conversation and some support. Also providing an anthology, a book, a movie, a reading, reading poetry, writing, whatever; giving that information to adoptees if they need it. [There are] also links on there [the Web site] on how to do [a] birth search, how to travel to Korea, what other agencies are out there, resources for you to utilize if you want this. It's just a good way to get people information.

The community provided the adoptees with a variety of ways to engage in their identities. Feeling a sense of family, they came to view the community as a place where they could connect with others like them. Some became fully engaged, while others dropped in occasionally to "get their fix." It appears that critically exploring their identities allowed them to develop a sense of security in their overall self-identity. No longer did they feel alone, because they were connected to others like them. No longer did they feel empty, because they had engaged in aspects of their racial and transracial adoptee identities. However, some still needed the answer to one of the biggest questions regarding their adoption—the location of their birth parents.

Birth Family Search

Once awakened to new information regarding birth family searches through connecting with other transracial adoptees, visiting adoption agencies and orphanages, and viewing adoption papers, some of the adoptees wanted to discover more about their lives prior to adoption. Eleven adoptees conducted birth family searches, while eighteen chose not to.[5]

Three adoptees, Abby, Kendra, and Michelle, wanted answers to questions that had been unanswered most of their lives.

ABBY: I just think it's important for me because I would like to know my medical history. But also because there's . . . this part of my life that's just blank, that part of the book is blank. I'd like to know what happened. The papers tell me about my parent's relationships but I just want to know more.

KENDRA: I think if I don't deal with it [being adopted] then I don't think I'm like a whole person. And part of dealing with it is going back to Korea. It will be my first time back. I want to go back and I want to at least try to conduct a [birth family] search. It's like the biggest question for me. I've come to peace with other aspects of it [being adopted], but this is something that I have not yet dealt with. I've been putting it aside and shying away from it and I think it's time to face it. And, whether it will answer questions for me, it may not. I mean, that question is going to forever remain unanswered if I don't conduct a search.

MICHELLE: It was more, why do you want to find them. And it was because I really wanted to know where I got my character, my facial characteristics. I really wanted to know just dumb stuff like when people say, "You got your eyes from your grandpa or you got your nose from whomever." I really wanted to see where I got all my physical features, but also I wanted to know where I got some of my personal features from. Like certain characteristics of my personality, just to see if that came from someone over there. And it was just really important that I at least have a picture [of my family,] and it [is] just as simple as [having a picture of my family] that could [make] me happy.

Adoptees at the stage of just thinking about conducting a birth family search seemed to have minimal expectations of what they really thought they would find. Keeping expectations low allowed them to keep their hopes alive. But it also appears that they feared becoming too emotionally attached to the idea of a birth family search. For some of the adoptees, saying that they want to know their medical histories or find out who they may look like appear as safe, surface, noncommittal reasons for conducting a search.

In the end, none of the eleven adoptees in this study who initiated birth parent searches was able to meet any family members (one adoptee spoke to a relative on the phone, but no meeting took place). This finding in some ways illustrates the difficulty in locating birth parents due to the numerous factors that the adoptees discuss throughout this section.

Eight adoptees made a connection with their birth families. Two were able to reconnect through the assistance of their adoption agencies. Three were reunited when birth family members reached out to them. And three remained in contact with their birth families. For those who were able to locate birth families, the reunions raised more questions regarding both their racial and transracial adoptee identities, especially when it came to developing relationships with the birth families. It seems that the birth searches and reunions disempowered the adoptees' identities because they created greater uncertainty regarding their histories. As they attempted to develop relationships with birth family members, they exposed the deep cultural divide between them.

However, accepting that cultural divide and the unanswerable questions allowed some to gain a sense of peace about their transracial adoptee identity. Katerina accepted that this was an integral part of her identities, and these uncertainties and cultural divides bound her to the transracial adoptee community.

> I met them [her birth family] my first year I was in Korea. I had written a letter before I left and was very open ended in saying this is where I'm going to be and that there wasn't any pressure to meet me, just putting the ball in their court. In the week of *Chusok*[6] I got a call and he [my brother] said, "I'll be down in the area and I'd like to meet you tomorrow." So that was all pretty quick. And then I met my brother and his daughter. I mean, it was awkward because at that branch office there was nobody to translate and it was just . . . a brief meeting. And then through communication, he wanted me to go spend the weekend with him for *Chusok*, which was for five days. . . . And of course all the relatives came, aunts and uncles and everyone. It was really hard because I didn't recognize them. Of course, they knew me because I was almost four and we had lived with my family until we were placed for adoption. And of course they were pinching me. My niece was the age that I was when I had left and that's where the connection was, because she's a spitting image of what I was like at that age; we have the same build [as] my brother. It was just really weird. It was probably the longest five days of my life because it was just me. I had no one to talk with, really, and nobody in my family really spoke English, except for a cousin who spoke really, really basic English. I mean, that's a connection, but that sense of not connecting and realizing that even though they're blood relation[s], we missed twenty-plus years, and that experience and time together really has a big part in a relationship. So, that was good and then I went back to teach in [name of city] and I would spend . . . one Sunday a month or something with them, but it was more from my initiation. I would call and say, "I'd like to come over." I'm glad I got to see them. Sometimes we would go out and go to a museum or something. He'd [her brother] always say, "I'd like to learn English." But it just never happened. We've attempted to use

e-mails once in a while, but it takes a really long time for me to type in Korean and so it just didn't seem worth it sometimes. . . . Also, I think they've got their own lives and I've got mine. My husband [who is Korean] says I should call them more. But it's like, what do I talk to them about? It's not like there are any big changes. It's hard to know what to say. I'm curious to know what it would be like with my husband, if and when we go there to live, because it's easier to be in their presence and not say anything. I think, either if I live in Korea or go back to visit, that will be more of a connection.

There is so much within Katerina's story, from issues of reuniting to developing a connection with her birth family. As with many reunions, language is one of the main barriers to building strong connections. While Katerina was studying the Korean language, she did not have a strong enough grasp to carry out a sustained conversation. She also expected to feel some sense of connection, a sense of recognition with her family, but it was not there. The language barrier and cultural divide made it difficult to develop a sustained relationship with her birth family. And even though she kept trying to reach out to them, there was too much time and space between them to make a strong connection.

In addition to being unable to develop sustained connections with their birth families, several adoptees, prior to meeting their birth families, believed that a reunion would answer all of their burning questions. It would allow them to resolve questions that had followed them throughout their lives. Many adoptees might think that a reunion with their birth families will answer the main question, "Why was I placed for adoption?" And, receiving the answer, they could then delve deeper into their lives prior to adoption. However, Hanna believes that having such expectations will lead to disappointment for most adoptees because the answers are not always easy to come by.

The thing is, the search or meeting is such an overwhelming thing. And new pieces come up really fast, before you can even know what's happening. I think it's important to know what you would like to get out of the encounter. That's one of the things that I would recommend first and foremost to adoptees thinking about searching. They need to question, "What is the purpose for doing this is?" And that was a question I answered for myself before I went at twenty-four years old because at nineteen I didn't have an answer for that except the fact that they had written me a letter. And that wasn't enough. That wasn't a personal reason to go. But at twenty-four, I was thinking about who I was as an adopted person, what's my identity. In the end, I just wanted to let them know that I'm okay. Again, this thing of letting them know I was okay, that's what I hung on to during the whole time I was meeting these half-sisters and half-brothers and aunts and uncles, this whole family drama that I just dropped into and was a part of twenty-some years ago. At times I had no idea of why . . . I [was there]. But then I remembered, "Oh yeah, I wanted her [birth mother] to know that I'm okay." But I think if you don't have that clear sense, then it's more difficult. The second time I went I had more questions. But I think that led me to realize that the more questions I had, the more questions that came up. The little truths I got, I was just chasing all of these little truths and never would get that big truth—the definitive answer and story. And there again was this personal experience of who we say we are is up to who we say we are. Because even meeting my biological family didn't make my story more solid. And ultimately it was for me to interpret all of this stuff. I could interpret it in a way that made me feel good or I could interpret it in a way that makes me feel pretty bad.

It is interesting to see how Hanna tried to remain calm amid all the emotional and identity turmoil by reminding herself that the reason for reuniting with her birth family was to let them know that she was fine. This appears to be a common approach for adoptees attempting to locate birth families; the adoptees wanted to remain in control of the situation by keeping the search and reunion under their terms.

However, Hanna realized that it is nearly impossible to remain emotionally detached when it comes to searches and reunions. Once they met with their birth families, the adoptees needed to navigate through a variety of issues regarding their identities. For example, the adoptees' birth families might attempt to have them solely identify with a racial identity, hoping that years of separation and cultural divide will be overcome if the adoptee became more Korean. The cultural divide, especially in terms of communicating, was a constant reminder to the adoptees that they are not Korean and that they are who they are because of their transracial adoptee identity.

Most adoptees were unable to locate birth families, which had a profound impact on their identity journeys. However, instead of becoming discouraged or overwhelmed with a sense of loss and abandonment, they took their experiences and shared them with other transracial adoptees. This ultimately allowed them to gain a sense of control over their adoption stories. Alex shared that by investigating his life history he was in turn able to tell his story not from the perspectives of his parents, the adoption agency representative, or the social worker, but from his own informed self-identity.

It was the third year I went back to Korea that I said [I] really wanted to do some searching. She [a Korean mentor] had gone back two weeks earlier and she told me that she did a lot of research but couldn't find anything. I was fine with that; at least I tried. But then I was talking to my friend and because I said I think I have her fingerprints . . . he said, "If you have fingerprints, you should be able to find them with no problem." So I've always thought about that, but I haven't been back to Korea since, and I think that's something that I would like to do myself. Not necessarily [to] put it into someone else's hands. I still haven't decided whether that is something for me that I really want to do or need to do. I know it's not something that I need to do. But there's always that part of you that's just, if you don't try, you are always going to look back and say, "I never tried."

As with the information gained about the transracial adoptee experience and connecting with other transracial adoptees, the exploration of their adoptee backgrounds provided a sense of wholeness. Through this exploration they discovered that they now owned their adoption stories; discovering parts of their past allowed them to come to terms with their life histories and future lives.

Their committed engagement in exploring their racial and transracial adoptee identities should be viewed as paths toward empowerment. The more the adoptees explored what it meant to be Korean and a transracial adoptee, the less they felt that they were living false lives, because their lives were now informed by knowledge they had gained from their explorations. Kianna and Joan realized that these discoveries produced an identity that included their racial and transracial adoptee identities.

KIANNA: At times, I still feel like I don't have an identity. And I'm trying to figure that out, and that's what this is all about. It is really focusing on who I am and it's just something that has to be done and this is just part of the whole process.

JOAN: I just needed to live. And so that's what came out of all of that. It just gave me motivation to continue going on. And I don't really know if this is really typical with a lot of adoptees. I've spoken to some adoptees about this, but I feel like living life was a struggle. I just felt like a survivor. That's definitely what my life felt like, where I was just surviving and every day was just another day, the grind. But after that trip [to Korea], I just felt different; I felt fortunate, I didn't feel so isolated, and I didn't feel so alone anymore.

Their critical engagement allowed them to feel whole as they uncovered answers to unspoken questions, connected with others who understood their lives, and accepted their racial and transracial adoptee identities.

Their discoveries ultimately led to a sense of empowerment. The adoptees no longer identified with the "poor little orphan" who had been "saved" from a harsh life in Korea. They were no longer cowed by fears of being called ungrateful or angry. They no longer viewed White culture as superior to Korean culture. They no longer felt ashamed of not knowing Korean culture. They took control of their lives and identities by engaging in what it means to be a Korean adoptee.

CHAPTER 5

Questioning What I Have Done

Dancing with Tensions, Conflicts, and Contradictions

> CONNIE: My whole experience was positive. I grew up in a healthy
> family and my parents treated me well. They basically spoiled
> me. I'll be the first to admit it. I'm not going to complain about
> that. . . . I don't want this to contradict what I said about
> having a happy childhood, but in the past couple of years I
> really wish that they had introduced me to the Korean culture,
> even just a little. They never really showed an interest in it.
> I'm not faulting them for it because they were doing what they
> thought was best for me. I don't want them to feel that I resent
> them in any way for not introducing me to any Korean culture.

If "dancing in between and nowhere at all" can be considered the opening of Pandora's box, then dancing with a racial and transracial adoptee identity should be regarded as rummaging around inside that box. The adoptees' explorations to discover their identities gave rise to tension, conflict, and contradiction, especially with the people who loved and knew them best. Many of the adoptees remarked that digging into their identities was the most tumultuous period in their lives. Some even wanted to end their journey as their discoveries were neither pleasant nor gave them the answers they sought.

While they took pride in being Korean and followed some aspects of the culture, they came to realize that no matter how hard they tried to be accepted as authentic Koreans, their White cultural ways would impede full acceptance. No matter how much culture these adoptees actively embraced in their lives, more often than not Koreans did not view them as authentic Koreans. Even when the adoptees returned to Korea to live and connected with the culture, they typically spoke Korean with a "foreign" accent and viewed the world from a White cultural standpoint. All in all in they were learning, but not living, the Korean way.

The adoptees discussed how their identity explorations were filled with uncertainties that sometimes caused much anxiety, trepidation, anger, and sorrow. Often they were unsure how to process these intense and overwhelming feelings. Some wanted to revert to a state of colorblindness, but found that once awakened, they could not deny the complexity of their racial and transracial adoptee identities. After confronting everything that they believed to be true and revealing some of the unknowns, some adoptees lashed out against their parents and adoption agencies and were deemed angry adoptees. Of course, such anger and resentment arose because many felt that they had been lied to their entire lives by their loved ones. For many adoptees these feelings of anger eventually subsided as they further explored their identities and became more aware of and connected to their identity journeys. Some believed that this anger is a natural part of their dance of identities.

Exploring their racial and transracial identities often led to dissociation and antagonism toward their White cultural identities. These tensions ultimately caused friction with their White parents, family members, and peers. For the adoptees who were married, particularly to White partners, their identity awakenings and explorations restructured their identities, which often led them to question if their partners could understand and accept their new identities. Their parents and partners knew only the culturally White informed person, who disregarded and denied their identities. During their explorations, these identities were at the core of their self-identity. This exploration then drove the adoptees further away from their culturally White informed lives, which naturally included their White parents and partners.

A significant amount of tension arose as they attempted to claim control of their identities. Conflicts within the Korean adoptee community, alienation from Koreans, and separation from their White family members and peers certainly caused the adoptees to critically question if their identity journeys were worth the pain and anguish that they had brought upon themselves and their loved ones. However, once they were engaged in a sustained and critical exploration, they were unable to return to a state of complete denial of their racial and transracial identities and thus were forced to struggle with the "necessary negative" outcomes.

Diversity and Tensions within the Korean Adoptee Community

Several attendees of the 1999 Gathering returned to their homes and began seeking other Korean adoptees in their communities. Some joined and became actively involved in established adoptee groups. Where such groups did not exist, some formed their own. And when adoptees could not find direct connections with other adult adoptees, they sought refuge in the Internet and attended mini-Gatherings and conferences to get, as Karina stated earlier, their adoptee "fix." Some referred to this community of Korean adoptees as their new families because they finally felt that they fully belonged to a community.[1]

What was also apparent at the Gathering was the fact that even though the attendees shared the experience of being transracial adoptees from Korea, they nevertheless were a diverse group of people. And the more they shared their stories, the more apparent it became how diverse they really were in their experiences as Korean adoptees. The acceptance of the group's diversity would allow for the development of a global Korean adoptee community; however, several issues transpired that caused small rifts within the community.

Diversity Related to Age and Age at Adoption

Probably the most diverse aspects within the Korean adoptee community are related to the ages of the adoptees and their ages at the time of adoption. The four adoptees who were adopted before the 1970s held different views and had dissimilar experiences from those who were adopted later. This first wave of adoptees tends to view their adoptions as necessary for survival due to the economic instability of Korea in the years following the Korean War. One of the major differences between the two generations, as Brian points out, is that the earlier adoptees were more likely to "accept" the reasoning for their adoptions and thus were able to assimilate into their White culturally informed communities with little resistance.

> One of the new [anxieties] that I know from other conversations is that the twenty- and thirty-year-old adoptees, they are not war orphans. The only negative things that I've seen is that when the younger ones do find their adoption reckoning, when they realize that they're adopted, and they think about doing birth searches or the Korean thing, they seem to have a different angst, a different kind of anger or a different kind of identity crisis. One of the things that new adoptees have to face is that it wasn't by a lack of choice that their birth parents gave them up—the war, I can't feed you, it's likely that I'll be dead, I need to put you in a good place, a better place, so I let the orphanage take care of you. The justification is, you will go to a better land and be healthy and stronger. [For the] new adoptees, it's a rejection—I don't want you, so I'm going to send you to the orphanage. So it's much more of a rejection. Some of them really face that and they really have a sense of anger.

The first wave of adoptees was inclined to view their adoption more as a necessity than abandonment. This certainly influenced their identity development, especially with regards to how they viewed their lives in adopted homes. They seemed to accept the fact that there was really no other choice for them; staying in Korea would have meant a life of economic and social struggle.

This is not to say that the adoptees who came after 1975 did not also think such things growing up. However, as Brian pointed out, when these adoptees realized that at the time of their adoptions Korea was no longer in an economic upheaval caused by the Korean War, some of them may have viewed being put up for adoption as abandonment for more selfish reasons rather than for the survival of the child (e.g., out-of-wedlock birth, too many female children in the family, divorce, or remarriage).

In addition, the two generations experienced racism (individual, institutional, and cultural) in different ways. Specifically, the civil rights movement of the 1960s and 1970s provided a more "welcoming" racial environment in the 1980s and 1990s. As Cindy explained,

> At the conference, there was a mix of older and younger adoptees, the twenty-something crowd. I began realizing that their [the younger adoptees'] experiences and the environment that they're growing up in are so different that we are alien to each other. They have culture camps. They live in diverse communities. The society as a whole is a . . . lot more tolerant. There are more people that have heard of adoption and inter-country adoption. And it's not so foreign to people. For those of us who were adopted before, we were the pioneers, so our experiences are very different. We talk about . . . things like racism and prejudice and the younger generation says, "I don't know what you're talking about. You're crazy; I didn't experience that at all. That's not my reality." And we're going, "It is our reality."

While racism continues to plague the United States, the civil rights movement and the multicultural movement have to some degree awakened the consciousness to tolerance and a celebration of the diversity of cultures (Sleeter and Bernal 2004). As Cindy pointed out above, these social movements directly influenced the lives of the second wave of Korean adoptees, most notably through the development of Korean culture camps and greater awareness of transracial adoption. Certainly, the United States is very different now, in terms of race relations, than it was in the 1950s and 1960s, and these societal differences played a major role in how the adoptees developed their racial and transracial adoptee identities.

Also significant within the Korean adoptee community is the age of the adoptee at the time of adoption. Seventeen adoptees in this study were adopted in infancy (prenatal to one year old) and thirteen were adopted in early childhood (one to four years old). Six were adopted in the middle childhood years (five to ten years old), and two were adopted as adolescents (eleven to twenty-one years old).[2] The age at which they were adopted influenced their experiences growing up and, of course, the development of their racial and transracial adoptee identities.

The childhood and adolescent adoptees were able to remember their lives in Korea prior to adoption, including time spent with birth families and in their orphanages. Brenda and Julie recalled the hardships of living in the orphanages or with their families and, like the older generation of adoptees, viewed their adoptions as salvation from their lives in Korea.[3]

> BRENDA: I came as a ten-year-old. I lived a lifetime in Korea, in the sense of being on the street and taking care of my younger siblings. I was the oldest of four kids and it was really difficult.

> JULIE: I know that when it was time to take a nap, if you didn't take a nap, they glued your eyes shut with this ointment. And all of us were underneath this one comforter on the floor. I just remember roaches and crickets on the floor and they always frightened me. They always had a light on and there were a lot of windows. I remember seeing a lot of bugs attached to those windows. I think I still have nightmares about that stuff. I have other memories of that place. I see it and I'm not quite sure if it was real, but it seems real. If I have the chance to go back [to the orphanage], I think I might remember more distinctly.

The adoptees who were able to remember living in orphanages or struggling within their homes certainly viewed their adoptions differently from those adopted as infants who did not have a sense of hardship prior to being adopted. This difference had an impact in that some adoptees were more understanding of the institution of transracial adoption and the desire to assimilate into their White cultural environments, whereas the infant and early childhood adoptees grew up without memories of adversity and experienced White culture as primary, and middle childhood and adolescent adoptees already possessed both memories and Korean culture as primary. Thus the differences caused some friction to arise within the Korean adoptee community, especially over political issues related to transracial adoption.

Diversity Related to Biracial/Multiracial Adoptees

Three of the adoptees self-identified as biracial/multiracial, two of whom were adopted prior to 1960. Following the Korean War, the biracial/multiracial war orphans were especially hard to place in Korea, which is why so many of the first wave of adoptees are typically biracial/multiracial. These adoptees discussed their experiences of growing up as different from those of "full-blooded" adoptees, especially with regards to their racial identity. Specifically, because Daniel and Charlotte were recognized as physically biracial/multiracial, they found they were often not accepted as racially Korean, and they concluded that those adoptees who are "full-blooded" in appearance[4] could at the very least be accepted as Korean.

> DANIEL: Most people look at me and they think I'm Hawaiian so they don't really think of me as being Asian. [City name] has a big Native American population and so then people started thinking I was Native American. And it's one of those things when kids tease you or say something, they name . . . anything else but Korean. I'd always felt the connection [with being Korean] because in my mind I could go to Korea and I felt Korean because I was the same height and my color was the same as everybody else over there. But when I get to Korea, everyone looks at me as being White because they don't accept mixed race in Korea. They assume everyone's Korean or . . . not. And I was the "not."

> CHARLOTTE: Mixed heritage is a tough one because when you obviously look mixed, as far as my own appearance goes, I've gotten every kind of response under the sun from "you don't look Korean at all" . . . to everything else in [the] middle, but never do people think I look completely Korean. Sometimes people say, "Are you trying to be White?" And that really pains me. In Korea it's not a privilege to be mixed race, believe me, because that's what landed me in the Amerasian orphanage. And what do you mean, I'm trying to be White? I get everything else in between and rarely do people think I'm Korean. I always get Filipino, Hawaiian, Native American, and all of that.

Biracial and multiracial identity certainly adds another aspect to the ways in which the identity journey is unique to each adoptee. These stories reflect the need to accept diversity and differences rather than shun and exclude those who do not "fit in."

The biracial/multiracial adoptees found it difficult at times to relate to other adoptees who look "full-blooded" Korean. Even though she found the Korean adoptee groups enlightening, Charlotte believed that some adoptees had difficulty understanding biracial/multiracial perspectives.

I think most people [Korean adoptees] are really open and accepting, but again, even though I thought this is the group I'd been looking for all my life, I'm still getting comments like "you don't look Korean at all" or "you look Korean to me, so why are you trying to be White?" I'm getting the same response that I've gotten from the rest of the world and I'm thinking that these people do represent the rest of the world. The only thing we have in common is that we grew up in White families, and the way they perceive me [is] pretty much the same, no different. In my own experience, as I look back, I feel like I've never been in one place or one group long enough to claim one as my own. So much so that I don't relate to some of the adoptees because they came at infancy, they look completely Korean. Part of me feels like they think I'm a little out of it or I don't fit in with them. I don't feel that close to them on some level because of all those differences, and the adoption is the only thing that links me to them. I don't know what I was expecting when I first joined [the Korean adoptee group], but for a while it was . . . a social group and that was fine by me. I was just happy to meet really interesting people who had some things in common with me. But on another level, when you come here as a teenager, and as a person of mixed heritage, and then dealing with people who came at an early age or at infancy who are full-blooded Korean, . . . there [are] some cultural barriers between me and them.

There was a strong sense among the biracial/multiracial Korean adoptees that they were placed in a separate category of the Korean adoptee experience. Both Daniel and Charlotte speak about feeling at times ostracized from all three communities—Korean, White, and Korean transracial adoptee—because of their physical features. They both felt as though their biracial/mixed-race features placed them in unique situations that "full-blooded" adoptees could not altogether relate to that often resulted in some tension within the group around issues of acceptance and recognition of biracial/multiracial adoptees' identities. (See Williams-León and Nakashima 2001 for expansive and diverse readings on "Mixed-heritage Asian Americans.")

Elitism in the Korean Adoptee Community

Since the 1999 Gathering it seems that more Korean adoptees are attending subsequent Gatherings and other transracial adoptee conferences, becoming involved in adoptee groups, forming adoptee groups in their own areas, returning to Korea, attending Korean culture camps, volunteering as mentors for younger Korean adoptees, and speaking on panels about their adoptee experiences. A variety of experiences related to the amount of critical engagement in exploring their racial and transracial adoptee identities was created. Even though all of these activities allowed for more adoptees to explore their identities, it also produced tension within the Korean adoptee community.

Specifically, some adoptees sensed elitism among those who deemed themselves superior to others who were just awakening to their racial and transracial adoptee identities. A small number of the more involved Korean adoptees appeared to maintain a sense of aloofness toward those who were just joining the groups or attending a Gathering for the first time. According to Charlotte, "Both [two leaders in the international Korean adoptee community] have this reputation of being extremely—I don't want to say power hungry, but they have to be better than everyone, they have to be in control, and they think that their opinions are somehow more valuable than others. That's what people say. And I don't think either one of them even has their MA in sociology or social work."

Some adoptees in the study attributed this sense of elitism to a natural part of the identity journey and believe that as adoptees become more immersed in their identity journeys they will confront White privilege and openly criticize transracial adoptees who have yet to awaken to their identities. Gay states, "When Afro-Americans become immersed in the search for a Black identity referent, it is with a vengeance. . . . As regards persona and style in interpersonal relations, immersed Blacks employ confrontation, bluntness, and an either/or mentality as the primary basis for interacting with both Black and Whites" (1987, 59, 61). A few adoptees pointed out that as Korean adoptees critically engage in exploring their identities, an "us vs. them" mentality emerges. The more engaged adoptees then view the newly awakened adoptees as contributors to transracial adoptees' oppression because they are not actively working against White institutional and cultural racism. Gloria realized that certain group members viewed adoptees who were not actively and decisively immersed in exploring their identities as outsiders.

> I remember talking with my boyfriend at the time and he said Black people went through it too; [that] is, if you're not with us, then you're against us. If you're not going to be political and proactive and you're just going to be submissive, then you're part of the people keeping us down. And I was just trying to figure out what's right here. Let me form my own opinion and then I'll let you know if I'm on board. I might be, but you've got to give me a little bit of breathing room. And they [the Korean adoptee group] didn't.

It appears that some adoptees within these groups are engaged in dialogues aimed at creating an authentic Korean adoptee identity. An authentic Korean adoptee, then, is one who has been to Korea, searched for birth parents, joined a group, volunteered at culture camps, spoken on panels, and, most important, is actively working to eliminate the institution of transracial adoption. The adoptees who are active within these communities have developed a sense of control over who is judged an "authentic" Korean adoptee. Gay continues,

> Black authenticity and purification are preached fervently, as if to say, "By convincing others of the validity of my ethnicity, I will convince myself." Testifying Blacks argue for the unification of all Blacks around consensual prescriptions of Blackness. The message of this demand seems to be, "If we all ascribe to identical definitions and expressions of Blackness, our unity will reinforce our claims to a common heritage, our sense of people-hood, and a communal destiny." (1987, 61)

Some of the adoptees in the study viewed active adoptees as bringing an unconscious society to a critical awareness of the Korean adoptee experience as well as other forms of racial oppression. These Korean adoptees were outspoken in a variety of venues (e.g., publications, panel discussions, online forums, and Web sites) about issues related to the transracial adoptee experience. Some felt these outspoken adoptees could be a negative force within the Korean adoptee community. They saw them as being so immersed in their identity discoveries that they were no longer able to critically reflect upon their identity journeys and were essentially silencing and disempowering Korean adoptees who had not yet reached that point.

Tensions Related to a Diverse Membership

Diversity within the Korean adoptee community is to be expected; as within any large group of people, there will be a wide array of personalities. Cliques and friendships are formed around a variety of sociocultural variables (e.g., gender, age, sexual identity, marriage status, level of education, socioeconomic class) as well as around areas of interests. Some adoptees recognized that the in-group diversity described above could lead to the exclusion of certain adoptees from the group.

The adoptees in this study were well aware of the "angry" adoptees. This particular label disempowered some Korean adoptees from awakening to their racial and transracial adoptee identities because they did not want to be considered ungrateful to their parents and adoption agencies. Angry adoptees soon discovered that they were viewed as immature, erratic, and psychologically unstable by adoption agencies, parents, and even parts of the Korean adoptee community.

The "angry adoptee" label not only disempowered these adoptees, but also created tension within the Korean adoptee community. For example, this mindset caused Gloria to turn away because she did not view herself as disgruntled.

> Most of the people that are vocal are a little bit disgruntled for some reason or another. They are either disgruntled because of being a person of color or because of being an adoptee who doesn't understand their culture or because they had a bad [visiting] Korea experience or a bad experience meeting their birth family. I didn't meet or talk to a lot of people who were like me who have issues but were happy, generally speaking. So hearing all these people that were disgruntled, it made me very bitter towards the group.

Most of the adoptees in this study recognized that some transracial adoptees have endured great hardship in their lives and may struggle with mental problems and need professional psychiatric assistance. Brenda understood that the Korean adoptee community is not prepared professionally to provide such services and should not feel obligated to offer them: "They've got some real emotional baggage and problems that they need some professional help with. I think most of these groups don't have the patience to really be there for them for the long haul. They really do need the psychological help. What happens is that it is a double rejection; the group starts withdrawing. So this individual then feels even more rejected." Brenda and others contend that adoptees with certain mental instabilities should not be entirely turned away from the Korean adoptee community, because doing so could be even more damaging to those individuals. Brenda also commented that the groups could instead provide referrals to professional psychiatrists, psychologists, and other therapists who have experience working with transracial adoptees.

Some adoptees also recognize that there are those who are unable to openly express their stories because of their painful experiences. Brian and Kris believe that some adoptees often do not feel secure enough to share their stories even with the adoptee community, and therefore the community needs to promote openness and understanding.

> BRIAN: Some of us who've had unhappier upbringings are trying to suppress it rather than . . . express it. Apparently, among others that I've talked to, there are unhappy situations: second-class

citizens in the adoption home, physical abuse, very strong religious repression, all kind of things like that. And unfortunately those are not the things that they can actually sit down and write with gusto. It's a very painful process.

KRIS: I've seen a lot of passive Asian adoptees. I've seen more adoptees who have [an] "I don't care" attitude or "I just ignore this part of my life" attitude rather than the angry adoptees who state, "I hate my life. I wish I wasn't adopted." They [passive adoptees] are actually more difficult to deal with because they refuse in their own minds to recognize where they come from or who they are. They're ignoring that part of themselves. I think the only thing you can do, really, is to provide them with tools to help themselves. You can't really force it on them. You can talk about it a lot, but essentially that's up to them whether or not they want to embrace the group.

While it seems that there is very little the Korean adoptee community can do for these particular adoptees, several believed that the community needs to remain open to all who take the initial step to reveal their deepest thoughts rather than write them off as unreachable.

As part of exploring their racial and transracial adoptee identities, most adoptees opted to share their stories with the Korean adoptee community. Some wrote autobiographies or filmed documentaries, several attended Gatherings and other conferences related to transracial adoption, and a number volunteered to sit on panel discussions for parents and prospective adoptive parents. Gay states,

Another necessary dimension of information acquisition and processing in the search for a Black identity referent is "testifying and sermonizing." Testimonials and secular sermons are given about the trials and tribulations of being Black in a non-Black world, the emotional mutilations of self-denial, and the psychologically redemptive power of the decision to reclaim and to embrace one's birthright of Blackness. (1987, 61)

There is a great deal to learn from the adult Korean adoptees' stories. The sharing and validating of these stories should be recognized as an important component of the identity journey. Brian and Woojung encouraged all adoptees to share their experiences and viewed the group as a source to validate these stories by accepting them as part of the whole.

BRIAN: Another adoptee apparently came here [to the adoptee group]. She had gone through some physical and sexual abuse. Those things led her to join our group for feedback, for reinforcement, or simply to have someone else listen to her problems as opposed to a cold therapist. There seems to be more, even if you have some kind of angst and you can't understand it or articulate it; when you join us, you slowly realize that we've all been through some degree of it. Maybe not as much as this person who had been physically abused, but some sense of alienation or identity crisis—we've all been through it.

WOOJUNG: One of the hard points in doing this [forming a Korean adoptee community] is the diversity of people who are all on a very different spectrum in regards to their identity. Because how many times do I have to repeat the whole, "It's okay to be angry; it's okay to be so resentful." We can try to go beyond that and say, "Okay, we've gone through this. What's next?" It's a fine balance that we try to figure out. Some people are much better than others about reaching out and trying to be supportive of those who are going through some of those emotions that we've [gone] through already. But I think at this point there are people who've been going through it for a long time and have heard this a million times and are now questioning, "Is there more to this than just going through the same emotions, the same steps? What's beyond this exploration? What can we do?

The Korean adoptee community was formed around the transracial adoptee experience (i.e., this is the reason they came together as a group). Therefore, it was disconcerting for most adoptees to discover the ways in which in-group diversity led to the rejection of certain adoptees who did not "fit" the profile of the authentic Korean adoptee. Some adoptees found it difficult to find acceptance in the Korean adoptee community based on, for example, their age, their age at adoption, attendance at culture camp, a biracial/multiracial background, or other variables. This challenges the notion of who possesses the power to say which adoptees are authentic and which inauthentic, thus causing tension within the community.

Even though some stories may seem incompatible with the larger group, the adoptees concluded that neither the happy stories nor the unhappy ones should be claimed as the entirety of the identity journey. If all stories contribute to the transracial adoptee experience, then all transracial adoptees will feel that they are welcome and can contribute to the community.

Conflict with the Institution of Transracial Adoption

During their identity journeys, many of the adoptees requested their papers from the adoption agencies, visited their orphanages and adoption agencies in Korea, and facilitated a birth family search. A major aspect of exploring their identities was a critical understanding of the institution of transracial adoption.

In sharing their experiences with other Korean adoptees, most discovered how the adoption agencies provided false information or withheld specifics from adoptees. The adoptees discussed the common excuses the adoption agencies offered when they came looking for answers about their lives. Some adoptees in the study believed that the agencies often discouraged them from searching for answers in a misguided attempt to protect the adoptees from the lack of information, as well as protect themselves from future problems with the adoptees. As Jamie and Abby delved deeper into this issue, they concluded that the adoption agencies were trying to protect themselves from their past mistakes and protect the birth families from being found.

> JAMIE: I came over as an infant. We were told that I was left at a police station in Seoul. Since then I found out that many adoptees were told [the same story], and sometimes it's true and sometimes it's not.

> ABBY: But she [a group member] was saying, "My parents were killed in a car accident." And people [other group members] were asking her, "Do you really believe your parents were killed in a car accident? That's what a lot of people are hearing from [adoption agencies]. A lot of people just made that up. Their parents weren't really killed. That's what they said about my parents, her parents, and his parents. All our parents weren't killed in a car accident." And it helped her think about it more. She never thought of it that way. And it really encouraged her to search and become interested in that, where she never would have before. . . . When you go to look for your records and they say, "There was a fire"—there's always a fire someplace that burns all our records.

These two accounts illustrate one way in which the Korean adoptee groups have become a source of information. While some may see these groups solely as a source of support in helping adoptees overcome their sense of loss, anger, and resentment, it became clear that they provided much more than that. The groups are able to address some of the myths of the Korean adoptees' stories and at the same time create a space for adoptees to address these issues.

It is also possible that these adoptee groups could encourage a sense of outrage toward the institution of transracial adoption. Sophie and Amber believe that one of the major mistakes of the adoption agencies was placing Korean adoptees in White, overtly racist homes.

> SOPHIE: I know for a fact that my parents should not have adopted a child of color. My father is working towards getting better, but he was very, very prejudiced and said extremely offensive things to my face. I mean, he is not someone who should have adopted a child of color at all. And that makes me wonder what was the adoption agency doing; what did they see when they okayed this family to adopt a child from Korea? I assume that they asked my parents, "Why did you choose Korea?" And did they reply, "It was a convenient thing" or "We did a lot of research" or "We wanted to pick a country that was in need" or "It was the easiest thing to do. The paperwork was the easiest. It was the fastest process and we wanted a kid"?

> AMBER: I went to . . . look at my adoption files while I was in Korea. I knew growing up that my grandparents were extremely racist people, but to actually see it in my adoption file was upsetting. The Korean adoption agency had copies of the home studies from the American adoption agency, and before the adoption they said, "There are concerns, the parents of the parents are racist, and they've said that they will disown them." Then they did their post-adoption studies and . . . said, "They've stopped speaking, they don't come around. We hope this continues to be a successful adoption placement." And I'm just like, "If this was a racist family, what the hell are they doing sending a non-White child to this family?" But [if] they have . . . good intentions [or have] the money and [have] a stable career, [it's] enough for placement of a Korean child in a White home.

In both statements there is the feeling that meeting the criteria of being White, middle class, and a U.S. citizen was enough to adopt a child from Korea (or any other developing or underdeveloped nation). In other words, Sophie believed that some White parents may have chosen to adopt from Korea because the process for adopting Korean children versus White children was less strenuous; the requirements to adopt White children far exceeded those to adopt children of color, and the demand for White children probably resulted in longer waits and greater expenses. R. Lee states,

> By the 1960s and 1970s in the United States, White couples, who were usually older and infertile, began to consider international adoption as more feasible than domestic same-race adoption and less controversial than domestic adoption. Today, Americans, still predominantly White, are adopting more than ever before infants and young children from more than 40 countries world wide. (2003, 714)

Adoptees in the study also felt that adoptive parents did not take into consideration the feelings of the children because they are immersed in their own issues or believe that raising a transracial adopted child would be the same as raising any other child. As Halle points out, some parents simply do not want to hear the adult perspective or at least the angry adoptee perspective, because these parents may feel somewhat threatened by anything that might challenge White adoptive parents' notions of why they adopt children of color.

> I get angry seeing all the White people adopting the Korean kids and I feel like they have no idea what they're getting themselves into. . . . I mean, they're cute now and everything, but . . . they might have problems when they grow up. I offered my advice to one of my friends who adopted a Chinese baby. I just feel like they don't really want my help or my advice. They just think they can handle it their own way. I feel like they don't know what they are getting themselves into. It angers me because someone asked the one woman who adopted the Chinese baby, "Why are you adopting out of the country when there are so many kids in America that need to be adopted?" And she said because she [would] rather not go through the problems with the parents changing their minds and wanting their children back. She'd rather not go through all of that.

Halle attempts to understand some of the underlying reasons why White parents engage in transracial adoption. The reply of the woman in Halle's statement reflects the attitude that transracial adoptees would be less likely to find their birth parents. Thus White adoptive parents would not have to worry about custody battles or "losing" their child to birth parents, which to some adoptees, like Halle, is a selfish motive for wanting to adopt transracially.

Some adoptees were also of the opinion that the reasons for White parents to adopt transracially were related to their White and economic privilege. R. Lee concludes, "Third world advocates similarly have argued that international adoption is a new form of colonialism and cultural imperialism that treats children as economic commodities" (2003, 714). Brenda and Halle openly question the institution of transracial adoption, especially the reasons and costs for adopting children from overseas.

> BRENDA: I hate the policy in China. [For] each child that comes out of a Chinese orphanage, every parent pays three to five thousand dollars directly to that orphanage. They call it a donation; I call it corruption. There's no way it should cost anywhere from twenty to twenty-five thousand dollars to adopt. So three to five thousand is a donation to the orphanage. Those kids should be living in a mansion. If an average teacher, a high school teacher in China, makes less than three thousand dollars a year and we're giving three thousand dollars to that orphanage directly for each child that we take out of an orphanage, something is wrong.

> HALLE: My husband has a bad outlook towards it [the institution of transracial adoption] too. He thinks that White people adopt Asians to show that they have money because it's the thing to do now. Because a lot of people around [here] have been adopting, and most of the people, well, all the people that adopt, . . . are White and have money.

For some adoptees, gaining more information about their adoptions and the institution of transracial adoption produced feelings of anger and frustration, which led them to advocate tearing down the institution. Amber's statement below illustrates this sense of disgruntlement toward the institute of international transracial adoption.

> God bless Korea for figuring out a fabulous way that they could get rid of their burdens and their shames and make a little money to help the country get back on its feet. I love my parents and I've had a good life, yet I still feel very strongly about this modern colonialism—White, rich parents that can't have babies, [so] they just buy them from another country. There's really no reason for it in some places, especially Korea.

Outspoken adoptees such as Amber are quickly identified as angry, and in many arenas their voices are silenced because they are seen as irrational extremists within the Korean adoptee community when they use negative vocabulary such as "exporting children," "buying babies," and "transracial abductees." Voicing this type of antagonism often creates tension not only with the adoption agencies, but also with their families and some members of the Korean adoptee community. However, it is important to listen to these voices, as they provide insight into where their identity journeys have led them and where they are trying to direct their identity explorations. If we are able to see their anger as a part of their identity journeys toward a sense of empowerment, rather than disregard it altogether, then we may gain a more complete understanding of their racial and transracial identities.

Certainly, not all of the adoptees were angry or disgruntled upon discovering some of the difficult issues attached to transracial adoption. Several adoptees traveled to Korea and, in discussions with their adoption agencies, were able to uncover some of the truths about the institution of adoption in South Korea. In their discoveries, Joan and Tori seemed to understand the decisions of the adoption agencies in their attempts to cover up their past mistakes.

> JOAN: When I went to Korea in 2001, I actually talked to some people at [the adoption agency] about it, and first of all, they said for a long time a lot of folks lied to the adoptees because they really didn't want them to look for their families or they didn't want them to see the records because [they were] just so minimal. They were ashamed. So they would rather tell the adoptee that they had nothing or the records were burned or whatever than actually disclose the truth.

> TORI: I also heard . . . a lot of times that they [adoption agencies] were just filling in the adoption papers. Of course if they didn't know how to spell somebody's name or they weren't completely sure or maybe feeling lazy that day; just writing "no data" was always the easy thing to [do]. There is also the idea of privacy and confidentiality and the fact that if you didn't want to mark that poor woman [the birth mother], [if] you want her to go on and live her life and everything, . . . it was better not to reveal who she is and let her actually have her privacy so that she can go on with her life.

It is especially interesting that Tori tries to justify the decisions of the adoption agencies to protect the confidentiality of the birth mother (note that she does not mention the birth father or the birth family). Several adoptees who engaged in understanding what their Korean adoptee identities meant showed signs of compassion or empathy toward their birth mothers, rather than resentment and anger (as seen in the adoptees who are just beginning their identity journeys). When adoptees encountered a lack of information or falsified information, it encouraged some to seek more answers. The more they searched, the more frustrated they became with the entire institution of transracial adoption as they realized the errors and oversights involved in the process. However, as they began to find answers for themselves, they began to understand Korean culture. And even though they could not fully accept these traditional notions of Korean culture that prohibited them from remaining with their birth mothers or reuniting with them, several adoptees eventually came to appreciate and, to some degree, forgive their birth mothers. This is a very potent aspect of recognizing the value of exploring their identities; it allowed them to feel empowered because they no longer felt diminished by the misunderstandings, lost information, and lectures on what their identities should look like. Instead, they make powerful their identities through their identity explorations.

Conflicts with (White) Spouses/Significant Others

Seventeen of the adoptees in this study were or had been married. Four were divorced and one remarried. Twelve married White partners, one married a Korean immigrant, one married a Korean American (born in the United States), one married a Korean adoptee, one married an immigrant from Latin America, and one married a European immigrant. A main issue related to marriage was the tension that materialized between the adoptees and their partners when the former began to explore their identities. Jennifer stated that following the 1999 Gathering, several adoptees returned to their homes and soon discovered that they no longer felt a strong connection to their White partners. She attributed this tension to an awakening to their racial and transracial adoptee identities. Specifically, she believed that some of the adoptees who were awakened to and subsequently began exploring their identities concluded that they were not the same person their partners had married, which resulted in some of these adoptees filing for divorce. Brenda talked about divorce among the Korean adoptees who investigated their identities later in life.

> What I find really surprising with this group is that many of the thirty- and forty-year-olds and even [ones in their late twenties], who should have been dealing with all this [identity] in their teens, are now

questioning it. So you find . . . a number of people that are divorcing. I don't know if that's a trend with other groups, but they're reevaluating their relationships and many of them are divorcing.

Of the four divorcees, none gave the reason for divorce as due to their exploration of their racial and transracial adoptee identities. They gave other reasons, yet they all seemed to be related to their identities. Kendra stated that the reason for her divorce was related to her inability to trust another person, which she directly correlated to her abandonment issues.

I was married to him for thirteen years and I just decided one day that I didn't love him anymore. And I walked away. And he was a wonderful guy and I still have great respect for him. But yet, I think I run because it's almost like I'm afraid of being left, and so I leave first.

While Tammy remains married, she discussed how she found it difficult to trust her husband in the beginning of her marriage, yet through conversation and opening up, she was eventually able to trust him.

I'm very fortunate to have [husband's name] because he's pushed me to do it [identity journey]. I've really held my emotions in pretty much all my life and so that's a big deal in our marriage. I mean it's a lot better because [I] finally am starting to trust him.

Brenda, still married, mentioned that she had had commitment issues in many of her relationships prior to her marriage because she had difficulty trusting others, which she traces back to her fear of abandonment.

I did have problems with staying in a relationship because I would get to a point right where they would want to marry me, we'd get engaged, and then I thought, "I know you're going to leave me just like everybody else." So I would do everything to jeopardize and sabotage that relationship. I know, looking back, [that] I really hurt some people. And so I think it was a process . . . where I came to the point of [thinking], I'm okay. I like who I am and I'm okay. But that was a long process.

While most married adoptees did not end up divorcing their partners upon awakening to their identities, this does not mean that such discoveries did not cause tension in their marriages. The adoptees spoke of how their

White partners could not understand what was happening partly because White privilege blinded them not just to their own privilege, but also to understanding their adoptee spouses' identity struggles.

At the same time, Tammy believed that the adoptees needed to accept their White partners' inability to completely understand the complexities of the adoptees' identity development and therefore felt the adoptees needed to actively include their spouses/significant others. Indeed, the further immersed some adoptees became in their identity journeys, Tammy assumed, the more their White spouses/significant others felt marginalized by their partners and the adoptee groups.

> He [her husband] has a problem with [the] group because he thinks that we are victimizing ourselves. That we aren't ever going to get ahead in life because we're always saying, "We're adopted," so he sees it as a cop-out. He said, "Maybe it's because I'm not adopted." I mean, he has abandonment issues because his parents divorced when he was five and his dad was never around. But he said, "I can identify with it on that aspect, but I don't have the identity confusion. There's a lot of stuff I don't have that I've heard you guys talk about. At the same time, I don't think your group is really empowering each other and moving past the point that you're adopted." I tried to explain [that] that's who we are and that's why we are the way we are. And I said, "I don't think that we're victimizing ourselves because we survived. We've found each other and that's just made us that much stronger." I still don't think he really gets it. I think it's very hard for him too. We [the adoptee group] had a movie night and we were all sitting in a circle and all of a sudden he just got pushed out. Obviously it wasn't on purpose, but he just got completely pushed out of the circle. And he was looking around and all of sudden he's sitting there by himself. And he said, "I don't really belong here." And I said, "Just remember this feeling." I mean, not that I want him to feel bad, but to just be familiar with this feeling because this is how I felt my whole life.

Tammy's reflections on her husband's thoughts are quite complex. She discusses how her husband views the adoptee group as a means to perpetuate their self-victimization. This view is quite common, especially when looking at issues of racism. Often the White privileged view the racially oppressed as using racism as an excuse for their own failures, or as Tammy's husband sees it, "as a cop-out," rather than just "moving past the point." However, Tammy sees the group as an affirmation of "surviving" their adoptions, their oppression, by coming together to rejoice in developing a new community—one that Tammy's husband feels he is not fully part of.

Karina was the most forthcoming in explaining her struggles with her husband, especially after returning from the 1999 Gathering. I use her voice to illustrate the tensions that emerged once the adoptees began exploring their identities. Karina's statement includes several ways of overcoming some of the uncertainties and conflicts that arise when adoptees begin this exploration.

> I got married when I was really young. I went from my father's home, really, to my husband's house. There was something that just told me that you need to do this [identity exploration]. And that's when I had started prior to even going to the [1999] Gathering, talking on line, reading other people's stories. I could sit there and read them and [say], "Yep, I'm feeling this. I'm experiencing this," that type of thing. My husband and my dad both [felt], "Oh my gosh, she's just thirty and all women go through this when they're thirty." When I got back from the Gathering, I was emotionally a wreck. But having four children and trying to live an already established life was really, really difficult because all I wanted to do [was] sit and cry or pull the covers over my head and just wish it would all . . . go away. But you can't do that because you have all these other people that are depending on you at this stage of your life.[5]

Conflict and tension developed in Karina's marriage when she began her identity journey.

> When that gay or Asian thing came out,[6] I was on a rampage. I showed him [her husband] the ad, and he chuckled and said, "Come on. You're taking this way too serious." I'm like, "No, I'm not. You're not a Korean male. You don't understand how society views Korean men. You have White privilege and you don't understand it." I have to keep beating him over the head . . . saying, "Honey, your family is the perfect Catholic American family. And you know who your parents are, you know where you come from, you can trace your family tree if you want. Your siblings all live very close. You live the White American dream. But you don't understand it."

As Karina delved deeper into her journey, she could see that her husband continued to remain detached from what she was experiencing. While she tried to accept her husband's attitude, she saw him invoking his White male privilege to remain disconnected from her explorations.

> My husband is not the most sensitive guy. I know that when we go to Korean adoptee events, there's one other White guy that shows up with his girlfriend and these two guys have the same personality. My husband says, "If so-and-so is going to be there, I'll go because he's cool and we can make jokes about being married to you Korean women." He does not respect the way that Koreans treat Caucasian men who married Korean women. It makes him very angry. He says, "Why would I want to go to Korea where people are going to look down on me for marrying somebody that they cast away anyway?"

Rather than criticizing Karina's husband's insensitivity and blaming it in part on his lack of awareness of White privilege, it should be noted that the two were able to come to an agreement regarding her journey; her husband accepted that her identity awakening and journey were not only important, but also necessary for them to continue in their marriage.

> He finally has come to an understanding. When I wanted to go to the mini-gatherings, he knew how important it was to me; he knew that his life would be screwed up for a month after that, but he knew how important it was [for] me to go. He always provides whatever means, and in that way I have to say he has been very supportive [of] my need to do it.

Karina also understood that her identity journey was not easy on her family members, especially her husband and children. She believed, however, that her explorations allowed her to develop much stronger relationships with her husband and children as well as her father and siblings because she felt she could incorporate her racial and transracial adoptee identities into her White cultural background.

> It was about Korea; I started trying to cook Korean at home. And I think my family . . . was like, "What is up with you?" And that was a big struggle because I was all about Korea. My husband was very threatened. He felt that his little security in life was being threatened. The whole Korea thing, that was a real struggle; you peak, you go way to the left, then you go way to the right, and then you're way Korean. I found a happy balance in the middle

where I could still have my Korean friends, and they weren't a threat to my husband or my family and I could . . . still be mom to my kids.

While Karina was able to work with her husband to overcome many of the tensions that arose during her exploration of her racial and transracial adoptee identities, she knew several Korean adoptees who were unable to make similar compromises with their spouses/significant others during such a tumultuous time. Several adoptees discussed how their sustained engagement in exploring their identities often led to a newly defined identity that caused tension in their marriages/relationships. In some cases White spouses/significant others were seen as oppressors of their newfound identity. Unable to join their new identities with their old, several Korean adoptees opted to exclude their spouses/significant others and family members from sharing in their explorations.

Confronting Contradictions with Parents

Throughout our conversations, at one point or another, all of the adoptees discussed their relationships with their parents. Most were quick to point out that they had loving parents who had done the best they could with the few resources available to parents who adopted transracially. It also became apparent that most adoptees had some resentment toward their parents, for a variety of reasons. Most had forgiven their parents, but a few remained resentful. Most adoptees believe that by not exploring their racial and transracial adoptee identities, these issues and contradictions will remain unspoken in their families. They conclude that it is important to begin these dialogues, even though it may mean hurting some feelings along the way.

Several of the adoptees realized early that some of their thoughts were best not shared with their parents. This silencing of their voices thus was not intentional on their parents' part. Abby and Connie felt it was necessary to withhold certain thoughts from their parents because they did not want to hurt them.

> ABBY: I know . . . in our conversations, a lot of my friends, and even myself, are scared to talk to parents about this type of stuff because you're so afraid that you're going to hurt them, which you really shouldn't be because your parents should have known what they were signing up for. But when you love somebody you want to be very careful about what you say.

CONNIE: This just could be me being paranoid, but I've also sensed some level of discomfort with my mom, which, from talking with other adoptees, is common for the adoptive parents to feel. . . . I mean, she didn't really seem to want to know too much, and for me it's fine because I think it would be a somewhat uncomfortable conversation for both of us. I don't want to make her feel insecure. She doesn't even know that I'm taking Korean-language classes because I think that would make her feel sad that I want to learn about my culture. So I don't want to make her feel insecure.

The desire to protect parents' feelings seemed to have developed at an early age for the adoptees. Several did not want to question their parents about why they chose to adopt from Korea or discuss some of their own feelings and insecurities about being adopted. They worried that their desire to investigate and question aspects of their racial and transracial adoptee identities would be regarded as renouncing their parents' love and openly exhibiting a lack of appreciation for all that their parents had done for them. Even though their thoughts about their parents' reactions may not be altogether true, because several adoptees did not give their parents the opportunity to understand, the resulting lack of trust did not allow their parents to share in the dance of identities.

Kara talked about adoptees feeling a strong sense of guilt in exploring their identities because they thought they were disavowing the good homes that their parents had provided.

I always felt so different from them [her parents], and they never thought that way. They never treated me that way. I don't want to give the impression that my family ever treated me any different, because they certainly never . . . did. I think by becoming more active in this [adoptee group], in some ways I feel guilty that I'm leaving my family, somehow separating myself from my family and denying that part of me.

It seems that parents are in a difficult situation when it comes to engaging in conversations related to their children's adoption experiences because while adoptees may want their parents to support their journeys, there is still some hesitation on how much the adoptees want to share.

This hesitation does not come only from feelings of guilt. As shown in the previous chapter, parents often silence the adoptees' inquiries by dismissing the issues. For example, parents viewed racism as something the adoptees needed to "get over," or they equated being "teased" for wearing glasses to the racial harassment their children were experiencing. Consequently, the adoptees felt a sense of mistrust or felt that their parents could not understand their true feelings, which is very similar to the tensions that arose in the marriages/relationships described above.

Amber took the issue of mistrust a step further, stating that some parents may view their children as "angry" when they question issues related to their adoption.

A lot of adoptees talk about how very little they ever talk about adoption issues with their parents. I was not really given an opportunity to vent [about] the negative aspects of being a Korean adoptee. I think with the younger adoptees, their parents are forewarned that this is going to happen. It's okay [for the adoptees] to be angry with them [adoptees' parents], but don't negate their [adoptees'] feelings. It doesn't mean that they [adoptees] don't love you [parents] just because they're angry. I wish that my parents had known that because I didn't get all of that out of my system until I was [an] adult. I feel bad when I get worked up and I'm talking to my parents about adoption and asking them, "Why did you lie to me about all this stuff?" So that's been very difficult for them.

Some adoptees consciously decided to keep their explorations to themselves, as they wanted to maintain control over their experiences. Even if their parents did or said nothing in regards to their exploration, these adoptees concluded that sharing their experiences would taint their overall identity journey. Sharing would in some ways restrain full exploration of their identities because, as Kris pointed out, most adoptees were fearful of hurting their parents.

I don't actually share much at all. I like to keep it private because I do share a lot with my parents, but not the adoption piece. I do share it with them, but it's difficult for me to talk about. I know they're very involved in it; they cut out articles for me. But it's awkward for me to talk with them about adoption in a sit-down conversation. I like to keep it more private just because I feel like it's something that I need to have for myself and not have it be a family thing. I share so much of everything else with them about school, about my profession, about my interests, what I like to do with my friends. I introduce them to different parts of my life and that part is just something that I feel like I can have for myself.

In addition, Alex commented that he often felt his parents did not encourage or support his investigation of his racial and transracial adoptee identities because they did not grasp the substantial influence his identity explorations had on his life.

> I just don't think they [his parents] understand. When I'm going to these culture camps [as a mentor], their biggest question is, "Well, can you afford it?" And I'm like, "Mom, even if I can't afford it, I'm still going to do it. It's that important to me and for the kids." She's always interested in what I'm doing, but she doesn't quite get the adoption stuff. I'm involved with [an adoptee group] and she went to the fundraising dinner and said, "Oh, it was really good. You guys did a good job." But [she does] not necessarily [understand] the impact it has on me and other adoptees. That's not their [parents] fault; they're not adopted. I love my parents and I know that they back me up . . . whatever I do. But when it comes to adoption stuff and my involvement in adoption groups, they just don't see it the way I see it.

Some adoptees came to realize that the more they explored their identities, the more distance they created between themselves and their parents. Alex did not blame his parents for not understanding because he accepted that this was something that possibly only adoptees could understand. However, Hanna struggled with her parents' detached and sometimes demeaning attitude toward her identity exploration, even if she knew that her parents could not fully connect with all the emotions she was experiencing.

> My parents have no idea what it means to be between two worlds. Not even my brother and my sister. Not a lot of people have had that experience. I struggle with that too. I'm thinking they should know this because they adopted transracially and they should know what it means to be an Asian woman. But I have no clue what it's like to be a White male. So what are these demands that I'm making on them and how realistic are these demands? But it doesn't mean that I don't have those thoughts about my parents' attitude.

Desiring to close the distance that had been created by their identity journeys, most adoptees tried to involve their parents as much as possible in their new experiences. Some shared their explorations out of guilt, because they did not want their parents to feel as though they were leaving them. Others involved their parents because they wanted them to understand how and why this was so important in their lives. Some invited their parents to adoptee group functions or transracial adoptee conferences (e.g., the Korean-American Adoptee Adoptive Family Network) that included parents. Others shared their own writings or literature by other adoptees.

In 2000, Deann Borshay Liem, a Korean adoptee, released her auto-documentary, titled *First Person Plural*. The issues and themes of the film have particular significance for transracial adoptees, birth families, and adoptive families. Many transracial adoptees could relate to Liem's exploration. As for Amber, this documentary served as a starting point for her to talk with her parents about her thoughts and feelings.

> We watched the documentary *First Person Plural*. I was watching it with my father and . . . I felt really embarrassed, getting all choked up over stuff. And my dad was trying to use it as an opportunity to open some dialogue between us, but it was very difficult. I don't even know how to describe it. My dad was asking me, "Do you remember anything from Korea?" And it was difficult for me to talk about that. It was something that was so personal that I always kept it pure [i.e., kept it to herself]. It had nothing to do with my adoptive parents that I always kept it hidden. And when it finally was being exposed, it was very difficult for me to share it with them. And it wasn't that I was worried about hurting their feelings; it was just awkward for me.

It is interesting that Amber blames herself for not opening up to her parents about her thoughts and feelings on adoption. She uses words like "embarrassed," "pure," and "hurting their feelings" to describe why she was unwilling to talk with her parents about these issues. She acknowledges that her father attempted to start a dialogue around the issues of adoption, which in some ways is quite rare. Tammy indicated that fathers in general seemed largely absent or detached from any dialogues and feelings related to adoption.

> The first thing that I really asked them [her parents] to pay attention to was Deann Borshay Liem's *First Person Plural*. It was on PBS a couple of years ago. I saw it for the first time at the [festival] and I said, "Mom, this is going to be broadcast on this day; please watch it. It's important for me for you guys to see this because this is how I felt all my life." And so they watched it and my mom [is] doing really well with it, but my dad is not doing so well. My mom called right after it ended and . . . was crying. She said, "That was such a good

movie." I said, "But did you look at her mom and her dad? They did a pretty good job of going back to Korea with her and meeting her Korean mom. It's very threatening for the American parents." And then my dad got on the phone and . . . said, "Yeah, that was good." And that was it. I said, "That's all you have to say?" And he said, "Well, it was very informative." And I said, "I'm going to go." And the conversation always ceases with him. It never ceases to amaze me that he can't tell me what he thinks.

While some adoptees concluded that their parents would not be able to share the same feelings, some wanted their parents to be able to connect with them and support their explorations. Some were met with misunderstanding and at times resentment from their parents as they explored and discovered their racial and transracial adoptee identities.

Parents were unprepared to engage in these dialogues. Parents found it difficult to understand and connect with the adoptees' identity awakenings and explorations because they may have believed that a colorblind and adoptee-blind philosophy was the key to acceptance and happiness. In other words, parents weren't ready to take on a critical dialogue about race, racism, and transracial adoption due to a lack of investigation of their own racial identity development. Gloria and Tori explained that when adoptees began to challenge their parent's colorblind philosophy, some parents continued to avoid dialogues and denied that identity issues exist.

> GLORIA: I like to call my parents well-intentioned White people because they are trapped in ethnic blindness, trapped in that place where they don't acknowledge that difference exists, and they believe that all people are alike and they truly believe [that] "If you treat people good, people will treat you good." And I remember coming out of college and saying to them, "What do you say when people are not good to you?" And they said, "We don't know." And I think that was the first time in my life when I really acknowledged that my parents were not omnipotent or knowledgeable about everything.

> TORI: My parents and I . . . don't have . . . great communication in the sense that I don't talk to them about a whole lot of different things. I still hold a real animosity in the sense . . . that they are the average racist. They don't see that they are because there's this notion that "I can't be racist because I adopted you." But let's remember, she [her mother] said, "You don't look any different

to me than your sisters do." Then this nullifies each other. So, yes, you can be a racist [by not accepting her racial and transracial adoptee identities].

These comments illustrate how parents are often awakened to their White racial identity journeys by their transracially adopted children challenging their colorblind, nonracist ideology. In this way, White parents are made aware of their White privilege and how this privilege acts to racially discriminate against their children. However, like their own children's awakenings to their racial minority status, parents often resist. Kendra suggests that parents become bewildered when their children discuss how they struggled with their identities growing up and now want to explore their racial and transracial adoptee identities, because parents have viewed the adoptees' lives as ideal.

> My parents still bring out the worst tantrums when I try to talk to them about it [racial identity], because they still live in this denial that there's any difference. I was trying to talk to them one time about growing up and dealing with the racism, and they were like, "Oh, you didn't really have to deal with racism. Nobody really gave you a hard time." And I'm thinking to myself, "Oh my God, how can you?" I just said to them, "I can't and don't want to talk to you about this because we are going to have a fight." The emotions are so close to the [surface]. There's no way that I could talk to them in a logical way about this. I would either cry or get pissed off. It's just not something that I can talk to them about and I don't think they really want to hear it.

The denial by some Americans that racism still exists is not new, especially with regards to Asian Americans, who are considered the "model minority" and "honorary Whites" (S. Lee 1996, Tuan 1998). Most adoptees in this study talked about how they were well liked and accepted by their school friends and were also academically, socially, and financially successful. It is therefore relatively easy to understand why parents would believe that Korean adoptees did not endure racism in school. However, this denial and inability to recognize racism caused Kara and Tess a great deal of angst.

> KARA: I've really blamed her [mother] for a lot. I blame her for not really recognizing the fact that I was upset and depressed because I was the only minority and it was difficult for me. And she said, "You were so popular and you had so many friends." And I said,

"Yes, but that doesn't mean I didn't have problems. How could you be so naive to think that was never an issue?" I think they [her parents] really had no idea I had such a difficult time growing up being Asian. I now see that she [her mother] really had no idea how difficult it was for me. . . . It's just something that they . . . don't get. They want to—they try—to listen, [and] they really care so much, but they just can't get it; they just don't know. So it's something that I have to do . . . for myself.

TESS: She [her mother] doesn't understand why we [Tess and her biological adopted sister] need to do this [join an adult adoptee group]. She thinks that all our lives, we've been raised in the perfectly healthy White, close-knit family and therefore we don't need this. She said, "You're White. You come from an Irish, Norwegian background. You're fine." It's hard for me to explain to her that, yes, I do feel totally accepted, but on the other hand the exploration of the Korean culture, my background, is necessary for me. I told her, when I have kids, they're going to want to know, and I think I have to tell them. I want them to have a better background. I want them to be in that diverse culture, not just coming from thinking that they are Irish. My family is Irish, but there are other things to my background. There are other puzzle pieces. It's hard for them to realize that. They see us as White. She said, "But you're White, you're American, you're an American citizen." I'm like, "I know I am but [I've] got to do this for myself. [I've] got to learn things. I want to learn things."

These two statements are very telling in terms of how some parents see their transracially adopted children. Kara sees her parents as naive, which in some ways protects them from being "bad" parents for not recognizing the difficulties she experienced growing up as a racial minority. Tess' account of what her mother said to her was not all that common among the adoptees; most parents did not say outright to their children, "You're White." And while this might be an extreme situation, because it is obvious that Korean adoptees are not racially White, it reinforces the belief that their parents did not want to accept that the adoptees were different from anybody else in the family—that their adopted children were loved in the same way as their biological (White) children.

Tess' mother also stated, "You're American. You're an American citizen," therefore holding to the belief that her children should not be considered Korean. It is hard to determine exactly what Tess' mother was trying to say to her, but her resistance to Tess' desire to explore her identities may lead Tess to distance herself. Both Tess and Kara stated that they have "got to do this for myself." This desire to investigate their identities absent their parents' influence often meant leaving their parents on the periphery of their lives because it appears that their misunderstanding might have impeded and limited their racial and transracial adoptee identity explorations.

Several adoptees attempted to involve their parents in certain activities related to their identity journeys because they believed it was important for parents to understand their desire to empower their identities. However, they were often met with resistance from their parents. Amber concluded that when parents and even White siblings sense a possible distancing from their children/siblings or feel unable to fit in with a group of Korean adoptees, they become defensive and at times hurtful in their comments to the adoptee.

> I started reflecting on my own family. I never talk about the adoptee issues with my siblings or my parents. So all of a sudden I went from being aware and interested to . . . almost being militant—we need to abolish adoption and the White man is evil. And they were like, "What happened to our sister? What did you do with her?" Unfortunately, that was sad. I've tried to make it up to my parents by making the point to talk more about the issues and everything that has been going on with this newer adoptee group. I tell my parents now about what we're doing, and this and that. I feel bad because I can feel my mother sometimes getting defensive. I start talking about things, and she'll be like, "These resources weren't available when you were young." And I'm like, "I know, but we're aware of them now and I want to make sure that the adoptive parents now know about it."

Throughout this section on tensions, conflicts, and contradictions, I illustrated Amber's friction with her parents. She states that her "angry adoptee" period was sad because it caused a rift in her relationship with family members. Once she was able to understand where her anger was coming from, mostly from discovering all that she once was oblivious to, she then wanted to share with her parents all that she was exploring and learning, because she did not want another rift to form. Now, when she wanted to share these events with her family, her mother became defensive because in some ways she felt she was being attacked. This defensive reaction is similar among other adoptees' parents. Angie concluded, "My mom felt really threatened by the fact that we were a part of this organization [an adoptee group]. And I asked my mom, 'Why don't you and dad try to become a part of it?' And she started to cry. She felt that we missed out on something because she forgot to bring it up while we were growing up and she didn't force it upon us."

Their parents' defensive reactions appear to come out of a sense of guilt, even though many of the adoptees do not blame their parents for not introducing Korean culture, and some admit that even if they had tried to introduce aspects of the culture they would have resisted. For some adoptees, their parents' feelings of guilt led to resistance to their children's explorations of their racial and transracial adoptee identities. Joining adoptee groups, visiting Korea, and indulging themselves in all aspects of their identities were clear challenges to their parents' colorblind philosophy— indeed; race still *does* matter in the United States, especially for people of color. As their children further engaged in aspects of Korean culture, these parents often felt ostracized, almost pushed out of their children's lives because they were unable to cross the cultural boundary. Angie's exploration of her identities was met with passive resistance from her parents.

> It got me mad because my mom . . . first started off with, "That group you belong to." And I'm like, "What group are you talking about? I belong to a few." And [she said], "Your adopted group." And I [replied], "Well, it's important. I don't necessarily understand right now everything [about] why I'm involved in it, but it's important that you guys become involved in it, because it's just who I am." I wish that they would take a bigger part, but it's going to take some time.

Similarly, in a discussion with his younger sister, who is a Korean adoptee, Alex came to realize his mother's passive resistance to his involvement in Korean culture camps.

> My little sister [and I] had a conversation once. This was one of the only times we really talked about adoption and our relationship with our parents. She sees a big difference between us and my brother and my sister, who are biologically linked to our parents. She said, "They send out all these e-mails to the rest of the family and they're always talking about [our sister's] activities and [our brother's] school, but they never talk about what you do. Some of the activities that you do, no one really talks about that. That's such a big part of your life and you would think that they would want to talk about it." So that definitely got me thinking about it too. It is true.

They send out these e-mails and they're telling what [my brother] is doing with his summer and what [my sister] is doing with her summer. I don't think it's ever been mentioned that I'm traveling across the country doing these culture camps. They don't get it. For them, it's, I'm a camp counselor—that's it. But for me it's something that I enjoy doing so much and I get a lot out of it and I think it's more important than . . . my brother's [activities].

Feeling threatened by their children's identity explorations, parents appeared to uphold a passive-resistant attitude. Angie stated that her mother "felt threatened that I didn't want my parents to be my parents anymore." Some parents felt that they were losing a connection with their children—something these parents may have feared all along. Alex and Kris recognized that this feeling of loss was even more pronounced when they initiated birth family searches or reunited with their birth families; their parents were both supportive and wary of these decisions.

ALEX: I first started really realizing that my mom maybe didn't understand . . . when I brought up the birth search. I expected to have a bigger response from her. I mean, that's a pretty big thing. I wanted her to talk about it. What I got instead was, "That sounds good; just keep me informed on what's going on with that." That was it. For me, it's like, "Come on, Mom, this is a big thing!" I wanted her to tell me what she's thinking. I wanted her to answer some questions: "Do you not want me to do this? Is this hurting your feelings somehow? Are you fine with it? Do you just not really care?" She's always interested in what I'm doing, but she doesn't quite get the adoption stuff.

KRIS: With the whole [issue of] meeting my birth mother, before I found her, my parents were very supportive: "Oh, go for it. Oh, go look. We're 120 percent behind you." But when I finally was in Korea . . . I told them, "Oh my God, I met my birth mother," because they weren't there with me. They were like, "Oh, how was it?" They were very neutral about it. They were like, "Okay, well, that's nice, dear. We'll talk to you tomorrow." They didn't know what to say, of course. I'm not really sure if anyone would know what to say at that point. But they were a little cold about it and they really didn't touch the subject at all. That was their way of dealing with it. I know now that my mom was very threatened by it [meeting her birth mother], my adoptive mom. I tried to tell her a lot. [I told her], "Well, it doesn't really change my feelings for you."

Several adoptees acknowledged that it was appropriate for their parents to remain somewhat disengaged from the birth family search and reunion. Certainly there is a threat to parents as adoptees begin searching for people who are biologically connected to them. Kris was not "sure if anyone would know what to say" and understood that this was her parents' "way of dealing with it." Alex stated, "She doesn't quite get this adoption stuff." Yet the majority of adoptees still wanted their parents to at the very least appear to be interested in their birth search and reunion.

Some parents felt threatened by their children's birth searches. Angie revealed that her parents perhaps possessed an underlying fear that someday they could lose her to her birth parents.

> My mom's very crushed by that [Korean adoptee sister who wants to conduct a birth family search]. She asks me, "Doesn't [your sister] love us?" At one point she was really negative. She's like, "Oh, well, that's because she doesn't love me. She doesn't appreciate me being a mom." When we were first adopted, she always worried that one day our birth parents would want us back. So she felt really threatened by that, because she's said, "Adopting you was like giving birth to you. I waited so long for you. I'm afraid of someone taking you away." I think she feels really threatened, because she feels like she's not truly our birth mom. My mom feels really threatened that we could be taken away from her and that bond that she has with us is going to be taken away.

Most adoptees were aware that this was a natural reaction from adoptive parents with regards to birth family searches. Brian suggested that adoptees can "make it a positive thing by involving their parents" in the birth family search. And upon finding his birth mother, Jackson told his mother, "You don't have to worry. She's not my mother; she might have given birth to me, but she's not my mother. You're the only mother I've ever had and you're the only mother I will ever have in my life."

Moreover, birth parent searches caused tension in the adoptees' relationships with their parents, as both the adoptees and parents were unsure of their feelings. Kara and Keiza realized that this tension was exacerbated by silence and a lack of understanding on both the parents' and adoptees' parts.

KARA: It's still isolating because my family still doesn't know anything about it and they still don't talk about it that much. I don't really expect them to show much interest in it. It's another way in which I separate myself from them. Even outside of being Asian, I'm very different from my family. And so it's actually me separating myself from them.

KEIZA: We never talked about how I felt about being Korean, but I may have just shut down. When I got back [from Korea] I had big issues with my parents. I felt like they really couldn't understand what I had been through and so I just cut them off emotionally.

Silenced dialogues and resistance from family members and other loved ones were common responses to the identity journeys. Failure to convince significant others of their need to understand and empower their identities often left some adoptees feeling misunderstood and isolated from their families and communities. Michelle and Woojung stepped back from their explorations in an attempt to reflect on their dance of identities.

MICHELLE: I was in fifth grade when I decided that I wanted to go back to Korea. But for awhile, especially after my Korean trip, I didn't care. I didn't want to learn anything about Korea anymore. . . . Then a couple years went by and now I'm interested again and that's how I started to go back as mentor [at a culture camp]. I mean, a lot has to do with maturity, growing up as a person.

WOOJUNG: I was immersed in this whole international adoption community and I found myself almost getting bored because I was hearing so many stories and . . . it felt like a lot of the stories were the same and I got to the point where I thought I learned all that I can at this point about international adoption and being Asian American. I felt like I need[ed] to do something different. So after about two years [of working] I decided to go and live in Korea for a couple of years and just take a break from the whole adoption issue. It had been such a central part of my life that by the time I turned twenty-four, I just needed to take a step back and get a fresh perspective.

In their times of reflection, some adoptees were able to recognize the tension that they had created in their families, the hurt they had caused significant others, the constant misunderstandings and unconvincing explanations.

However, most adoptees were unable to walk completely away from investigating their identities. In their reflections they saw how their explorations were a means for them to understand what their identities meant to them. Rather than feeling inadequate in their knowledge of Korean culture and their adoptee experiences, they felt a sense of confidence that enabled them to acknowledge and accept the knowns as well as the unknowns in their lives. Their explorations were authenticated by a group of people who provided them with a sense of comfort and understanding that had been absent most of their lives. In spite of the in-group diversity that resulted in fluctuating affiliations and vacillating theories, they understood that an established Korean adoptee community could act as a catalyst for adoptees to awaken to and critically engage in explorations of their racial and transracial adoptee identities. They believed that this community could encourage and support the need for transracial adoptees to empower their identities.

CHAPTER 6

Empowering Identities

Dancing with Empowerment and Executing Social Change

HANNA: I made a lot of metaphors for myself and one of them was the yin and the yang. How many parts are there in the yin and yang symbol? Most people would say two. But [there are] actually . . . four: There's the yin and the yang, there's a line in between, and then there's the whole. Where I saw myself was that line in between. And that's a force that's so moving and powerful. The yin and the yang press against the line and they connect at that one point. That's where I saw myself between these two kinds of worlds. And then I thought either I could lament that I'm not the status quo or I could take this experience and change things.

The previous chapters illustrate how the participants' identity journeys ultimately led some to gain empowered identities. Indeed, I described the process and the initiating factors that allowed the adoptees to develop these identities. This chapter discusses in further detail the characteristics of these empowered identities and, more important, the social justice agendas these adoptees initiate within the transracial adoptee community. By engaging in critical and sustained explorations of their identities, some adoptees were able to take control of them. They no longer felt that their identities were boxed into certain racially defining categories. They neither felt obligated to explain their unique identities nor compelled to adapt them for the sake of others. They were able to control their identities. Hanna further delineates the characteristics of an empowered identity.

I saw myself as a potential bridge. I could help people understand and encourage [them] to go through the process, and then they'll ultimately be empowered. How can you feel empowered by being adopted if you think that everything wrong in your life is because you're adopted? That's not going to leave you in a very empowering position. That was really more of what the stand of the group was— you feel empowered by your experiences. Giving people a space where they can claim their own identity enables them to feel empowered.

Adoptees like Hanna viewed their unique identities as "in between and nowhere at all" as a powerful position because they were able to construct bridges to connect others and at the same time advocate for other Korean adoptees to engage in a critical dance with their identities. Through the process of empowering their identities the adoptees could understand what their racial, cultural, and transracial adoptee identities meant to each of them.

Rather than believing that they were victims of racism and oppression, which often caused tension with Whites (including their parents), the empowered Korean adoptees saw themselves as active agents of change who could directly impact, for example, the institution of transracial adoption and social constructions of race. Some came to realize, through their engaged identity journeys, that in order to transform the institution of transracial adoption, they needed to build bridges to other transracial adoptees, to parents and adoption agencies, to other oppressed groups, and to the larger society. This does not mean that they accepted an inferior role or felt obligated to educate everyone about transracial adoption; instead, they chose when and how to forge relationships with those who acknowledged and were respectful of their self-defined racial and transracial adoptee identities.

Consequently, from their sustained exploration of their identities and through dialoguing about their unique experiences as people of color growing up in culturally White informed homes, there emerged new theories related to race, racism, and racial identity development. They then executed these theories to transform and challenge the boundaries of racial identity development theory and static notions of race, racism, and White privilege. Through empowering their racial and transracial adoptee identities, they became social justice activists for both transracial adoption and race politics.

Nevertheless, some adoptees understand that it could take years of seeking cultural knowledge and answering the unknowns before Korean adoptees can gain a sense of empowerment over their racial and transracial adoptee identities. They also concluded that even when adoptees are able to empower their identities, they continue to explore other facets of these identities as new elements and quandaries arise.

Last, only a few adoptees in this study could be identified as possessing empowered identities. The large majority was still critically exploring their identities, and a few were just awakening to their identities. However, all of the adoptees in one way or another possessed aspects of empowered identities, of seeing how the multiple characteristics of their identities connected them to the whole. They were able to articulate a foundation for how to develop empowered identities and how those identities could enact social change.

Empowered Identities

Throughout their lives, the adoptees were constantly asked to explain their identities. Whether it was related to their names, which did not sound Asian, their ability to speak fluent English, or their inability to speak Korean, people, even strangers, felt it was their right and privilege to ask such personal questions. Ellison referred to this as "constantly being bumped against by those of poor vision" (1952, 1). Some adoptees resisted being placed in rigid racial identity boxes by either ignoring these inquiries or "going off on a verbal tirade" (envision the "angry adoptee"), hoping it would make them feel better. Some tried to explain their unique identities, usually without success, which often left them feeling both empty and more confused.

When the adoptees took control of their racial and transracial adoptee identities, the intruders' questions were no longer sources of anguish or reminders of uncertainties. Hanna and Tori could speak with certainty and confidence about their lives, or they simply refused to entertain such prying questions.

> HANNA: I think of being empowered [as,] you can push all my buttons, you can ask me all these questions, and I don't have to react anymore. I can just be me. For example, [before,] somebody would ask, "How did you get that name?" And I would [say,] "I'm adopted" and then go into my whole story. And I don't have to do that anymore. I could share it, but I don't have to, because that's a little button right there—"How did you get that name? Are you married?" And now I can say, "No, I'm not married." But before, I felt an obligation to explain who I was. And now, I know who I am and so I can share with you what I want to or what I don't want. And I can see that this is a question that triggered a feeling that I have to be sorry and apologetic and therefore . . . explain why my name doesn't match my face. And that was my reaction. That's just an example to illustrate my feeling of empowerment, of being whole. I know all of who I am. I don't have to be apologetic anymore for it. It's just who I am.

> TORI: I always have to explain myself, meaning, when I meet new people, I always have to reveal. Other people don't have to reveal

these things. I have to reveal and then tell them I was born in Korea and I was adopted. I've been dealing with this my . . . entire life. Other people don't ever have to do that. And it is a point of vulnerability. When I was younger, I didn't really want to think about these things. Now, I'm fine with it. I no longer have shame about it.

The adoptees also discussed how people, often strangers, would tell them how they should feel, think, and behave. When they told their stories to complete strangers and sometimes to people they considered friends, they were often told that they should be grateful for the wonderful opportunity to escape their destitute lives in Korea, that their parents were absolutely wonderful people (and they "knew" this without ever meeting them), and, sometimes, that they should feel ashamed at not knowing their Korean cultural heritage. Ellison continues, "You ache with the need to convince yourself that you do exist in the real world, that you're a part of all the sound and anguish, and you strike out with your fists, you curse and you swear, to make them recognize you. And, alas, it's seldom successful" (1952, 3).

When adoptees attempted to "strike out" against these intruders, some discovered that their voices were often dismissed as unreal or abnormal, and they were then labeled an angry or ungrateful adoptee. By allowing the adoptees to engage in critical dialogue with others like them, the adoptee groups validated their voices, and this authentication was a major part of the process toward self-empowerment. Amber added,

I think a lot of adoptees are angry because they haven't had a voice until more recently. I mean, there's been all that great self-empowerment through the adoptee groups. Now they step up and say, "You can't tell me how to feel. You're an adoptive parent, you might be the best parent in the world to your little Bobby or Suzie from whatever country, but you never have been in our position. You do not know what it's like to be us. You can't tell us how to feel, how to think, what we should do, what we shouldn't do." We've got that network right there with the other Korean adoptees.

Another facet of the process of empowering their identities involved destroying the image of the "poor little orphan that needs to be saved." Several adoptees felt this was the most disempowering and most difficult notion to wrest from their oppressors. Daniel and Hanna were adamant about tearing down this image and wanting the same for other transracial adoptees.

HANNA: I would yell at people about the whole idea of adoptees as orphans and we need to be saved. I was always fighting against the perception that all adoptees are these wounded animals [and] we're always searching because we're lost and we don't know who we are. That's something also that I've railed against.

DANIEL: I really think that empowerment is one of the basic premises behind the [2004] Gathering. All of the adoption agencies have wanted to help and they've gotten upset at us because we've said no. Adoptive parents want to speak at the [2004] Gathering and we've said no. We want the adoption community to realize that we are adults. When they [the adoption agencies and parents] talk to us, they really think of us as children still.

Both Daniel and Hanna pinpointed certain perceptions that have been disempowering to their identities and were able to work directly against the image of "lost children" that parents and adoption agencies have used to maintain control over the adoptees. Hanna was active in her adult adoptee group in educating people about the harm of viewing adoptees as disempowered, and Daniel made clear that he wanted people working within the adoption agencies to see the self-empowerment that came out of organizing the Gatherings by and for transracial adoptees.

This image of being "lost" in their identities became a starting point for adoptees in discovering their racial and transracial adoptee identities. Some no longer wanted to feel that others controlled their identities. They took it upon themselves to fill in the missing pieces in their lives. Specifically, prior to and during their identity journeys, some adoptees felt that something had always been absent in their lives, which caused them to feel disconnected from the world. This sense of disconnection then pushed them to find answers, to fill the gaps in their lives, and ultimately to come to an understanding and empowerment of their identities. Keiza and Hanna discussed this:

KEIZA: Over the past three and a half years I have become more comfortable with thinking that I am Korean, that the culture is mine too if I want it. I've made efforts to learn Korean. I've met other Asian people in my professional life that I probably never would have even approached before. I feel less like an imposter now. I feel like I have something to back it up now because I've been there [Korea], I've experienced it; if people are speaking Korean, I know it right away. I'm a lot more comfortable in identifying myself as being Korean.

HANNA: In research studies, adoptees often talk about missing a piece. And in essence it's about lacking that wholeness, knowing all of who you are. And that's often translated as, I have to know the . . . facts of what had happened. But to become whole, it can be a state of mind as well; you can do an internal journey. That's why I think that a process of [a birth family] search isn't really about finding these people; it is about searching for self and searching for who you are in the wholeness of everything that has happened to you.

Even if they were not able to uncover all of the unknowns, the explorations led to a place of comfort in their racial and transracial adoptee identities because they no longer felt lost or disconnected. In the process of becoming whole the adoptees gained control of their life stories. A few of the adoptees no longer felt that they were living inauthentic lives or seeking the validation of others, because they had explored their multiple and complex identities. Sophie and Charlotte were able to accept their White cultural, Korean racial, and transracial adoptee identities.

SOPHIE: I think I have a pretty good grasp of who I am now. I don't have a sense of loss. I don't have real anger. I mean, there are still some issues, but it's not as if I feel troubled or sad about the situation that I'm in. It's more a sense of this is how it is and I'm okay.

CHARLOTTE: I just began realizing that my whole life feels like having a huge rubber band wrapped around my chest and I'm trying to go forward, but all the past events that took place are taking me right back to that place, and the harder I try to forget, the more those memories pop up. Finally, at this point in my life, I just accept everything. It's okay to grieve or cry from time to time. I think just in the last few years I actually began looking at things the way they actually happened with full knowledge. Because in between the beginning of this whole thing and now, there were so many pieces of information missing, so I couldn't really understand what had happened. But now, I'm okay.

Embarking on the journey to discover their identities allowed them to reach a point where they could understand the complexities associated with living with these identities and know that in the end there were no definitive answers to their identity questions. Moreover, their identity journeys made it clear that an empowered identity can never really be fully achieved, as some of the adoptees came to realize how their identities are constantly being challenged—when they enter into marriage and parenthood, or when they connect with birth parents. In short, as they experience life, their identities are challenged. Hanna illustrates that in order to feel a sense of empowerment, Korean adoptees need to find a way to claim their identities.

> And for most adoptees, we often question, "Who am I, because I don't even know if I was really born the day that I was told. . . . I don't even know what my biological family looks like." For adoptees, we're punctured with a lot of holes because we don't really necessarily know. . . . I came to realize that there was no truth with a capital "T" that was going to answer everything. All I had were little facts. In that way I gained a freedom, because I accepted that I will never know and therefore I will create my own story. This is where I have freedom. I get to say who and what had happened. If I'm in a good mood, maybe I'll twist my story this way and if I'm in a bad mood, then I'll twist my story another way. I finally claimed my own adoption story. I claimed for myself who I am; I am a transcultural, transracial, hybrid person.

Feeling empty or lost was a significant part of their disempowered identities. Hanna therefore concludes that the empowering of one's identities comes from exploring these identities in an attempt to find answers. Once they were able to claim a sense of ownership of their identities, some realized that by raising their empowered voices, they could construct cultural bridges that could lead to social change.

Constructing Bridges: Executing Social Justice Agendas

Through the development of their empowered identities, several adoptees discussed how they reached out and educated others about the transracial adoptee experience. They saw the need to share with the transracial adoptee community so that they too could connect to and understand the importance of the identity journeys. Some adoptees wanted to educate parents and prospective parents about their experiences and offered advice on developing the racial and transracial adoptee identities of younger generations of adoptees. Some saw the need to challenge the institution of transracial adoption by reaching out to and working with adoption agencies as well as the Korean population.

Hanna viewed her empowered identity as being a cultural bridge between

Korean and White, Asian American and White, Asian American and other racially oppressed groups, and, most important, racially oppressed groups and oppressors.

> Building cultural bridges is taking my experiences of being between these two worlds; navigating my adopted family and my Korean side and then using it as a strength. I saw myself as a potential bridge because I could help people understand. You feel empowered by your experiences and you feel empowered because you are a bridge, you are somebody who can make changes. I feel empowered by being a bridge.

Their empowered identities provided adoptees with insight into how their lives crossed several cultural boundaries. By seeing themselves as in between cultures as well as part of the whole, they could bridge these cultural differences.

Building Bridges to Transracial Adoptees: Forming and Sustaining Adoptee Groups

The leaders of the adoptee groups talked about the initial need to create a space for adoptees to come together and engage in an exploration of their identities through a dialogue about their experiences. From her empowered identities, Kris realized the pressing need for a space for transracial adoptees to not only awaken to their racial and transracial adoptee identities, but also break the silence surrounding their identity journeys.

> I started my own club and basically it encouraged any adoptee to come be with other adoptees and encouraged dialogue, openness and self-exploration. A big thing of it was teaching other people about what adoption is and what it's about and breaking down stereotypes about adoptees. I don't remember word for word what our mission statement was, but essentially it was just to bring together a group of people who were adoptees from all different backgrounds in a forum to discuss issues that are relevant in the media, in our lives, to educate others and ourselves about issues that are relevant to us. We got together to share our experiences, to encourage others, and to promote awareness.

Even though there is the hint of a desire for the groups to be active in challenging issues related to the transracial adoptee experience, the majority of the groups had neither a strong political agenda nor a belief in establishing a social justice stance. The groups were more interested in creating a place where adoptees could gather to discuss issues related to being a transracial adoptee.

> BRENDA: So it [the adoptee group] came out of [the idea] [that] the adult adoptees didn't feel that they had any sense that there were others out there. There were five of us that got together and we decided to form a group of adult adoptees that would focus on creating an avenue for other adoptees to get together, to know that they were not by themselves. Our focus wasn't so much on all these adoptees getting together to talk about their problems. It was to allow a means where these people can get together and feel like there are other people in their situation.

> KELLY: I think one of the greatest [things that] groups can do is provide a space and a support network. . . . I always talk about the larger issues that we could have an impact on adoption or the way people talk about it and having a set of ideas that you want people who are adopting now to think about.

At the same time, these groups were not formed so that Korean adoptees could come together and solve their personal issues. Many of the adoptees mentioned that this was one of the major misconceptions about the groups—they were not therapy groups where adoptees complained about the evils of the world (i.e., to victimize themselves). The members viewed it as a place to meet others like them, to engage in free dialogue about their lives and issues related to transracial adoption, and to create opportunities for more transracial adoptees to get together.

Hanna, on the other hand, was the only founder I spoke with who began a group with a specific social justice foundation. She believed that the group would encourage individuals to construct bridges between and among their identities. She felt that the group would promote and provide assistance to members who had awakened to their identity complexities and are actively exploring these identities.

> I wanted to create a community of people who I define as transcultural people—where they encompass more than one race, culture, or creed. And so, that was the transformation piece of our mission— building cultural bridges. Looking at how I [can] take my experience of being between these two worlds—navigating my adopted family and my Korean side—and asking myself, "How can I use that as a

strength?" . . . In the end I think that the mission [of the group] is broad enough and I think it encompasses many of the needs that I think most adult adoptees need to have to feel empowered or connected to their adoption experience. I want them to be able to create bridges with their birth cultures, whether it's with other Asians here or whether it's going to their birth country.

Even though Hanna was the only founder to recognize how the group could be an empowering force for many of the members, most others believed that these groups should be developed as platforms for Korean adoptees to launch explorations of their racial and transracial adoptee identities. These leaders reflected on their own identity journeys and strongly believed that a space was needed where all transracial adoptees would be free to dance with their identities. Sophie stated that such a space would ultimately allow other adoptees to claim control over their identities.

I just hope to provide for people who are coming to ask some questions. That to me is important; I need to take the initiative to talk to them, be open to them, not judge them, not tell them what to do or how to feel. That there is a connection of knowing that we have that shared bond and that I'm not going to judge you on how you think or feel because you may see things differently or you feel differently [than I do] about adoption. But that doesn't mean that we still don't have that bond. That is the best way to dialogue. Of course, I can recommend this book or I can recommend this movie, but I think dialogue is just as important—the most important, really.

In spite of their desire to provide opportunities for transracial adoptees to explore and dance with their identities, the leaders in these groups understood that they needed to be careful in how they presented the group to potential members and nonmembers. Specifically, Brenda was aware of the possibility of abusing certain members within the groups.

If people . . . see you as a helper or mentor, then the person who is always giving will get tired of it and either they're going to stay in the group and change the dynamics or they're going to leave. Also, you have college students [who] don't want to be mentored. They want to be accepted as equals too. When we come into this group we are here to have fun. All my labels should get left at the door.

In establishing these groups, the leaders felt it was necessary to present a philosophy that there are no defined roles within the group. They wanted people to feel free within the group and to use it as a space to explore their identities.

Adoptees in the study acknowledged that certain adoptees may harbor more angst about their racial identity and therefore need to establish a strong connection with it. Some may have more trouble understanding their transracial adoptee identity and will need to uncover parts of their lives prior to adoption. Keiza and Amber decided that there is no perfect time for the journey to begin, no one activist agenda to follow, and no completely authentic White cultural, Korean racial, or transracial adoptee identity.

> KEIZA: I didn't know that there was a journey to be had. I now know that some of the people have done that already and some have not. That's what I find so interesting about meeting other adoptees . . . how we're all at different stages and just even learning that it is a journey to be taken because I didn't know there was one. I was clueless and believed that everything is all great and fine in the world. That was my upbringing.

> AMBER: One of the things that I've learned from other adoptees is that my experiences are normal. I mean, you're going through basically a big void where you don't know what to expect. There's no straight path. Nobody does it the exact same way. People are hitting different milestones at different points and maybe they don't even hit all of these in their [lives]. I think that there is a small percentage of adoptees who choose to go to Korea because they think, "If I can't fit in here, maybe I'll fit in better there." And some of them do, but some of them don't. I mean, I talked to some adoptees who [said], "I'm never talking to my adoptive parents again." Some of them [say], "I'll never go back to the U.S." And some are like, "I'll never date a White person again." It's so hard to lump them all together.

The diverse experiences within the adoptee groups led to a variety of identity journeys. Realizing and accepting this allowed Woojung and Charlotte to appreciate the different meanings that the adoptee groups offered each of its members. Acceptance of these differences was a key aspect of the way the group was able to encourage empowered identities.

WOOJUNG: I think it's an interesting dynamic because there are old timers who have been around for four or five years and then [there are] always new people coming in. It's the new people who I see that are going through a lot of the same emotions that I went through earlier—the whole sense of "I'm the only Korean American adoptee and this is the first time being exposed to all of this. There are so many emotions that are coming up and this is the group that can really understand me and help me along with this process." Some of them are searching for biological families, so that's what they are looking for from the group. And then for some people, this group and the whole Korean American adoptee experience is so central to their lives. So the group is a social network for them.

CHARLOTTE: Just because we are grown up and have jobs doesn't mean our stories ended. We now have to start thinking about the next generations and how the issue of adoption affects each of our lives. When I was younger, I pretty much thought that one story just said it all—sadness and reunions and peers. How many times can you tell the same story over and over? And every time some graduate student approached me about writing a thesis on Korean adoptees, I thought, "Why don't you just go out there and make a copy [of the previous theses]?" But just having more exposure to other people really opened up my mind. I think we could write an encyclopedia full of stories. It definitely [broadened] my horizons.

In this way, the group's diversity allowed Gloria to understand that her identity journey was never ending, and with each new discovery there were new avenues to pursue, more questions to answer, new experiences to reflect on, and group feedback to absorb: "There are so many issues and they're so enmeshed, and it's so overwhelming, and you only can pick one and deal with that and then maybe when you've gotten some understanding of that, you move to the next thing. No one can try to conquer it all, because it's just so intense and immense."

The acceptance and recognition of in-group diversity allowed for the creation of subgroups that could meet needs related to specific adoptee experiences. Katerina joined a group of adoptees who had reunited with their birth families because she felt that those who had not reunited would not only feel left out of these conversations, but also could hinder the conversations, since the focus was solely on reunions, not birth parent searches.

I participated in a group of people who had met their birth families. We started up with the local people here who were interested. We met on a monthly basis. It's a pretty small group, but . . . it's very quaint and I get this opportunity to talk about a lot of issues without having to explain a lot of things because we already know and can understand some of the experiences, even among the differences. Some people in our group had lived in Korea for various amounts of time and some had lived with their birth families. And we're still evolving and figuring out where we want to go with that. We've talked about adoptive family relationships and a sense of displacement within our homes. . . . We all have that connection with both families. So we are having discussions that give us the opportunity to talk about our struggles with living here [in the United States] with these family dynamics.

Another issue that came up within the larger groups was the number of adoptees who had married White spouses. Within this subgroup they not only discussed their relationships with their spouses, but also the need to dialogue about raising biracial children. Karina clarified:

There needs to be a group out there for couples who are biracially married and trying to all of a sudden in mid-marriage discover their Korean identity. I'm sure you heard a lot of this and how you get through it. . . . I would have picnics at my house for a couple of people that I knew that had biracial children. And once the word got out that it was really a family setting, I had what started out to be ten to fifteen people from [the local Korean adoptee group] that then turned out to be thirty people because there was such a need for these families where one of the adoptees was married to a Caucasian and they had biracial kids.

What is so dynamic about these offshoot groups is that they tend not to completely dissociate themselves from the larger Korean adoptee community, yet at the same time realize that there is a need for focused groups within the larger group. These offshoot groups also represent the larger group's ability to overcome some of the identity elitism by recognizing the diversity of experiences and issues.

The adoptee groups and their offshoots not only had an impact on the group members, but also significantly influenced family members. Family members, including parents, siblings, and spouses, were invited to special events where the issue of transracial adoption was not the focus. These events allowed family members to feel that they could be a part of the Korean adoptees' experiences. More important, it allowed them to connect with other Korean adoptees and their families. It gave family members the opportunity to share their experiences with other non-adoptees who, in some way, could validate their feelings and concerns. Several of the adoptees, especially those with White spouses, commented that having family members interact and share with one another allowed them to further understand and confirm the transracial adoptee experience, rather than constantly question the role of the group and feel ostracized from it.

Building Bridges to Younger Adoptees: Mentoring Transracial Adoptees

Reflecting on their identity journeys, many of the adoptees stated that they wished they had had the opportunity to meet older Korean adoptees when they were younger. They discussed how a role model in their teenage years would have provided them with, at the very least, a positive older image of themselves. Specifically, they felt that an adult adoptee mentor would have provided an opportunity to talk about issues that they felt they could not discuss with their parents. Therefore, Amber and Joan saw the need to give back to the Korean adoptee community by volunteering as mentors for the younger generation of transracial adoptees.

> AMBER: I wish I had [had] something like that [a mentorship program run by adult adoptees] when I was a teenager. We all know how painful adolescence is and it's ten times more painful if you're a minority and you've got this whole adoption issue hanging over you.

> JOAN: I just want to make sure that the next generation of kids who are adopted from abroad, be it Korea or China, . . . have adult adoptee mentors. Because if you can nip it in the bud at an earlier age, there will be less internal struggle, there will be less emotional stress one needs to go through. I would have loved to have had these mentors when I was younger.

Both statements reflect the belief that an adult transracial adoptee mentor would allow the younger adoptee to express her/his pain and internal struggle. This mentor would enable the adoptee to begin exploring her/his identities at an earlier age, which many of the adult adoptees viewed as a positive step toward developing an empowered identity.

These interactions and dialogues did not necessarily have to encompass issues related to their racial and transracial adoptee identities. Alex and Tonya understood the benefits for younger adoptees to simply be around Korean adoptees, especially older ones.

ALEX: I think it's good because it sets a time and a place for them to interact with some of their friends and they're going to see us [mentors]. We are just friends. So it's just nice to show up and . . . hang out with them. . . . For example, with the teen group, some of the older boys sat down and . . . just started asking me all these questions. The first thing they wanted to know was about girls. "Do you date Asian girls? Do you date White girls?" Those were some of the questions I had in my head when I was their age, but I didn't know any adult adoptees. I had to answer them by myself or just let it go. I think all [these] kids need adult adoptee role models.

TONYA: Especially in places where they don't necessarily see another Korean every single day, I think it's good to say to them, "I went through that experience and this is what I did," or maybe, "This is how you could do it." Some say to me, "I'm going through this and I feel so left out," and I just let them know that they're not alone.

The most important aspect of connecting with these issues seems to be that the older adoptees were able to normalize the younger ones' experiences. The younger adoptees then could feel that they were not alone in their experiences, which Daniel, Amber, and Sophie discussed as being one of the most difficult facets of growing up as a transracial adoptee—feeling that no one could understand.

DANIEL: I think the biggest thing is for the teens, they're at that age where they feel different anyway. And it's tough to not fit in with the crowd if you look different. A lot of these kids think that nobody else in the world has ever had these thoughts or feelings. I think it just gives them an opportunity to be able to bounce those things off of people and realize that all of us have gone through similar things that they're starting to experience now. Sometimes it's just being able to look at some of the adult adoptees and see that we do grow up and we have jobs and we are just like anybody else. It's just providing an opportunity for teens to let

them know it's okay to ask questions and to see if we can help
with whatever questions [they've] got.

AMBER: There's a part of me that believes . . . this is how I'm going
to make a difference for the future generation. I want to be here
for them. I want them to know about the resources that are out
there. I want them to know that they're not alone. That's what
motivates me in all this.

SOPHIE: I've been gearing my life towards being a positive role model.
I really enjoy doing the volunteer work and just interacting with
the younger adoptees. It doesn't have to be about sitting down
and having intense conversations. I am an Asian American adult,
but I'm just as normal as you are. I may have the same issues and
if you need to talk to me about it, then you can.

The adoptees also wanted to show the younger adoptees what an empowered identity could look like by offering advice on how to explore and dance
with their identities. Karina reflected,

There's this one kid that I've mentored for a couple of years. He
lives in a very White town. I asked him to come and hang out with
me even though I'm a . . . mother of four. He'll come over and I'll
cook Korean food for him. I think it's his own way of trying to get
his Korean fix. He can't get it at home, so he comes out and hangs
out with my family. . . . I took him to a Korean restaurant for the
first time. When we went in there and sat down, there were a lot of
Koreans there speaking Korean. He said he felt odd and he didn't
really fit in there because these people were all speaking Korean. He
didn't know what to expect. So we talked a lot about that and how
it's okay to feel a little uncomfortable at first, because I felt that way
too at first.

Most adult adoptees saw the need to create spaces for the younger ones
to be able to talk about their racial and transracial adoptee identities. Alex
and Abby believed that these dialogues needed to address the issues of race,
racism, and White privilege, which challenge the colorblind philosophy pro-
claimed in many transracial adoptees' households.

ALEX: These adopted kids . . . are coming from towns of 250 people
and they're the only person of color there. With the older kids,

the thirteen- to sixteen-year-olds, we really talk about racism and identity and what those words mean to them. Some of these kids are really quick to open up and some of them don't so much. But at the end of it, there are a lot of kids that come up and say, "Thanks, I never would have talked about this with my parents or even my friends at school. It's nice that we can talk to you about this because you have a sense of what we're going through."

ABBY: Children are dealing with issues of race. When you can't ever address that issue when you're growing, [it] just gets held back and it builds up inside you. Especially if you are feeling insecure about your appearance, as a lot of teenagers do, and then they are unable to express to anybody who understands them in these predominantly White communities. I think it's extremely difficult to grow up Asian American. We live in a racist country. I think with Asians, there is some institutionalized racism, but it's more blatant personal racism that we experience. And many of these children experience personalized racism in these all-White communities, but they don't have an outlet. They don't have anybody to talk to about these things.

By creating an outlet for the younger adoptees to discuss issues of race and racism, the mentors recognized the importance of dancing with their racial, transracial adoptee, and White cultural identities during adolescence. While some may agree that addressing these topics at a younger age will eventually allow the individual to develop an empowered identity earlier on, Michelle and Sophie discovered that teenagers really were not all that interested in talking about issues of race, racism, and identity.

MICHELLE: I started discussions with . . . the teenagers about dating and racism. I had the seventh and eighth grade at the time, so topics like racism or finding yourself as far as identity goes really didn't strike an interest [in] them. They were more interested in, "What did you do since last year? I haven't seen you in years." It was a little hard with the seventh and eighth graders. I did spark some interests with those topics and talking about hometown experiences, but not much overall.

SOPHIE: There were attempts to discuss and do some journal writing about what it feels like to be adopted and have discussion about adoption. We also watched a movie about adoption with the campers. I had the oldest girls, fourteen-, fifteen-year-olds, and they were not longing to have in-depth conversations about identity. They were more interested in, "Whose cute over at the guy's side of the camp?" I found my campers to be unwilling to talk about those issues. They said, "I'm good. I have no problems."

These statements address two important aspects of mentoring teenage transracial adoptees. First, the teenage adoptees expressed the desire to be treated as any normal American teenager. They did not want to be burdened with in-depth and critical discussions on race. Second, the mentors needed to be aware that forcing dialogues on racial issues could ultimately have a negative impact on the teenagers' identities. Indeed, the teenagers might conclude that all the adult adoptees want to talk about are the negative issues associated with being a transracial adoptee. This could result in the teenagers labeling their adult mentors "angry adoptees." Therefore, several of the adult adoptees realized that while they may strongly believe in the importance of discussing issues related to transracial adoption and identity development, they needed to allow the teenagers to open the dialogue, and not push it to the point where the adolescents were turned off.

Another problem some adoptees discovered with the mentorship program involved parents who wanted to send their children to adult adoptees as a means to solve their children's problems, even though some "problems" could be classified as normal teenage dilemmas. Conversely, some younger adoptees needed professional guidance—something that Gloria believed adult adoptees either did not feel qualified for or, for those who were social workers, did not believe it was their role outside of their professional practices (these professional counselors strongly urged parents to go through their offices rather than the adoptee groups or culture camps for such services).

I had offered to meet with groups of younger adoptees and what I got instead was this woman whose child was becoming very disturbed by his adoption. She wanted me to meet with him but I felt like she wanted me to counsel him. I wasn't equipped to do that. So I declined. She got very bitter and bad-mouthed me. But I said, "Look, lady, if you want free therapy, that's not what I'm about to do." . . . That's not appropriate.

Throughout many interactions with younger adoptees, some older adoptees encountered or heard about parents who wanted to attribute all of a teenager's problems to their Korean adoptee identity. Rather than dismiss the parents as hopeless or even racist, Tori was able to see the need to reach out to parents and prospective adoptive parents as well as adoption agencies as a way to assist the younger adoptees in their identity journeys.

> I think that adult adoptees, those who have at least tried to work through some of these identity issues [i.e., empowered adoptees], really need to be there to help educate parents because we have an adult perspective. We can share things in a way that will be more understandable to the average parent. Some parents may think it's just being a stupid teenager. But [for] the adoptee who is being a stupid teenager, [it] may be directly related to self-esteem. I think we, as adult adoptees, have an obligation to try to educate parents as much as possible.

By working through their tensions with their own parents, some adoptees realized that many parents and adoption agency workers are essential players in assisting (or hindering) transracial adoptees in their identity journeys. These adoptees realized that forcing parents and adoption agencies out of the conversation, due in part to their racist and White-privilege ideologies, would prolong the oppressive state of transracial adoption. Therefore, several adoptees began to reach out to parents and adoption agencies with the intent of educating them about issues related to transracial adoption from a transracial adoptee perspective.

Building Bridges to Parents, Prospective Parents, and Adoption Agencies

While mentoring younger adoptees certainly was a primary component of most Korean adoptees' activist agendas, they also realized that they needed to bridge the divide between themselves and parents and adoption agencies. Several adoptees volunteered to speak on panels arranged by adoptive parent groups and adoption agencies. Some worked directly with them as social workers, board members, and culture camp directors. These interactions eventually opened up dialogues where both sides listened to each other, instead of telling each other how to think and what they should do about transracial adoption.

Within these interactions, some tensions arose. Adoptees were weary of the parents' attitude toward transracial adoption; they often viewed parents as being unaware of how White privilege and entitlement play a major role in transracial adoption. Cathy and Halle discuss this point:

CATHY: It's healthy for their kids to have a connection with Korean adoptees, but the parents are just oblivious. I run into a lot of oblivious parents who think that taking their kids to culture camp is more than enough. And there are some parents who really believe that their child will never be one of them [angry adoptees] and they'll grow up perfectly and fit into the White community.

HALLE: They [parents] just think they can handle it their own way. I just feel like they don't know what they are getting themselves into. They don't know that it's not easy being a Korean adoptee in a predominantly White environment.

Parents and adoption agencies were often quick to resist and dismiss the adoptees' voices, because they largely viewed them as either "poor little orphans" or "angry adoptees." Some adoptees believed that a struggle over power and control was a major barrier in these groups coming together.

However, several adoptees came to these dialogues hoping to share the explorations of their racial and transracial adoptee identities in an attempt to get parents and adoption agencies to better understand these experiences. Because they were able to develop an empowered identity, Bettina and Karina no longer felt a sense of angst and ire. While they believed the angry adoptee story needed to be heard by all, they also understood that this story could ultimately silence the dialogue around transracial adoption, since parents and adoption agencies would not be willing to openly listen to tirades about the evils of transracial adoption.

BETTINA: I mean, there are people who have not had a good experience being adopted, but they're still willing to sit on panels because they want to make sure that parents know there is another perspective. As long as they do it in a—I don't want to say in a good way—but as long as they present it in a noncritical way to the parents, I think that can be a good resource of information too. Just so that adoptive parents have an idea that it's not easy for every adoptee to grow up being adopted.

KARINA: I wish that more adult adoptees who are in a good place would speak on this panel. It can't be somebody that's still searching for the answers to life. It needs to be someone who has been one way, gone to the right, gone to the left, and then found a happy balance in between and have pride in being a Korean American and [an] adoptee. These adoptees need to share their

experiences with these parents. I wish more adult adoptees were
at that point in their [lives] and would give their time.

Understanding the fine line between informing parents of the adult perspective and not completely bashing the institution of transracial adoption,
some adoptees spoke with an empowered voice about their experiences and
beliefs about transracial adoption. They were then able to convince the parents and adoption agencies that sharing their reflections of their own experiences would ultimately make a major difference in the lives of all transracial
adoptees. Tori wanted parents, prospective parents, and adoption agencies
to recognize and acknowledge the importance of their identity journeys:
"Parents are soliciting advice and opinions. These are folks who want to
learn and help their children. We really need to educate parents. It has to
be a partnership because the kids who are dealing with this cannot vocalize
their thoughts. I, as an adult adoptee, have the power, then, to educate all
of these parents."

While many of the adoptees stated that they had difficulty talking with
their own parents about some of these issues, they found that speaking on
the panels allowed them to reflect on their dance of identities, especially as
they pertained to their parental issues. Robby and Karina were able to see
the reciprocity in building bridges (partnerships) with parents and adoption
agencies.

> ROBBY: It dawned on me that I had an opportunity to ask parents
> why they adopted. I got close to a lot of the parents that way by
> being able to see why they decided to adopt. It's pretty much the
> same story as my parents of why they decided to adopt, and so it
> was nice to hear that I don't have weird parents.

> KARINA: It [speaking on a panel] gave me a different perspective on
> adoptive parents because we, as adoptees, don't really understand
> what adoptive parents go through: the waiting, all the paperwork
> they have to go through, the emotional strain. There are so many
> different pieces to that that we don't even try to see because it's
> all about us. When I was up there, I realized that I couldn't go to
> my mom and ask, "Why did you adopt me?" So I was learning
> from the adoptive parents about why they adopt and a little bit
> about the adoption process from the parents' perspective.

These open dialogues between parents and adoptees took time to foster,
as each side typically came to the table with preconceived notions of each

other. However, it appeared that the empowered adoptees were able to open up and listen to the parents' perspectives and at the same time not feel attacked by parents. The adoptees' open and less defensive attitude allowed parents to let down their guard and listen to the negatives and positives of transracial adoption from adult adoptees. The dialogues were no longer about attacking each other, but about understanding each other.

The general advice that most adoptees gave to the parents revolved around issues of exploring their racial and transracial adoptee identities. They talked about how they wished that they had had more exposure to Korean culture as children because it would have allowed them to better understand their racial and transracial adoptee identities, especially during their identity awakenings and explorations. Sadie and Amber stressed providing Korean culture in their lives.

> SADIE: Teach them anything: food, dress, language, traditions. Some families who adopt from Korea . . . do the traditional first birthday with all the presents out on the table.[1] They [parents] try to follow through as much as possible.

> AMBER: The adoptive parents don't have an excuse anymore for assimilating them to the point where they're ashamed of being around other Korean people. There are too many opportunities for their children to know Korean culture.

In addition, most adoptees felt that interactions with Korean culture had to be an ongoing aspect of the adoptees' lives. Kendra and Cathy concluded that single engagements could perpetuate the belief that White is "right" and "normal," while Korean culture is something else and less important.

> KENDRA: What I always tell the parents is, "You can't once a year dress your kid up in a *hanbok* or just take them to [the] Asian Festival. It has got to be more than that."

> CATHY: I know that they love their children, but that's not enough because there are going to be things they won't be able to understand. I think these parents have in mind that just by going to camp they can become part of whatever their kids are experiencing. I know it makes them very happy to think that they fulfilled this cultural part and now they're fully in their child's place. They believe they can direct their children to become happy

and productive young people. But this is not enough. They have to do much more.

The adoptees wanted the parents to understand that including Korean culture in the daily lives of their children was imperative to getting their children to be positive about their identities. More important, they wanted the parents to realize the power that White culture has over their children's dance of identities, especially how children can easily develop a negative, almost self-hating perception of their racial and transracial adoptee identities. Therefore, several adoptees who work with adoptive parents stressed the importance of accepting Korean culture as a significant part for the entire family. Rather than viewing Korean culture as solely for the Korean adoptee, the family needs to participate in and accept the culture as a "normal" facet of the family structure.

However, several adoptees were quick to note that while it is important for parents to accept Korean culture into the family, they should neither claim it as their own nor push the culture too much on their children. Reflecting on their difficulties in reconciling the desire to fit into White culture with the need for acceptance of their racial and transracial adoptee identities, Tonya and Amber realized that adoptive parents must understand the multiple forces that promote assimilation and simultaneously present opportunities to their children to continually engage in exploring their identities.

TONYA: I tell the parents to encourage their child to explore their history. But don't push it and don't hide it. Getting to know their background should come naturally, and if parents try to disclaim their child's history or are too pushy about it, it makes it harder for that child. The parents can watch for signals to determine when the child is interested in getting more information. But they also need to encourage them to study the culture instead of just saying to them, "You're in America and you're going to do as Americans do."

AMBER: No parent can ever do too much for their child. However, there is the issue about finding the balance. That's something I always tell the prospective adoptive parents. If you want your children to be proud of their cultural heritage, then it's important to present the opportunities to them. It's important that parents are aware of all the opportunities and . . . present them to their children without force-feeding them, without making it . . . a chore. I mean, if the kid wants to learn Korean, then the whole family should go learn Korean. It shouldn't just be the one child being punished for having been from Korea.

It is clear that there is a delicate balance between providing opportunities and forcing cultural awareness upon adoptees. Amber believes that the child should not feel as though s/he is being singled out and suggests that the whole family study the Korean language together. However, embedded within this advice is the point of ownership and control of the identity journey.

The adoptees talked about parents going too far in their involvement with Korean culture—for example, mothers wearing a *hanbok* or fathers taking taekwondo. While it is agreed upon that parents should share with their children aspects of Korean culture, the empowered adoptees realized that there was a fine line between sharing and claiming Korean culture that parents needed to be aware of. Moreover, Sophie and Kendra encouraged parents to engage in an exploration of their own White racial identities, including investigating their own White privilege.

> SOPHIE: This is the one thing that I say when I [participate on] prospective parent panels: "If you adopt a child of color you have to see yourself as a person of color but also draw that line of saying, that's also not my group to join. If you are saying that you are so open-minded that you can adopt a child of color, then I want you to think about your own life." Because how many of these parents have friends who are Indian? Who are Chinese? Who are Black? Who are Spanish speaking? Many of them don't. But some of them do. I then say to them, "You don't have to have your token friend of color, but if you really are open, then it should be reflected in your life." People say that they're so open but if you look at these parents' lives, sometimes they're very White. They may say, "I'm open, I have no problem with Black people," but none of their close friends are Black people. That doesn't mean that they should latch on to the next Black person. This is the complication of race relations in the United States.

> KENDRA: I think that, more than anything else, parents have to recognize the importance of racial differences in the family. They may not see it because, of course, they believe that family is the most important thing and that they love all their children equally. If we could live in an insulated world where all we dealt with was our families for the rest of our lives, then this thinking would be okay. However, as soon as we step out the door, other people

see these racial differences and usually want to bring [them] to our attention. Therefore, I think it's important that parents understand and recognize that racism exists. What I find is that most of them live in rural areas. . . . It's hard for White parents to move into the more diverse neighborhoods because they don't deal with their own fears of living next to minorities. For them to actually move into a neighborhood that's more diverse they have to put aside their own fears. They have to put aside their stereotypes and their own negative perceptions. A lot of them aren't willing to do that.

As well as wanting parents to awaken to their White racial identity by acknowledging their fears and stereotypes of people of color, several adoptees advised parents to challenge their existing beliefs that racism is an individual phenomenon. In other words, White parents' attempts to "connect" with their children's experiences of racism were not critical examinations of race. Often, parents would claim they were not racist by talking about a "Black" friend or colleague or an incident where they, too, were discriminated against. Tori and Gloria were adamant about destroying the belief that parents could empathize with their children over acts of racism because of parents' claims of experiencing individual acts of unkindness.

TORI: Parents were saying things like, "I try to explain to my child that when I was a kid, I wore glasses and I got picked on for wearing glasses," or "I had red hair." I understand that they were trying to relate. I don't want it to sound like I'm just White bashing because that's not the case here. I seek to bridge and create understanding. That's my whole . . . life. But racism is not the same thing as getting picked on for wearing glasses. It's not the same thing as having red hair. It's not the same thing as being the fat kid. It's not any of those things. I mean, just that one statement of saying, "Why don't you go back to where you came from," it's racial stereotyping and the fact that we're always made to feel like foreigners in this land. No matter how long your family has been here, you are still a foreigner. It's always, "Go back to where you came from."

GLORIA: I think my parents were so overwhelmed, they didn't know what to say. And that's where part of the rift existed. That they could never just concretely say to me, racism isn't okay and it happens and we're sorry that it happens and we'll help you to develop a way that you can handle it. Their method was [to] turn the [other] cheek. What I heard as a child was, accept your fate as a minority in this country; accept it with a smile on your face and eat spoonfuls of bull****. What they were saying is, don't cause any unnecessary drama, lead by example and with dignity, and don't think on the level of those ignorant people. I think we all know that names hurt and sometimes the scars and wounds from a name linger with you . . . longer than any bruise on your face or any stick or stone scar will heal, but . . . names hurt. When somebody calls you a "gook" or a "chink," you feel it with all the power and history of what those words represent, and it wounds you.

Even though some adoptees accepted the fact that White parents were unable to truly empathize with the impact of racism in their children's lives, this does not mean that the parents were exempt from engaging in critical dialogues about race, racism, and White privilege. Some adoptees wanted parents to critically engage in discourses about these issues in an attempt to help them in raising their children as racially conscious people.

In addition, these adoptees wanted to recruit parents as allies in the struggle against racial oppression. Certainly, White parents of transracially adopted children can provide a unique insight into the dynamics of racism. However, the adoptees concluded that parents need to first awaken to their White racial identity, rather than hide behind a colorblind philosophy.

As an example, several adoptees believed that parents who consistently shared in the experience of learning Korean culture allowed their children to accept it as a natural part of their lives. Some also believed that being given regular opportunities to engage with Korean culture allowed children to view Korean culture as equal to White culture. Sharing in these experiences allows Korean adopted children to feel that Korean culture is important for the whole family, which then enables them to feel like full members of the family.

Some adoptees also advised parents to be aware of their child's development when presenting opportunities to engage in her/his birth culture. Through their identity journeys, adoptees realized that the pressure to assimilate could cause resistance to learning Korean culture. Julie and Sadie believed that pushing too hard could engender feelings of resentment.

> JULIE: It is really clear for me that each child is going to be different in wanting to know about their Korean culture. That's why we're telling the adoptive parents to be aware of what their child's

feelings [are] because some kids want to know and others don't want to know. I think it's always good to expose them as kids to their culture, to who they are as Koreans, but parents need to be sensitive.

SADIE: What some people are finding is that as the kids get older, they just don't want to do it [learn about Korean culture] anymore and the parents shouldn't shove the culture down their throats. They just want to put it on the plate for them. Just say it's out there if you want to get involved.

Maturity level was also something the adoptees wanted parents to consider with regards to providing opportunities for their children to explore their racial and transracial adoptee identities. This was particularly the case in advising parents about visiting Korea and birth family searches. Tess believed that younger adoptees are not emotionally prepared to comprehend what a birth search entails or the impact a trip back to Korea could have on their identities.

There are some parents that feel that they have to take their children right back over to Korea . . . to visit their homeland. But I think there's a level of maturity that goes along with that, a level of understanding that the children need. I think it's great that they go to these camps and they want to learn about the culture; they want to seek it out for themselves. But, on the other hand, having to immerse themselves directly as a young child into the Korean culture by going to Korea—personally, I don't think it's all that good. I talked with a couple of campers that went back when they were still in junior high. I think that it is a difficult period of growing up mentally, physically, and socially and therefore it can be the wrong time to go back. I think parents should really think about it and wait until they are mature enough to talk about it. Because some kids aren't even mature enough to talk about their adoption and they aren't even thinking about that. They're thinking about school or the next dance. I don't think the parents should push them to do that. It should be up to the child. When they're ready, they'll decide to go.

In addition to reaching out to parents and prospective parents, adoptees believed it was necessary to work with adoption agencies. Some worked for the agencies as social workers and advisers; they discussed how they were advocating for change from the inside. Others were working within their adoptee groups to raise their voices to transform aspects of the institution of transracial adoption. And like their relationships with adoptive parents, these adoptees strongly believed that they needed to work with adoption agencies in order for the institution to begin to recognize and address issues of race and racism as well as other forms of oppression.

Hanna and Charlotte believed that working with adoption agencies was necessary because transracial adoption was not, at least in the near future, going to come to an absolute end.

> HANNA: A friend of mine works in an adoption agency and she was talking about her own conflict with perpetuating the practice of transracial adoption. My take on it is that whether you agree with it or not, it doesn't mean that it is going to go away. If that's the situation, then what are you going to do with it? It's like you can be . . . angry, you can talk about the baby business, you can talk about all that stuff, but is it going to go away? And as long is there's supply and demand, I'm sorry, it's not going away. So then how can you make the process as good as you can?

> CHARLOTTE: I felt the need to tell my story to others. I want them to know that adoption is not all fun and games and for every well-adjusted, successful, happy individual, there are children who [have] dearly paid a price in the name of adoption. And I want them to be aware and see that balance. I'm not against international adoption, and I'm so happy that some of us are doing really well and lived in a loving environment. I have a hard time making up my mind, but I still support international adoption; . . . you [just] have to reform it a little.

Recognizing that there is a need to question the institution of transracial adoption, these adoptees acknowledged that the institution is not going to be destroyed overnight, and therefore they needed to challenge aspects that could be immediately affected by their voices. Instead of working against the institution of transracial adoption completely, they believed that they could have a profound and lasting impact by informing the agencies of their life experiences and their critical insights. For example, Brenda and Abby found it necessary to enact immediate changes to areas such as placement, post-adoption services, and birth family searches.

> BRENDA: When I got involved with the adoption work, I probably wasn't the best because I questioned every one of these parents'

motivation for adopting because my mother's motivation was so bad. When people used to tell me, "God laid it on my heart to adopt this little orphan," I would just fly off the handle. In many ways, maybe I was really good because I really grilled these parents. I said to them, "You are taking a child into your home; you're not adopting a cause, and it's not some project."

ABBY: These adoption agencies make people believe they can just adopt this child, this beautiful little baby, and it will be fine. They'll be this happy family. But that's not enough. And no one tells these people how to raise these children. And then there are all these adults who have issues for the rest of their lives and children who are suicidal. I mean, it's because of the lack of education. It is horrific.

Some adoptees believed that one way to transform the institution of international adoption would be to promote Koreans adopting Korean children. Amber and Daniel saw the need to reach out to Koreans and educate them about their lives because they were aware of a cultural emphasis on keeping family bloodlines "pure" creates a social stigma that hinders Korean families from adopting (unrelated) Korean children.

AMBER: I'm firmly about trying to abolish international adoption. I honestly can say I don't really believe it ever is going to end, but [I'll do] anything I can do to try to help curb that, especially for Korean adoptees. I just think it's so much more beneficial for these Korean children to be able to grow up in their own country, in their own culture. But they have to change the mentality there. And so I'm working towards making sure that happens.

DANIEL: I've always felt that, ideally, Korea could take care of its own, and no one would have to be adopted out of the country. That, to me, would be ideal. But I know enough of the Korean culture that it's just not going to happen anytime soon. I know a Korean woman who adopted domestically. For two months she wore pillows under her shirt so the people would think [she was] pregnant. Still to this day, nobody outside of her immediate family knows that her daughter is adopted, and she refuses to tell anybody. I was telling her that it's great that you adopted, but it would be so much better if you told people. This kid is exactly like anybody else. She's born in Korea. She's growing up in Korea, she speaks Korean, she eats Korean, everything. And she loves her just like her own birth daughter. And unless people see that, they are always going to look down on somebody who's adopted. . . . Even some of the people at the adoption agencies [in Korea] would never consider adopting. I was talking with [a] lady that's in charge of the post-adoption services there and she's been in the agency for forty years, and I said, "With all these kids coming through, why didn't you ever adopt?" And she was like, "No, no, I couldn't do that. There's so many, how would I choose?" That made me realize that their attitudes will change slowly, but it's going to take a while.

Korea policies based on a traditional adherence to bloodlines remains the leading excuse for the continuation of allowing Korean children to be adopted by non-Korean families. However, when Korean adoptees place nearly all of the blame for intercountry adoption on Korean culture, the Korean government is largely exempt from responsibility. In response, some adoptees were trying to break down Korean stigmas about adopting children by reaching out to the Korean government and voicing their opinions about transracial adoption. The 2004 and 2007 Gatherings in Seoul brought Korean public attention to the issue of transracial adoption. In 2004, much of South Korea's media was present at the five-day Gathering. Front-page stories ran in major newspapers, as did headline news reports on the major television networks. People protested against transracial adoption outside the conference site. There was also a strong sense of pride among some attendees, and they wanted to share it with the Korean public.[2] Daniel stated, "We want them to realize that we are as normal as anybody else. We may have started at a disadvantage, but we're not there anymore. We've moved on. They don't need to look at us as poor little adoptees."

Continuing to push for more awareness, some adoptees reached out to Koreans to let them know about the diverse experiences of Korean adoptees. Amber and Hanna wanted Koreans to be fully aware of the positive and negative sides of adoption.

AMBER: Korea's slowly moving towards getting adoptees into the popular conscious[ness]. They are trying to let people know that there are a lot of adoptees and they are our brothers and sisters, so we can't ignore them anymore. That's the first step. But it would be nice if they started really having their eyes opened to the fact [that there are] a lot of Korean adoptees who will never go back to Korea because they just can't handle it. They only hear about the success stories or the stories about the Korean adoptees who go and kill their parents. I meet Koreans who are genuinely interested in the whole adoption thing and they recognize that it's not easy, but we have to educate them more.

HANNA: On the tours to Korea, . . . we've had encounters with college kids and they were saying, "Wow, you guys are so normal and happy." In Korea there's a perception of all of us as being sad and lost. Almost every story in the news is about somebody looking for their biological family because they're so sad and lost. And we're always searching and we're lost. We don't know who we are. Koreans love that drama anyway, but for us to give them an offering of encountering adoptees who aren't in that much pain, that's important.

These empowered adoptees no longer felt the need to hide their identities. They wanted to share with others their life stories so that stereotypes and misconceptions would not linger in the minds of not only Koreans, but also parents, adoption agencies, peers, teachers, and nearly anyone who has come into contact with transracial adoptees. By sharing their stories, their highs and lows, these adoptees were hoping to break down the misunderstandings associated with transracial adoptees.

I have attempted to conclude how dancing with and exploring their identities ultimately led some adoptees to empower their racial, transracial adoptee, and White cultural identities. I intended to use the dialogues to illustrate the identity journey toward empowerment, the characteristics of empowered identities, and social justice agendas through the thinking of the adoptees. The adoptees concluded that an empowered identity meant feeling whole and complete as well as taking ownership of their identities. And with this empowered identity, several adoptees felt the desire and obligation to give back to the transracial adoptee community. They set out to develop adoptee groups and gatherings, to mentor younger adoptees, and to create open and honest dialogues with parents and adoption agencies. And through these activities lay the underlying challenge to cultural racism. These particular adoptees were able to utilize their critical investigations of their dance of identities to assist others in their journeys toward empowering their identities.

CHAPTER 7

Linking the Dance of Identities Theory to Life Experiences

TORI: I felt [a] much . . . deeper self-love, self-confidence, self-esteem the moment I realized that I didn't need somebody else's validation and approval and the moment I realized that I was chasing myself down this road I was never going to get to the end of because I realized that the end of the road is the fact that we are never going to blend, because we're never going to be White. The reality is that, as adoptees, we are always going to be naturally forced in these polar ways where either you blend and [are] like everybody else or you're shoved out. I do say "shoved" because I've felt I was shoved repeatedly. There is that sense that so many folks shake their head and say, "If you just got some Korean culture, you would feel so much better." What I mean is, you need to accept yourself or otherwise you're self-hating. I think you need to accept yourself as who you are and what you look like. That has to be the central piece.

The dance of identities theory appears to resemble Cross' (1971) established racial identity development model that includes the stages of pre-encounter, encounter, immersion/emersion, internalization, and internalization-commitment. The pre-encounter stage is evident in the ways the Korean adoptees assimilate into their White cultural identities; the encounter stage is similar to the "awakenings" and the opening of Pandora's box; immersion/emersion resembles the engaging and reflecting of their racial and transracial adoptee identities; and internalization and internalization-commitment reflect their empowered identities.

By critically examining the lives and reflections of Korean adult adoptees, it was my intent to bring attention to the lives of transracial adoptees by providing a space for them to freely express their thoughts, concerns, and theories. Through their voices, I wanted to break through the stigmas attached to transracial adoptees so that people could see them as more than "poor little orphans." I was adamant about portraying their identities from their perspectives so that others could see them for their accomplishments as well as their struggles. I aspired to reveal the intricacies of their identities by asking them to critically analyze their life experiences and future endeavors.

It was evident that their unique racial and cultural backgrounds had much to offer to the dialogues on race, racism, White privilege, racial identity, and social justice activism. Their very nature of being racially Korean and culturally White challenged the notions of racial categories and racial identity development. And through their words a theory emerged that represented how they danced with a White cultural identity, a Korean racial identity, and a transracial adoptee identity. Even though their identity journeys took them on painful paths toward discovering their multiple and complex identities, several eventually were able to claim ownership of their identities, while others remained on the course toward empowerment.

The adoptees shared how they were raised in culturally White informed homes and were quick to assimilate and sustain notions of cultural racism and colorblind philosophy. They were allowed special entrance into their White communities based in part on their status as the model minority and honorary Whites (S. Lee 1996, Tuan 1998). In turn, some Korean adoptees desired aspects of Whiteness and wanted the world to view them as White. In their dance with a White cultural identity, they typically disregarded and denied their racial and transracial adoptee identities by adhering to a colorblind philosophy.

However, they looked Asian physically, and the world saw them as such. And as they attempted to ignore the racist comments from their peers, and as their parents sent them off to Korean culture camps, their colorblind philosophy was put to the test because they realized that while those in their lives advocated such a philosophy, it was not actually practiced. Some were then able to understand that race was a defining aspect of their lives, yet they did not know what it meant to be Korean; and in their attempts to discover that, they were at times resistant because they possessed a "fear of people of color, based on stereotypes learned from friends, family, or the media" (Tatum 1992, 13). They realized that some Koreans did not accept them as "authentic" Koreans and that some people of color identified them as "sellouts" and "White wannabes" because they lacked the knowledge and acceptance of their racial identity.

When their racial identity collided with their White cultural identity, they discovered a dance that was all their own. Feeling isolated led some to return to denying their race because "withdrawal (accomplished by avoiding contact with people of color and the topic of racism) is another strategy for dealing with discomfort" (Tatum 1992, 14). Through the emergence of a vibrant and dynamic Korean adoptee community, some adoptees were given opportunities to engage in explorations of their racial and transracial adoptee identities with the validation and support of other Korean adoptees. They no longer felt isolated as they began to see the similarities in their experiences as transracial adoptees. They were then encouraged by the Korean adoptee community to discover what their identities meant to them.

Some took trips to Korea as a way to feel whole. Others chose to live in Korea to discover what it meant to be Korean. Some initiated birth family searches in an attempt to reveal their life histories. Some took Korean-language courses. Several engaged in critical dialogues with others in the Korean adoptee community. The explorations depended on the individuals and what they felt was relevant to understanding their own identities. The adoptees soon realized that there was no single journey that led to empowering these identities.

By claiming and making their own decisions about their racial and transracial adoptee identities, some adoptees found it necessary to give back to the Korean adoptee community. They developed groups in an attempt to encourage other adoptees to awaken to and engage in exploration of their identities. Realizing the freedom that empowered identities brought to their lives, they enthusiastically wanted to share with other Korean adoptees their theories of empowerment.

They set out to mentor the younger generation of Korean adoptees in an attempt to provide them with interactions and insights that would help them in their identity journeys. Some volunteered at culture camps and insisted on including critical dialogues in the curriculum around race, racism, and racial and transracial adoptee identity development. Others developed mentorship programs within their adoptee groups to give younger adoptees opportunities to interact with those like them. They realized that the younger generation needed role models who could truly relate to their lives and answer their questions and concerns.

Through their empowered identities these adoptees constructed bridges to parents and prospective parents. They realized that parents are influential in developing racial and transracial adoptee identities; therefore, they wanted to educate parents on both the positives and negatives of identity journeys as a way of assisting them in rearing the younger and future generations of transracial adoptees.

The adoptees wanted parents to awaken to their White privilege and engage in explorations of their own racial identity development. They wanted parents to understand that a colorblind philosophy is both unrealistic and contradictory: unrealistic in that racial differences are visible, and contradictory in that the parents constantly viewed and acted upon racial differences. These adoptees wanted the parents to know that such contradictions can cause mistrust, which ultimately leads to silenced dialogues between parent and child around the issues of racial and transracial adoptee identities. In order to create the extraordinary conversations around these issues, they wanted to work and speak with parents to get them to understand the adoptees' perspectives (Fine 2003).

Adoptees also recognized that they needed to include parents and adoption agencies in their endeavors in order to transform the institution of transracial adoption. From challenging placement decisions to post-adoption services, the empowered individuals encouraged these people to recognize how White privilege is the underlying force that facilitates and perpetuates the institution of transracial adoption. And while they accepted that transracial adoption was not going to end anytime soon, they believed it was imperative to transform existing practices.

Some empowered individuals were able to bridge relationships with the larger, global community. They set out to educate Koreans about their life experiences in an attempt to destroy the image of the "poor little orphan" and the disgruntled adoptee. The 2004 Gathering in Seoul was organized solely by Korean adoptees because they wanted Koreans as well as parents and adoption agencies to acknowledge their empowered voices. They wanted the world to see the positives and negatives of transracial adoption. They were also able to connect their experiences with the larger forces of global oppression. Some shared their insights with the global community through their work as social workers, educators, writers, and researchers.

Dance of Identities: Transracial Adoptee Identity Development Model

I strongly believe that the Korean adoptees' dance of identities could serve as a paradigm for people of color and members of other oppressed groups, as well as Whites, to reflect upon and further understand the journey toward empowered identities. In order to move from disempowerment to empowerment, people must first awaken to their disempowerment. Then they must engage in explorations of their individual identities to determine what they mean to them. In taking control of their identities, they will see the need to execute social justice agendas. Therefore, I contend that educators and mentors of people of color and members of oppressed groups could use the Korean adoptees' dance of identities as a foundation for educating future social justice advocates. They could advocate for identity awakenings, guide identity explorations toward empowerment, and then illustrate how social justice activists become members of a global community, while at the same time retaining their own identities.

Another important aspect embedded within the dance of identities theory is in the description of the characteristics of an empowered identity. Within the theory, I described an empowered identity as the moment when one takes ownership of her/his identity; a person with an empowered identity ultimately chooses when and how to identify. For example, prior to empowering their identities, most adoptees felt that they needed to apologize for their confused identities and were embarrassed for not knowing what it meant to be Korean. People were able to challenge their identities with simple questions about them, which often led to discomfort and, ultimately, the silencing of their identities. However, once the adoptees critically engaged their racial, transracial adoptee, and White cultural identities, they were able to determine for themselves what their identities meant to them. An empowered identity no longer seeks approval from others.

I also found it interesting that engaging in their identity journeys allowed adoptees to feel comfortable in all of their identities. An empowered identity provided them with the reassurance that they could go on living in a White cultural identity and not feel that they were "sell-outs" or "White wannabes," that they could engage in their racial identity without feeling that they were not "authentic" enough, and that they could develop relationships with other Korean adoptees not solely as a means to support their Korean transracial adoptee identity, but because they truly enjoyed their company. Their empowered identities gave them the freedom to identify with all three at once, separately, or not at all. An empowered identity was possible because they engaged and reflected on all three and discovered for themselves what they meant to them.

Several adoptees brought up the point that there is an identity journey to be had, yet the one who determines this journey is the individual her/himself. The dance of identities theory allows for an individual to move from identity to identity as s/he discovers what each one means to her/him. Thus as an individual explores her/his identity, dancing back and forth between identities should be a natural process because the racial boundaries become less rigid as the individual begins to see that there is no one "authentic" racial identity and no true sellout identity.

A few of the adoptees were aware of how a sense of elitism could develop within the adoptee groups where those who had explored and empowered their identities might look down on those adoptees who were just beginning their journeys. In an attempt to understand this elitism with the Korean adoptee community, the dance of identities theory clearly points out how adoptees seek their own paths to understanding and determining aspects of their multiple and complex identities in their own time and way.

One of the main reasons for investigating identities is the belief that educators can then better connect with themselves and their students. Gay (1985) believed that teachers who possess a deeper and more complex understanding of their students' identities may improve academic achievement and quality of life, especially for culturally and linguistically diverse (CLD) students. A static and singular perception on "specific cultural material practices can lead to beliefs about [CLD] students that are simpleminded and stereotypic" (S. Lee 2001, 118), which may then result in CLD students feeling invisible, isolated, and silenced. Teachers need to develop a deeper and more varied understanding of all of their students so that they can be more effective in their work (Darling-Hammond and Cobb 1996). It is my hope that by illustrating the Korean adoptees' dance of identities, educators will be able to assist all their students in their identity development.

Working with and Understanding Adoptive Parents

The adoptees in this study often reflected on how their identity journeys were directly related to their parents' influences. In these dialogues, it was apparent that the adoptees wanted parents and future parents to recognize that assimilation is damaging and, at the same time, sporadic and negligent associations with their child's birth heritage (e.g., culture camps once a year or occasional visits to the local Korean restaurant) are not enough. A colorblind philosophy is destructive to adoptees' racial and transracial adoptee identities, especially when parents profess this philosophy but do not implement it in their daily lives (e.g., claiming colorblindness but living in predominantly White communities).[1] While assimilation into the White culturally informed home might seems like the best way for children to feel accepted in the family and surrounding community, when that family and community contradict this philosophy in any way, the children are left wondering where they fit in.

Parents need to recognize that their families are no longer White families. Once they adopted transracially, the family dynamics changed to biracial/multicultural. The children should be made to fit in by a family connection to both the White and Korean cultures. When both are integrated into their daily lives, the children can begin to recognize not only the importance of accepting both cultures, but also that one is not superior to the other. This allows the children to see that both cultures are viable in their lives and may enable them to bypass some of the insecurities associated with appearance and interactions with other Koreans and people of color.

I also recognize that this is not an easy task for the parents to take on. The dilemma rests in the fact that they have limited knowledge of Korean culture, most of which typically pertains to visible aspects such as food, celebrations, traditional dress, and language. Parents need to be aware that they should not take Korean culture as their own; it is not theirs to possess or control. More important, I strongly believe, as did the adoptees, that parents need to awaken to and engage in explorations of their own racial (White) identity. This does not mean that they should investigate only their ancestry (certainly this could be a part of their dance of identities); rather, they need to critically investigate their own White privilege and racial stereotypes.

This exploration will not be easy because it will force the parents to critically reflect on their life decisions and, in particular, why they chose to adopt transracially. They will feel uncomfortable with some of their discoveries because they may see how their philosophy on race and racism allowed them to remain oblivious to their own White privilege. They may realize the hypocrisy of their colorblind theory: the irrationality of their belief that since they adopted transracially, then they cannot be racist; the absurdity of comparing harassment for, say, wearing glasses to racial taunts; and the futility of their advice to "turn the other cheek" in the face of racial discrimination.

Parents will need to face their own fears and stereotypes of people of color. They will need to force themselves outside of their comfort zones. This does not mean that they must move to a more racially diverse area, but it could help. They need to make meaningful relationships with people of color to show their children that being bicultural involves sincere and sustained interactions with another culture, not colonizing another culture.

The parents can set a strong example of the importance of being a member of a bicultural/multicultural family. Their critical engagements and reflections will enable them to see that race matters and that, as members of a multiracial family, they, too, need to become anti-racist. This ultimately could prevent the strong desire for adoptees to want to "be like White" and instead encourage them to engage in explorations of their own racial and transracial adoptee identities.

Working with and Understanding Adoption Agencies

Some adoptees may advocate for the complete elimination of the institution of international and transracial adoption. And while there is an ongoing debate on its continuation, several adoptees offered suggestions for adoption agencies when placing children for adoption and post-adoption services that could have a profound impact on transracial adoption. These adoptees feel that placement of adoptees into homes needs stricter guidelines. It is not enough to be White, Christian, and wealthy. Adoptees also revealed that racists existed in their own families. A few questioned the motives for transracial adoption: moral obligation, fighting for a cause, status in the community, or looking for the quickest and most convenient way to adopt a child were not valid reasons.

When it came to post-adoption services, many adoptees encouraged more opportunities for children to engage in activities with other transracial adoptees. Attending just once-a-year culture camps that teach the same curriculum over and over is not enough. These children need spaces throughout their lives to engage in dialogue about their racial and transracial adoptee identities.

Adoptees also advocated honesty and sincerity from the adoption agencies. They wanted these agencies to understand and accept that adoptees deserve and are strong enough for the truth. Lying about birth families or hiding important information in a misguided attempt to protect their psychological stability was not a valid excuse. They wanted the adoption agencies to cast aside their perception of adoptees as poor little orphans.

Beyond the Dance of Identities

Throughout my research I realized that several areas need further investigation. The topic of birth family searches and the impact they can have on transracial adoptees' identities needs its own study, as there is an overabundance of psychological and social issues involved. Also, I am aware of the need to include parents' observations and reflections in this study because it would provide insight into the identity journeys. Similarly, it would be interesting to include the thoughts of the transracial adoptees' White siblings in an attempt to understand how the siblings' identity development is affected by the family's decision to adopt transracially.

The transracial adoption community continues to grow, especially with the dramatic increase of Chinese adoptees in the United States. Their lives will continue to have an impact on communities in rural, suburban, and urban areas. It is important to recognize their lives not only as unique, but as major contributors to the structures of race and racism. As people of color who grow up in culturally White homes, they provide a certain insight into the dynamics of race and culture. They should be encouraged to voice their thoughts and offer paradigms for understanding race, racism, and racial identity.

Concluding Thoughts

I believe that this book illustrates the complexities and multiple facets that Korean adoptees must navigate on their journeys toward empowering their identities. When I began my research one of the main audiences I had in mind was the transracial adoptee community. First and foremost, I wanted them to know that they are not alone and that there are thousands of transracial adoptees also navigating and reflecting on their identities. I wanted them to become aware that they can own their dance of identities.

I recognize that certain negative images of transracial adoptees prevent some transracial adoptees from exploring and reflecting on their racial and transracial adoptee identities. Most may view their lives as healthy and stable, since they are well adjusted in their families and communities. They are loved by their parents and accepted by their communities, hence they do not feel angry or disgruntled, and they see no need to explore where there is nothing to explore.

I also understand that there is fear in exploring the unknown. In this study I have examined the tensions that arose when the adoptees awakened to and explored their racial and transracial adoptee identities. I wanted to show that the journey toward empowerment is not easy and is fraught with pitfalls. I want transracial adoptees to realize that these tensions are natural. Through open and critical dialogue, such conflicts can add to a more complex understanding of one's identity journey. Thus by empowering their own racial and transracial adoptee identities, these adoptees could alleviate many of the uncertainties and dilemmas.

I would like all transracial adoptees to realize that an engaged identity journey can lead to empowered identities. These explorations allow the adoptee to gain a sense of ownership and control over her/his identities. Empowered identities are created by discovering what those identities mean to the individual adoptee. Moreover, adoptees can come to realize that their White cultural identity does not necessarily have to be separated from their racial and transracial adoptee identities; all are essential aspects of the overall self-identity.

Transracial adoptees also need to acknowledge that their identity journeys are under their control. Through the adoptees' voices I attempted to illustrate the varied identity journeys and highlight that there was no single path toward empowering their racial and transracial adoptee identities. There is no set age when things are supposed to happen, there is no established set of rules of engagement, and there is no dominant voice that promotes one identity journey as superior. Adoptees just starting their journeys should not feel inadequate or inferior to those who are farther down the path.

Last, I want transracial adoptees to know that it requires a tremendous amount of courage and persistence to reflect on and explore their racial and transracial identities. There will be times when they may want to give up or when they feel that the emerging tensions may lead to silencing. But it is worth the struggle to finally empower their identities. Indeed, I want all transracial adoptees to awaken to their identity journeys, engage in identity explorations, and empower their identities through these explorations—and in the end, their empowered identities will provide them with the knowledge, experience, and confidence that they can make a difference in their lives and communities.

Notes

Preface

1. The phrase "to be like White" refers to the desire to fully assimilate into the White middle class. I altered the phrase "to be like Mike" from Michael Jordan's Gatorade commercials.

2. My family includes nine children, two by natural birth and seven transracial adoptees: two Korean, two Vietnamese, and three biracial Korean-White children. My oldest brother Michael Christopher passed away in 2006. I would like to point out that I always hated the way in which I described my siblings as either adopted or biological; however, for the sake of clarification, I use these terms here.

3. Danico (2004, 1) defines the 1.5 generation as "a concept that originated in the Korean community to describe immigrant children who are not quite first- or second-generation Korean."

4. *Bulgogi* is a thinly sliced, marinated, barbecued beef dish that is very popular in Korea. Kimchee is a cabbage side dish most commonly fermented in red pepper, red pepper paste, and garlic and typically served at every Korean meal. *Buchaechum,* the traditional Korean fan dance, involves female dancers who elegantly use fans throughout the performance; it originated during the Chosun dynasty (1392–1910).

5. The culture camp still exists today.

6. *Kimbap* is a popular dish in Korea where rice, thinly sliced vegetables, and sometimes meat are rolled into a sheet of laver (similar to a sushi roll). Street-food vending carts selling *kimbap* are quite popular in Korea.

7. The official name of the 1999 Gathering is the "Gathering of the First Generation of Korean Adoptees: 다함께."

Chapter 1. Dance of Identities

1. Parents were specifically prohibited from attending any of the sessions at the Gatherings. Although the first Gathering was partially sponsored by Holt International Adoption Agency, the subsequent 2001 Gathering featured no adoption agency involvement in the planning or structuring of the conference.

2. This particular dilemma of elitism is raised by several adoptees; they acknowledge that there are some within the Korean adoptee groups who attempt to portray an identity that is more advanced and better than those who have yet to explore. However, this is a small minority within their formed adoptee groups.

3. This is similar to Valverde's exploration of mixed-race class typology within the Vietnamese American community, in which she states, "I, and others like myself, have learned to negotiate our identities within the complex class typology that exists for multiracial Vietnamese within the Vietnamese American community. I liken this dynamic labeling process to a dance" (2001, 131).

4. Some Korean adoptees, as well as Asian Americans, have also used the terms "twinkie" or "golden pear" to describe their identity as racially Asian (yellow on the outside) and culturally White (White on the inside) (Trinh 1995).

5. For statistics on immigrant orphans admitted to the United States, see Immigration and Naturalization Service, U.S. Department of Justice, *Statistical Yearbook of the Immigration and Naturalization Service,* tables 14 and 15; U.S. Department of State, Immediate Relative Visas Issues, FY 1958–2001, FY 1971–2001, and FY 1991–2001.

6. Even before Bishoff and Rankin (1997), Janine Bishop's account as a Korean adoptee was published in *East to America: Korean American Life Stories* (1996).

7. One leader denied my request; I was told that too many researchers had been soliciting interviews from this particular group with no real results, and therefore felt that I would waste the members' time.

Chapter 2. Wanting to Be Like White: Dancing with a White Cultural Identity

1. I chose four as the cutoff age between the child and infant adoptees because I believe by that age a child has acquired language skills, obtained some aspects of Korean culture, and maintained some memories.

2. Other participants also talked about mothers with emotional and psychological problems and how they adopted out of the belief that the love of a child, especially one who would be grateful for the opportunity to leave the orphanage for the comforts of a loving home, would fix their problems.

3. Prior to, during, and after this study I had several conversations with Korean adoptees who came to the United States when they were children (older than four years old). Most were amazed at how quickly they were able to assimilate into their White families and communities. A close friend described her assimilation as going to sleep one night speaking only Korean and waking up in the morning speaking only English. These adoptees now regret losing their Korean-language skills.

4. In a previously published study (Palmer 2001b, 183), a teenage female Korean adoptee stated something very similar: "I tell my friends that I'm having trouble at school because I don't think people accept me because I'm different. And [they say,] 'Why [Ana]? Everybody thinks of you as not being Asian.' I'm always telling them I don't feel as good as everyone else because I'm Asian and they're always telling me, 'But we don't look at you as Asian. We just look at you as [Ana] and you're like us.' "

5. Throughout the Chosun dynasty and into the twenty-first century Korea has often been referred to as the Land of the Morning Calm.

6. For example, in their schools White culture dominates the everyday curriculum, while the cultures of people of color are often given only chapters, months, or special days of the year. Whiteness is thus portrayed as beautiful, elegant, and elite, while people of color are often portrayed as exotic, stereotypical, and inferior.

Chapter 3. Opening Pandora's Box: Dancing in Between and Nowhere at All

1. Gay uses the term "ethnic awakening" to describe a time when students of color "experience a conscious confrontation with their ethnicity during the early adolescent years" (1978, 650). "Identity awakening" is derived from Gay's "ethnic awakening."

2. Hangul is the official Korean language.

3. I was honored that these Korean adoptees chose to share with me this powerful awakening, and as I wrote this book, I was blessed with my first child—David Mingyu. This event allowed me to relate to many of the issues these Korean adoptee women were trying to address about their identities when they discussed their children.

4. It seems obvious that Michelle was uncomfortable with the fact that people recognized her solely on the basis of her racial identity. Because she did not see herself as Korean, she used a colorblind rhetoric that she may have learned in her White cultural environments (e.g., "it sounds terrible" and "I hate saying this"). Therefore, when her race is recognized by others, she feels she is being misidentified—that people see only her racial identity and are thus unable to recognize her cultural identity.

5. I recognize that some adoptees attend Korean culture camps. However, I view them as providing only surface cultural artifacts, hence the Korean adoptees who attend these camps may develop stereotypical notions about Korean culture and are not critically reflecting on their identities.

6. *Soju* is an alcoholic beverage that is very popular in Korea.

7. At first I decided that their trips to Korea should be placed in the following chapter, related to their committed engagement in exploring their racial and transracial adoptee identities. However, the more I reviewed the interview transcripts, the more apparent it became that their first trips to Korea were awakenings to both their racial and transracial adoptee identities.

Chapter 4. Engaging and Reflecting: Dancing with a Racial Identity and Transracial Adoptee Identity

1. I chose these years as the dividing line based on the even split of adoptees at nineteen to each side.

2. *Hanbok* is the traditional Korean attire. It is currently worn on special occasions and holidays.

3. Culture camps are a relatively new phenomenon, and their influence has yet to be determined as many of the adoptees who grew up attending culture camp are just now entering their adult years. I strongly believe that research

on the influence of culture camps on adoptees' racial and transracial adoptee identities is needed. The wave of Korean adoptees who are growing up with Korean culture camps today also needs further research.

4. Adopted Koreans' Association, Sweden, 1985; Forum for Korean Adoptees, Norway, 1990; Minnesota Adopted Koreans, Minneapolis, 1990; The Korea Club, Denmark, 1990; Arirang, The Netherlands, 1991; Euro-Korean-League, Belgium, 1992; Dongari, Switzerland, 1994; Adopted Korean Association, Los Angeles, 1994; Racines Coréenes, France, 1995; Kobel, Belgium, 1996; Also-Known-As, Inc., New York City, 1996; Asian Adult Adoptees of Washington, Seattle, 1996; Global Overseas Adoptees' Link, Seoul, 1998.

5. The focus is not on birth family searches and reunions; rather, I am investigating the identity journeys of Korean adoptees, hence the importance of birth family searches and reunions is solely related to the exploration of their Korean racial, Korean adoptee, and White cultural identities.

6. *Chusok* is Korean Thanksgiving.

Chapter 5: Questioning What I Have Done: Dancing with Tensions, Conflicts, and Contradictions

1. What is interesting here is that, for some of the participants, the concept of family is questionable. This can be traced back to being first abandoned by their birth families and then feeling that they do not completely belong in their adoptive families, because no matter how loving their families are, they do not fit in racially or biologically.

2. These developmental stages are outlined by the American Academy of Pediatrics (www.aap.org). I strongly suggest that further research is needed in this area regarding transracial adoptees' identity development. I believe that age of adoption has a profound impact on the transracial adoptees' identities, as they are associated with primary and secondary cultural awareness (Ogbu 1992) as well as memory and identity.

3. Charlotte remained in contact with her birth family and is fluent in Korean. She therefore has many memories of living in Korea. Life in her adoptive family home was not positive for her, especially with regards to her adoptive parents' attempts to stifle all contact with her Korean family. All of these factors greatly influenced her identity development, and this is why many of her views do not match those of other adoptees in this study.

4. I state "in appearance" because some do not know the full extent of their backgrounds and possibly could be biracial/multiracial yet appear to be full Korean.

5. Her husband first sees her identity changes and uncertainties as related to a midlife crisis—that is, turning thirty years old. In some ways he seems to be employing his White male privilege by associating her racial and transracial adoptee identities with an event that he believes all women experience at this stage in their lives.

6. In April 2004, *Details* magazine published a spread that compared

the "physical and fashion" characteristics of an Asian male to homophobic stereotypes. This particular piece caused quite a stir in the Asian American community; *Details* magazine claimed "satire" as their reasoning for publishing such a racist and homophobic piece. (See Sakai 2004 for more details.)

Chapter 6. Empowering Identities: Dancing with Empowerment and Executing Social Change

1. *Dol* is the first birthday celebration. The child is dressed in a *hanbok*. One of the major activities during the celebration is when the child "determines" her/his future. The parents place the child in front of a variety of objects. Then the child is encouraged to grab one of the objects. The first object that the child grabs is believed to hold the child's future—a pencil means s/he will become a scholar, money foretells economic fortune, a thread means a long life, and rice means the child will eat good food throughout her/his life.

2. I was asked to write an opinion piece for the *JoongAng Ilbo,* which I titled, "우리 해외 입양인은 강합니다" (We overseas Korean adoptees are strong).

Chapter 7. Linking the Dance of Identities Theory to Life Experiences

1. See Lewis 2001 for further explanation of the contradictions in a colorblind philosophy.

References

Apple, Michael W. 1997. "Consuming the Other: Whiteness, Education, and Cheap French Fries." In *Off White: Readings on Race, Power, and Society*, ed. Michelle Fine et al. New York: Routledge, 121–128.

Banks, James A. 1984. *Teaching Strategies for Ethnic Studies*. 3rd ed. Boston: Allyn and Bacon.

———. 1994. *Multiethnic Education: Theory and Practice*. 3rd ed. Boston: Allyn and Bacon.

Bartolome, Lilia I., and Donaldo P. Macedo. 1997. "Dancing with Bigotry: The Poisoning of Racial and Ethnic Identities." *Harvard Educational Review* 67: 223–320.

Bergquist, Kathleen Ja Sook, M. Elizabeth Vonk, Dong Soo Kim, and Marvin D. Feit, eds. 2007. *International Korean Adoption: A Fifty-Year History of Policy and Practice*. Binghamton, N.Y.: The Haworth Press, Inc.

Bishoff, Tonya, and Jo Rankin, eds. 1997. *Seeds from a Silent Tree: An Anthology by Korean Adoptees*. 3rd ed. San Diego: Pandal Press.

Bishop, Janine. 1996. "Adopted." In *East to America: Korean American Life Stories*, ed. Elaine H. Kim and Eui-Young Yu. New York: The New Press, 306–313.

Brian, Kristi. 2004. "'This Is Not a Civic Duty': Racial Selection, Consumer Choice and the 'Multiculturalist' Bind in the Production of Korean-American Adoption." Ph.D. dissertation, Temple University.

Brownell, Shawn C., and Carol A. Peacok. 2000. *Mommy Far, Mommy Near: An Adoption Story*. Morton Grove, Ill.: Albert Whitman.

Buchanan, Emily. 2006. *From China with Love: A Long Road to Motherhood*. New York: John Wiley and Sons.

Choi, Keum-Hyeong. 2002. "Psychological Separation-Individuation and Adjustment to College among Korean American Students: The Roles of Collectivism and Individualism." *Journal of Counseling Psychology* 49: 468–475.

Clement, Thomas P. 1998. *The Unforgotten War (Dust of the Streets)*. Bloomfield, Ind.: Truepeny Publishing Company.

Cox, Susan S., ed. 1999. *Voices From Another Place: A Collection of Works From a Generation Born in Korea and Adopted to Other Countries*. St. Paul, Minn.: Yeong and Yeong Book Company.

Cross, William E. Jr. 1971. "The Negro to Black Conversion Experience: Toward a Psychology of Black Liberation." *Black World* 20(9): 13–17.

———. 1978. "The Thomas and Cross Models of Psychological Nigrescence: A Literature Review." *Journal of Black Psychology* 4: 13–31.

———. 1991. *Shades of Black: Diversity in African-American Identity.* Philadelphia: Temple University Press.

Cross, William E. Jr., Thomas A. Parham, and Janet E. Helms. 1991. "The Stages of Black Identity Development: Nigrescence Models." In *Black Psychology,* 3rd ed., ed. Reginald L. Jones. San Francisco: Cobb and Henry, 319–338.

Danico, Mary Yu. 2004. *The 1.5 Generation: Becoming Korean American in Hawai'i.* Honolulu: University of Hawai'i Press.

Darling-Hammond, Linda, and Velma L. Cobb. 1996. "The Changing Context of Teacher Education." In *The Teacher Educator's Handbook: Building a Knowledge Base for the Preparation of Teachers,* ed. Frank B. Murray. San Francisco: Jossey-Bass, 67–101.

Demers, David. 2004. *China Girl: One Man's Adoption Story.* Spokane, Wash.: Marquette Books.

Derman-Sparks, Louise, and Carol B. Phillips. 1997. *Teaching/Learning Anti-Racism: A Developmental Approach.* New York: Teachers College Press.

Dorow, Sara. 1997. *When You Were Born in China: A Memory Book for Children Adopted from China.* St. Paul, Minn.: Yeong and Yeong Book Company.

DuBois, W. E. B. 2004 [1903]. *The Souls of Black Folks.* Boulder, Colo.: Paradigm Publishers.

Eastman, Philip Dey. 1960. *Are You My Mother?* New York: Random House.

Ellison, Ralph. 1952. *The Invisible Man.* New York: Random House.

Evans, Karin U. 2001. *The Lost Daughters of China: Abandoned Girls, Their Journey to America, and the Search for a Missing Past.* New York: Putnam Publishing Co.

Fabos, Bettina. 2004. *Wrong Turn on the Information Superhighway: Education and the Commercialization of the Internet.* New York: Teachers College Press.

Fine, Michelle. 1997. "Witnessing Whiteness." In *Off White: Readings on Race, Power, and Society,* ed. Michelle Fine et al. New York: Routledge, 57–65.

———. 2003. "Silencing and Nurturing Voice in an Improbable Context: Urban Adolescents in Public School." In *Silenced Voices and Extraordinary Conversations: Re-Imagining Schools,* ed. Michelle Fine and Lois Weis. New York: Teachers College Press, 13–37.

Flower Kim, Katherin M. 2005. "We Are Family: Trans-Racial Adoption and the Work of Assembling and Practicing Family (Korea)." Ph.D. dissertation, Syracuse University.

Freundlich, Madelyn, and Joy Kim Lieberthal. 2000. "The Gathering of the First Generation of Adult Korean Adoptees: Adoptees' Perceptions of International Adoption." The Evan B. Donaldson Adoption Institute, <http://www.adoptioninstitute.org/proed/korfindings.html>.

Fujimoto, Etsuko. 2001. "Korean Adoptees Growing Up in the United States: Negotiating Racial and Ethnic Identities in White America." Ph.D. dissertation, Arizona State University.

Gay, Geneva. 1978. "Ethnic Identity in Early Adolescence: Some Implications for Instructional Reform." *Educational Leadership* 35: 649–655.

———. 1985. "Implications of Selected Models of Ethnic Identity Development for Educators." *Journal of Negro Education* 54: 43–55.

———. 1987. "Ethnic Identity Development and Black Expressiveness." In *Expressively Black: The Cultural Basis of Ethnic Identity,* ed. Geneva Gay and Willie L. Baber. New York: Prager, 35–73.

———. 1994. "Coming of Age Ethnically: Teaching Your Adolescents of Color." *Theory into Practice* 33: 149–155.

———. 2000. *Culturally Responsive Teaching: Theory, Research, and Practice.* New York: Teachers College Press.

Gee, James Paul. 2001. "Identity as an Analytic Lens for Research in Education." *Review of Research in Education* 25: 99–125.

Goldstein, Rebecca A. 2007. "Who You Think I Am Is Not Necessarily Who I Think I Am: The Multiple Positionalities of Urban Student Identities." In *Teaching City Kids: Understanding and Appreciating Them,* ed. Joe L. Kincheloe and Kecia Hayes. New York: Peter Lang Publishing, 97–107.

Gray, Deborah D. 2001. *Attaching in Adoption: Practical Tools for Today's Parents.* Indianapolis, Ind.: Perspectives Press, Inc.

Hardiman, Rita. 2001. "Reflections on White Identity Development Theory." In *New Perspectives on Racial Identity Development: A Theoretical and Practical Anthology,* ed. Charmaine L. Wijeyesinghe and Bailey. W. Jackson III. New York: New York University Press, 108–128.

Helms, Janet E. 1984. "Toward a Theoretical Explanation of the Effects of Race on Counseling: A Black and White Model." *Counseling Psychologist* 12: 153–165.

———, ed. 1990. *Black and White Racial Identity: Theory, Research, and Practice.* New York: Greenwood.

Higginson, Joanne. 2003. *Unlocking the Past.* Flat Rock, Mich.: Anyo Publishing Co.

hooks, bell. 1992. "Representing Whiteness in the Black Imagination." In *Cultural Studies,* ed. Lawrence Grossberg, Cary Nelson, and Paula A. Treichler. New York: Routledge, 338–346.

Hübinette, Tobias. 2005. "Comforting an Orphaned Nation: Representations of International Adoption and Adopted Koreans in Korean Popular Culture." Ph.D. dissertation, Stockholm University.

Huh, Nam-Soon. 1997. "Korean Children's Ethnic Identity Formation and Understanding of Adoption." Ph.D. dissertation, University at Albany, State University of New York.

Kallgren, Carl A., and Pamela J. Caudill. 1993. "Current Transracial Adoption

Practices: Racial Dissonance or Racial Awareness." *Psychological Reports* 72: 551–558.

Kim, Dong Soo. 1977. "How They Fared in American Homes: A Follow-up Study of Adopted Korean Children in the United States." *Children Today* 6 (March–April): 2–6.

————. 1978. "Issues in Transracial and Transcultural Adoption." *Social Casework* 59: 477–486.

Kim, Eleana. 2001. "Korean Adoptee Auto-Ethnography: Refashioning Self, Family, and Finding Community." *Visual Anthropology Review* 16: 43–70.

————. 2004a. "Korean Adoptee Status in the United States." In *Korean Americans: Past, Present, and Future,* ed. Ilpyong J. Kim. Cambridge, Mass.: Harvard/Hollym Publishing, 180–202.

————. 2004b. "Gathering 'Roots' and Making History in the Korean Adoptee Community." In *Local Actions: Cultural Activism, Power, and Public Life,* ed. Melissa Checker and Maggie Fishman. New York: Columbia University Press, 208–230.

————. 2005. "Wedding Citizenship and Culture: Korean Adoptees and the Global Family of Korea." In *Cultures of Transnational Adoption,* ed. Toby Alice Volkman. Durham, N.C.: Duke University Press, 49–80.

————. 2007a. "Our Adoptee, Our Alien: Transnational Adoptees as Specters of Foreignness and Family in South Korea." *Anthropological Quarterly* 80: 497–532.

————. 2007b. "Remembering Loss: The Cultural Politics of Overseas Adoption from South Korea." Ph.D. dissertation, New York University.

Kim, Elizabeth. 2000. *Ten Thousand Sorrows.* New York: Random House.

Kim, Jean. 1981. "Processes of Asian American Identity Development: A Study of Japanese American Women's Perceptions of Their Struggle to Achieve Positive Identities as Americans of Asian Ancestry." Ph.D. dissertation, University of Massachusetts.

————. 2001. "Asian American Identity Development Theory." In *New Perspectives on Racial Identity Development: A Theoretical and Practical Anthology,* ed. Charmaine L. Wijeyesinghe and Bailey W. Jackson III. New York: New York University Press, 67–90.

Kim, S. Peter, Sungdo Hong, and Bok Soon Kim. 1979. "Adoption of Korean Children by New York Area Couples: A Preliminary Study." *Child Welfare* 58: 419–427.

Kim, Wun Jung. 1995. "International Adoption: A Case Review of Korean Children." *Child Psychiatry and Human Development* 25: 141–154.

Kinney, Aaron. 2005. " 'Looting' or 'Finding'? Bloggers are outraged over the different captions on photos of blacks and whites in New Orleans" (September 1). *Salon,* http://dir.salon.com/story/news/feature/2005/09/01/photo_controversy/index.html.

Klatzkin, Amy, ed. 2001. *A Passage to the Heart: Writings from Families with Children from China.* St. Paul, Minn.: Yeong and Yeong Book Company.

Koh, Frances M. 1981. *Oriental Children in American Homes*. Minneapolis: East-West Press.

———. 1993. *Adopted from Asia: How it Feels to Grow Up in America*. Minneapolis: East-West Press.

Ladson-Billings, Gloria. 1994. *The Dreamkeepers: Successful Teachers of African American Children*. San Francisco: Jossey-Bass Publishers.

Landerholm, Lotta. 2001. "The Experience of Abandonment and Adoption, as a Child and as a Parent, in a Psychological Motivational Perspective." *International Forum of Psychoanalysis* 10: 12–25.

Lee, Richard M. 2003. "The Transracial Adoption Paradox: History, Research, and Counseling. Implications of Cultural Socialization." *The Counseling Psychologist* 31: 711–744.

———. 2004. "The Coming of Age of Korean Adoptees: Ethnic Identity Development and Psychological Adjustment." In *Korean Americans: Past, Present, and Future*, ed. Ilpyong J. Kim. Cambridge, Mass.: Harvard/Hollym Publishing, 203–224.

Lee, Stacey J. 1996. *Unraveling the "Model Minority" Stereotype: Listening to Asian American Youth*. New York: Teachers College Press.

———. 2001. "More than 'Model Minorities' or 'Delinquents': A Look at Hmong American High School Students." *Harvard Educational Review* 71: 505–528.

———. 2005. *Up Against Whiteness: Race, School, and Immigrant Youth*. New York: Teacher College Press.

Lewis, Amanda E. 2001. "There is No 'Race' in the Schoolyard: Color-Blind Ideology in an (Almost) All-White School." *American Educational Research Journal* 38: 781–811.

Lieberman, Kira. 2001. "The Process of Racial and Ethnic Identity Development and Search for Self in Adult Korean Transracial Adoptees." Ph.D. dissertation, Massachusetts School of Professional Psychology.

McCabe, Nancy. 2003. *Meeting Sophie: A Memoir of Adoption*. Columbia: University of Missouri Press.

McCutcheon, John, and Julie Paschkis. 2001. *Happy Adoption Day!* Boston: Little, Brown Children's Books.

McIntosh, Peggy. 1992. "White Privilege and Male Privilege: A Personal Account of Coming to See Correspondence through Work in Women's Studies." In *Race, Class, and Gender: An Anthology*. 2nd ed., ed. Margaret L. Andersen and Patricia Hill Collins. Belmont, Calif.: Wadsworth Publishing Co., 70–81

Meier, Dani Isaac. 1998. "Loss and Reclaimed Lives: Cultural Identity and Place in Korean American Intercountry Adoptees." Ph.D. dissertation, University of Minnesota.

Melina, Lois Ruskai. 1986. *Raising Adopted Children: A Manual for Adoptive Parents*. New York: HarperCollins Publishers.

Nakashima, Daniel A. 2001. "A Rose by Any Other Name: Names, Multiracial/

Multiethnic People, and the Politics of Identity." In *The Sum of Our Parts: Mixed Heritage Asian Americans,* ed. Teresa Williams-León and Cynthia L. Nakashima. Philadelphia: Temple University Press, 111–120.

Ogbu, John U. 1992. "Understanding Cultural Diversity and Learning. *Educational Researcher* 21(8): 5–14.

Omi, Michael, and Howard Winant. 1986. *Racial Formations in the United States: From the 1960s to the 1980s.* New York: Routledge.

———. 1993. "On the Theoretical Status of the Concept of Race." In *Race Identity and Representation in Education,* ed. Cameron McCarthy and Warren Crichlow. New York: Routledge, 3–10.

Oparah, Julia Chinyere, Sun Yung Shin, and Jane Jeong Trenka. 2006. "Introduction." In *Outsiders Within: Writing on Transracial Adoption,* ed. Jane Jeong Trenka, Julia Chinyere Oparah, and Sun Yung Shin. Cambridge, Mass: South End Press, 1–15.

Palmer, John D. 1999. "From the 'Yellow Peril' to the 'Model Minority': Asian American Stereotypes from the 19th Century to Today." *American Educational History Journal* 26: 33–42.

———. 2001a. "In the Midst of Two Cultures: 1.5 Generation Korean Americans' Acculturation Process and Ethnic Identity Development." Ph.D. dissertation, University of Iowa.

———. 2001b. "Korean Adopted Young Women: Gender Bias, Racial Issues, and Educational Implications." In *Research on the Education of Asian Pacific Americans,* ed. Clara C. Park, A. Lin Goodwin, and Stacey J. Lee. Greenwich, Conn.: Information Age Publishing Inc., 177–204.

———. 2004. "우리 해외 입양인은 강합니다" (We overseas Korean adoptees are strong). 주앙일보 오피니언 (JoongAng Daily—Opinion page), vol. 12314, no. 43 (August 7), 22. Invited editorial for the JoonAng Daily.

———. 2006. "Negotiating the Indistinct: Reflections of a Korean Adopted American Working with Korean Born, Korean Americans." *Qualitative Research* 6: 473–495.

———. 2007. "In the Midst of Competing Identities: Korean Born, Korean American High School Students' Negotiations of Ascribed and Achieved Identities. *Journal of Language, Identity, and Education* 8: 297–317.

Pang, Valerie Ooka. 1997. "Caring for the Whole Child: Asian Pacific American Students." In *Critical Knowledge for Diverse Teachers and Learners,* ed. Jacqueline Jordan Irvine. Washington, D.C.: American Association of Colleges for Teacher Education, ERIC Clearinghouse on Teaching and Teacher Education, ED 413292, 149–188.

———. 2004. *Multicultural Education.* 2nd ed. New York: McGraw Hill.

Parker, Lonnae O'Neal. 1995. "Adopted Korean Children Rediscover Their Roots: Camps, Other Events Explore Common Ground" (October 26). *The Washington Post,* <http://www.lexisnexis.com/us/lnacademic/search/homesubmitForm.do>.

Partridge, Elizabeth. 2002. *This Land Was Made for You and Me: The Life and Songs of Woody Guthrie.* New York: Viking Press.

Patton, Sandra L. 2000. *Birthmarks: Transracial Adoption in Contemporary America.* New York: New York University Press.

Petertyl, Mary Ebejer, and Jill Chambers. 1997. *Seeds of Love: For Brothers and Sisters of International Adoption.* Grand Rapids, Mich.: Folio One Publishing.

Phinney, Jean S. 1989. "Stages of Ethnic Identity Development in Minority Group Adolescents." *Journal of Early Adolescents* 9: 34–49.

———. 1990. "Ethnic Identity Adolescence and Adulthood: A Review of Research." *Psychological Bulletin* 108: 499–514.

———. 1992. "The Multigroup Ethnic Identity Measure: A New Scale for Use with Diverse Groups." *Journal of Adolescent Research* 7: 156–176.

———. 2000. "Identity Formation across Cultures: The Interaction of Personal, Societal, and Historical Change." *Human Development* 43: 27–31.

Rager, Kathleen B. 2005. "Self-Care and the Qualitative Researcher: When Collecting Data Can Break Your Heart." *Educational Researcher* 34(4): 23–27.

Register, Cheri. 2005. *Beyond Good Intentions: A Mother Reflects on Raising Internationally Adopted Children.* Minneapolis: Yeong and Yeong Book Company.

Robinson, Katy. 2002. *Single Square Picture: A Korean Adoptee's Search for Her Roots.* New York: Berkley Books.

Rosaldo, Renato. 1993. *Culture and Truth: The Remaking of Social Analysis.* Boston: Beacon Press.

Said, Edward. 1993. *Culture and Imperialism.* New York: Knopf.

Sakai, Karen. 2004. " 'Gay or Asian?' Spread Causes Minority Uproar. *Asian Pacific Arts Magazine.* Los Angeles: University of California, Los Angeles Asian Institute, http://www.asiaarts.ucla.edu/article.asp?parentid=9755.

Scheurich, James Joseph, and Michelle D. Young. 1997. "Coloring Epistemologies: Are Our Research Epistemologies Racially Biased?" *Educational Researcher* 26(4): 4–16.

Sleeter, Christine, and Dolores Delgado Bernal. 2004. "Critical Pedagogy, Critical Race Theory and Anti-Racist Education: Implications for Multicultural Education." In *Handbook of Research on Multicultural Education.* 2nd ed., ed. James A. Banks and Cherry A. McGee Banks. San Francisco: Jossey-Bass, 240–258.

Sue, David, Winnie S. Mak, and Derald W. Sue. 1998. "Ethnic Identity." In *Handbook of Asian American Psychology,* ed. Lee C. Lee and Nolan W. S. Zane. Thousand Oaks, Calif.: SAGE Publications, 289–323.

Sue, Stanley, and Derald W. Sue. 1971. "Chinese-American Personality and Mental Health." *Amerasia Journal* 1: 36–49.

Sunny Jo. 2005. *From the Morning Calm to Midnight Sun.* Bloomfield, Ind.: Truepeny Publishing.

Takaki, Ronald. 1989. *Strangers from a Different Shore: A History of Asian Americans*. Boston: Little, Brown and Company.

———. 1993. *A Different Mirror: A History of Multicultural America*. New York: Little, Brown and Company.

———. 2003. "Why Multiculturalism Matters in America." Lecture given at the 2nd Annual Race and Education Lecture Series, Colgate University, Hamilton, New York, April 10.

Tatum, Beverly Daniel. 1992. "Talking about Race, Learning about Racism: The Application of Racial Identity Development Theory in the Classroom." *Harvard Educational Review* 62: 1–24.

———. 1997. *Why Are All the Black Kids Sitting Together in the Cafeteria? And Other Conversations about Race: A Psychologist Explains the Development of Racial Identity*. New York: Basic Books.

———. 1999. "Color Blind or Color Conscious?" *School Administrator* 56(6): 28–30.

Trenka, Jane Jeong. 2003. *The Language of Blood: A Memoir*. Minneapolis: Minnesota Historical Society Press, Borealis Books.

Trenka, Jane Jeong, Julia Chinyere Oparah, and Sun Yung Shin, eds. 2006. *Outsiders Within: Writing on Transracial Adoption*. Cambridge, Mass: South End Press.

Trevor, Terra. 2006. *Pushing Up the Sky: A Mother's Story*. Seoul: Hollym International Publishers.

Trinh, Tram Mai. 1995. "Banana: To Be One of 'Them.'" *VietNow Magazine*, 20.

Trolley, Barbara C., Julia Wallin, and James Hansen. 1995. "International Adoption: Issues of Acknowledgment of Adoption and Birth Culture." *Child and Adolescent Social Work Journal* 12: 465–479.

Tuan, Mia. 1998. *Forever Foreigners or Honorary Whites? The Asian Ethnic Experience Today*. New Brunswick, N.J.: Rutgers University Press.

Valk, Margaret A. 1957. *Korean-American Children in American Adoptive Homes*. New York: Child Welfare League of America.

Valverde, Kieu Linh Caroline. 2001. "Doing the Mixed-Race Dance: Negotiating Social Spheres within the Multiracial Vietnamese American Class Typology. In *The Sum of Our Parts: Mixed Heritage Asian Americans*, ed. Teresa Williams-León and Cynthia L. Nakashima. Philadelphia: Temple University Press, 131–143.

Vance, Jeannine Joy. 2003. *Twins Found in a Box: Adapting to Adoption*. Bloomington, Ind.: 1st Books.

Wadia-Ells, Susan, ed. 1995. *The Adoption Reader: Birth Mothers, Adoptive Mothers, and Adopted Daughters Tell Their Stories*. Seattle: Seal Press.

Watkins, Mary, and Susan Fisher. 1995. *Talking with Young Children about Adoption*. New Haven, Conn.: Yale University Press.

West, Cornel. 1993. *Race Matters*. Boston: Beacon Press.

Whang, Min Sung. 1976. "An Exploratory Descriptive Study of Inter-Country

Adoption of Korean Children with Known Parents." Master's thesis, University of Hawai'i at Mānoa.

Wilkinson, Sook, and Nancy Fox, eds. 2002. *After the Morning Calm: Reflections of Korean Adoptees.* Bloomfield Hills, Mich.: Sunrise Ventures.

Williams-León, Teresa, and Cynthia L. Nakashima, eds. 2001. *The Sum of Our Parts: Mixed Heritage Asian Americans.* Philadelphia: Temple University Press.

Wise, Tim. 2006. "Disasters Natural and Otherwise: What Hurricane Katrina Tells Us about Race, Class, and Privilege in the U.S." Lecture given at the 7th Annual White Privilege Conference, University of Missouri, St. Louis, April 28.

Woodard, Sarah L. 2002. *Daughter from Afar: A Family's International Adoption Story.* Lincoln, Neb.: Writers Club Press.

Wu, Frank H. 2002. *Yellow: Race in America beyond Black and White.* New York: Basic Books.

Young, Michelle D. 2000. "Considering (Irreconcilable?) Contradictions in Cross-group Feminist Research." *International Journal of Qualitative Studies in Education* 13: 629–660.

Zhou, Min. 1997a. "Growing up American: The Challenge Confronting Immigrant Children and Children of Immigrants." *Annual Review of Sociology* 23(63): 63–96.

———. 1997b. "Social Capital in Chinatown: The Role of Community-based Organizations and Families in the Adaptation of the Younger Generation." In *Beyond Black and White: New Voices, New Faces in the United States Schools,* ed. Maxine Seller and Lois Weis. Albany: State University of New York Press, 181–206.

Zuniga, Maria E. 1991. "Transracial Adoption: Educating the Parents." *Journal of Multicultural Social Work* 1: 17–30.

Subject Index

See the separate Index of Korean Transracial Adoptee Participants for specific adoptees cited in the text.

Index of Korean Transracial
Adoptee Participants

ABOUT THE AUTHOR

JOHN D. PALMER was adopted at the age of thirteen months from South Korea. He grew up in Iowa with his four brothers and four sisters, five adopted from South Korea and two from Vietnam. Throughout much of his early life his main contact with other Koreans and Korean adoptees was through an annual Korean culture camp established by his mother and Dorothy Mattson. After teaching at the elementary school level, John journeyed to South Korea in search of a closer attachment with his racial and ethnic identity. Over the course of three years he earned his Master's degree in Korean studies from Yonsei University and was granted the privilege of working as a research associate at Iwhajang, the late President Syngman Rhee's private residence and archives under the tutelage of Dr. Young Ick Lew. John then returned to Iowa, where he earned his Ph.D. in educational planning and leadership studies from the University of Iowa. John currently is an associate professor at Colgate University in the Department of Educational Studies. He resides in upstate New York with his wife Woolim and sons David Mingyu, Jonathan Minhoo, and Henry Minjoon and continues to visit Korea on a regular basis to conduct research and visit family and friends.

Production Notes for Palmer / THE DANCE OF IDENTITIES
Jacket designed by Julie Matsuo-Chun
Interior designed by Josie Herr in Sabon
Composition by Terri Miyasato
Printing and binding by Sheridan Books, Inc.
Printed on 60 lb. House White, 444 ppi